THE IRISH POLITICAL SYSTEM, 1740–1765

The Irish Political System, 1740–1765

The Golden Age of the Undertakers

EOIN MAGENNIS

FOUR COURTS PRESS

Set in 10.5 on 12.5 point Ehrhardt for
FOUR COURTS PRESS LTD
Fumbally Lane, Dublin 8, Ireland
e-mail: info@four-courts-press.ie
http://www.four-courts-press.ie
and in North America for
FOUR COURTS PRESS
c/o ISBS, 5804 N.E. Hassalo Street, Portland, OR 97213.

A catalogue record for this title
is available from the British Library.

ISBN 1–85182–484–7

Printed in Great Britain
by MPG Books, Bodmin, Cornwall

For Clare and Siobhán with much love

Contents

List of Abbreviations

Add. Mss.	Additional Manuscripts
BL	British Library
BNL	*Belfast News-Letter*
CHOP	*Calendar of the Home Office Papers*
CJI	*Commons Journal of the Irish Parliament*
ECI	*Eighteenth Century Ireland*
FDJ	*Faulkner's Dublin Journal*
FJ	*Freeman's Journal*
HMC	*Historical Manuscripts Commission*
IHS	*Irish Historical Studies*
NAI	National Archives of Ireland
NLI	National Library of Ireland
PRO	Public Record Office, London
PRONI	Public Record Office of Northern Ireland
RIA	Royal Irish Academy
TCD	Trinity College, Dublin.

Acknowledgments

In writing a book you acquire innumerable debts. First, I want to thank the keepers, archivists and librarians for their assistance and, where appropriate, permission to quote from manuscripts in their care: Armagh Public Library, Belfast Central Library, Boston Public Library, British Library, Derbyshire Record Office, Dublin Corporation Public Libraries: Gilbert Library, House of Lords Record Office, the Council of Trustees of the National Library of Ireland, National Archives of Ireland, Northumberland Record Office, Deputy Keeper of the Public Record Office of Northern Ireland (special thanks to A.P.W. Malcomson), Public Record Office, Royal Irish Academy, the Board of Trinity College, Dublin, University of Nottingham Library, Yale University Beinecke Library. Access to the Harvard University Library, Ipswich and East Sussex Record Office, Kent Record Office, Magee College Library, Presbyterian Historical Society, West Sussex Record Office was also gratefully received. Last, and far from least, the staff of the Irish and Local Studies departments in Belfast Central Library (especially Linda Greenwood), the Linen Hall Library (in particular Ciaran Crossey and Mary Delargy) and Queen's University Library were always prepared to go out of their way for obscure requests.

With regard to academic assistance, Peter Jupp has provided the inspiration, supervision and criticism for over a decade, without which this book would be much the poorer. The School of Modern History in Queen's University possesses a welcoming Irish history circle that provided supportive colleagues at many points during my postgraduate and lecturing days. Special mention here for the contributions of David Hayton, Mary O'Dowd, Alvin Jackson and the research students of the early 1990s. The Linen Hall Library has been a research-friendly refuge and, lately, my day-job, where Ophelia Byrne and John Killen have made it a better place to work. Others have been kind enough to invite me to come and speak to them, as individuals or groups, about my research and special thanks are due to James Kelly, Paddy McNally, Toby Barnard and the committee of Cumann Seanchais Ard Mhaca. Ronan Gallagher and the staff of Four Courts Press deserve an award for patience, while Marie Moore provided the editing skills. Also, I want to thank the staff of Belvoir Park Hospital in Belfast for cancer care above and beyond the call of duty at a time of great uncertainty about their own future.

Beyond work, family and friends lie behind a collective work. Those, among many, who deserve a special mention for the offers of free dinners and an escape from the undertakers include Pat Clarke, Hugh Warden, Chris Marsh, Fionnuala Vallely, John Fotheringham, Eithne Flanagan, and the Wells family. Above all, my parents, brothers, Feidhlimidh and Lochlann, and sister, Caitriona, have been supportive at every point. While they are not responsible for any errors in this book, it is they who made it possible.

Introduction

In May 1758 a former viceroy, Lord Chesterfield, wrote wearily about the state of Irish politics. By that date the Money Bill crisis was over and several less than successful settlements had been attempted. After all of the political excitement, the viceroy still seemed bound to a cabal of undertakers (Boyle – now Lord Shannon – Ponsonby and Stone). In Chesterfield's eyes this was to the detriment of government. What is more, the apostasy of Henry Boyle in 1756 and the return to power of the key 'Castle man', Primate George Stone, in February 1758, made political integrity seem a quixotic notion. Thus both the public good and public service appeared to be in terminal decline in Ireland. Little wonder then that Chesterfield was so acerbic:

> The Lord Lieutenant may, if he pleases, govern alone, but then he must, as I know by experience, take a great deal more trouble upon himself than most Lord Lieutenants care to do, and he must not be afraid. But as they commonly prefer *otium cum dignitate*, their guards, their battle-axes, and their trumpets, not to mention perhaps the profits of their post, to a laborious execution of it, they must necessarily rule by a faction, of which faction for the time being they are only the first slaves ... Thus from that moment these undertakers bury the governors alive, but indeed pompously.[1]

This cynicism is not surprising given his knowledge of Ireland between 1744 and 1758. There seemed to be few redeeming features in this 'age of the undertakers' where patronage, lazy officialdom, lack of significant political principle and a feckless elite all combined to create little worth studying. The Money Bill crisis of 1753–5 in a sense summed up this corruption as opposition politicians adopted patriotism in an opportunistic way and then dropped it when their old offices or new pensions and peerages were dangled before them. In 1930 T.J. Kiernan concluded, when analysing the crisis, 'that the Irish parliament produced a single member who was not corrupt is its glory'.[2] While

1 Chesterfield to Chevenix, 23 May 1758, in B. Dobree (ed.), *The Correspondence of Philip Dormer Stanhope, fourth Earl Of Chesterfield* (5 vols, London 1932, hereafter *Chesterfield Correspondence*), v, pp. 2303–5. 2 T.J. Kiernan, *History of the Financial Administration of Ireland to 1817* (London, 1930), p. 180.

early nineteenth-century Irish historians had some sympathy with the Patriots of 1753, this was later to disappear. Lecky chose not to look closely at the period before 1760 and characterised the 1750s as a decade of struggle over the spoils, though with some principle thrown in.[3] It should be remembered that in the period of Home Rule agitation, half-hearted Patriots were much less fashionable than those, like Charlemont or Grattan, who pursued opposition politics with a vengeance.[4]

By the 1900s there was some change in perceptions after the work of C. Litton Falkiner, a leading Unionist historian. He produced a much more sympathetic version of the government's position in mid-century, something close to Chesterfield's view above. Falkiner relied on the correspondence of Archbishop Stone and the Stopford-Sackville papers for his sources, but found the key to his understanding of the period in the 1757 pamphlet by Edmund Sexton Pery, *A Letter to the Duke of Bedford*. From these different perpectives this historian was able to reconstruct circumstances where the undertakers, specifically Boyle, had an absolute hold on Dublin Castle and parliament during the 1740s until this was challenged by Stone and the Sackvilles.[5] Thus the Castle had most of the principles during the Money Bill crisis, rather than the venal Patriots.

This view of both the undertaker system before 1750 and the crisis in it during the 1750s proved an influential one until amended by J.L. McCracken in the 1940s. His view was hardly more sympathetic: the Money Bill crisis reflected the factionalism of Irish politics as Stone and Boyle fought over control of government and legislature.[6] Once more, in the 1970s, the undertaker system and the 1750s received more specialist interest and the McCracken view was challenged in its details and also its conclusions.[7] Yet the factional approach, much influenced by Lewis Namier's work, still dominates views on Irish politics before 1782, particularly in the general overviews:

---

3 W.E.H. Lecky, *A History of Ireland in the Eighteenth Century* (5 vols, London, 1892), i, pp. 465–6. **4** D. McCartney, *W.E.H. Lecky: Historian and Politician, 1838–1903* (Dublin, 1994), chapter 1. **5** C. Litton Falkiner, 'Archbishop Stone', in idem., *Essays relating to Ireland* (London, 1909), pp. 32–63; idem., 'Correspondence of Archbishop George Stone and the Duke of Newcastle', *English Historical Review*, xx (1905), pp. 509–42, 735–63. **6** These views were developed in J.L. McCracken, 'The Undertakers in Ireland and their Relations with the lord lieutenants, 1727–1771' (MA thesis, Queen's University Belfast, 1941); idem., 'The conflict between the Irish administration and parliament, 1753–1756', *IHS*, iii (1942–3), pp. 159–79; idem., 'The Irish Viceroyalty, 1760–1773', in H.A. Cronne, T.W. Moody and D.B. Quinn (eds), *Essays in British and Irish History in honour of J.E. Todd* (Dublin, 1949). **7** Among others see D. Hayton, 'The Beginnings of the "Undertaker System"', in T. Bartlett and D.W. Hayton (eds), *Penal Age and Golden Era* (Belfast, 1979, hereafter *Penal Age*), pp. 32–54; E.M. Johnston, *Ireland in the Eighteenth Century* (Dublin, 1974); T. Bartlett, 'The Townshend Viceroyalty, 1767–1772' (PhD. thesis, Queen's University Belfast, 1976).

> From the 1720s the Irish House of Commons was a Namierite para-
> dise: factions, families, interests, connections, 'friends of government'
> (inconstant) and 'independent patriots (inconsistent) ... And with the
> establishment of factional politics came the age of the great individual
> who could monopolise 'undertaking' a successful parliamentary passage
> for government business.[8]

The major dissenting voice from this consensus has been Declan O'Donovan.
As he has published little and his thesis is perhaps more often quoted than read,
it is worthwhile to explain his theory about the undertaker system.[9] In essence, the
1753 crisis was caused less by a factional dispute than by an attempt to destroy the
chief undertaker's political interest and take over management of the Irish Commons. The reason for this was that parliament was the last bastion of the 'Irish
interest' and the Castle sought to bring it under its control as it had done to the
judiciary, bishop's bench and army since 1690. This was the reason why the
Patriot opposition could generate a belief that the interests of Ireland were in
danger. The conflict was made sharper by an economic slump, which meant that
any tampering with the Irish Treasury was seen with an even more jaundiced eye.
O'Donovan's conclusion that 1753 proved something of a curtain-raiser for the
Patriot glory days of 1779–82 is close to Lord Charlemont's own views on the
effects of 1753:

> By them [the opposition of 1753] the people were taught a secret of
> which they had been hitherto ignorant, that government might be
> opposed with success, and, as a confidence in the possibility of victory is
> the best inspirer of courage, a spirit was consequently raised in the
> nation, hereafter to be employed to better purpose ... In a word, Irishmen
> were taught to think, a lesson which is the first and most necessary step
> to the acquirement of liberty.[10]

I have taken O'Donovan's work as a starting point for this book and the thesis
whence it came but have come to slightly different conclusions.

---

8 R.F. Foster, *Modern Ireland, 1600–1972* (London, 1988), p. 231. 9 O'Donovan's thesis
proved impossible to get from University College, Dublin. Much better-known is the summary
in D. O'Donovan, 'The Money Bill Dispute of 1753', in *Penal Age*, pp. 55–87. 10 *HMC 12th
Report, Appendix V: The Manuscripts and Correspondence of James, First Earl of Charlemont* (2
vols, London, 1891, hereafter *Charlemont Mss.*), i, p. 7.

When researching the PhD thesis on which this book is based, it struck me that there would be no 'discoveries' or 'revelations' on a par with the seminal work of the 1970s.[11] What ended as a study of Ireland during the Seven Years War (1756–63) began as a search for the 'Aftermath of the Watershed' of 1753–5. This proved quite fruitless, though when taking a longer term view of the 1740s, 1750s and 1760s several points may be made.

First, that the 'undertaker system' of parliamentary management was much less an ascendancy than Archbishop Stone maintained between 1748 and 1754. Far from emulating William Conolly's position, Henry Boyle actually had less influence with the Castle because of his opposition traditions. Despite this, he proved a largely successful undertaker between 1733 and 1750 because of his standing with MPs. After Boyle's retirement from the Speakership in 1756 the problems were different. The undertaker system had fractured and no one manager could be entirely relied upon to dominate the Commons in the way that Conolly and Boyle had done. It did not help that John Ponsonby was a much less convincing Speaker. Rather than holding the viceroy in bondage, the undertakers after 1755 led the Castle and its business to be more open to public opinion. It was the failure of parliamentary management, rather than the ability of the undertakers to cow successive viceroys, that led to increasing ministerial frustration with the system.

The second point is connected to the first. James Kelly has argued that 'the broad thrust of English thinking on Ireland from the mid-eighteenth century was integrative.'[12] If one limits this to thinking and starts the action timeline with the later years of the Townshend viceroyalty then it is largely true. Taking the 1740–68 period as a whole, however, there was little in the way of sustained interest in changing the existing system of governing Ireland. For one thing the Castle executive was successful in plodding along and meeting the needs of government (men and money) up to the end of the Seven Years War. It was the same when the undertaker system was viewed from London. Ministerial frustration or resentment with Irish politicians certainly grew during the 1750s, though to little practical effect, in terms of policy, until 1765. Then the decision of the Grenville ministry, in February 1765, that the next viceroy should reside in Ireland, was taken with the opportunity provided by the deaths of the two leading undertakers, Stone

---

11 The essays in *Penal Age* are one sign of the productivity of that decade. Other important works are A.P.W. Malcomson, *John Foster: The politics of the Anglo-Irish Ascendancy* (Oxford, 1978) and, more recently, James Kelly, *Henry Flood: Patriots and Politics in Eighteenth Century Ireland* (Dublin, 1998). 12 James Kelly, *Prelude to Union: Anglo-Irish Politics in the 1780s* (Cork, 1992 hereafter Kelly, *Prelude*), p. 7; Martyn J. Powell, 'The reform of the undertaker system: Anglo-Irish politics, 1750–1767', *IHS*, xxxi (1998, hereafter Powell, 'Reform'), pp. 19–36.

and Shannon, in December 1764 and the ill-health of the then viceroy, Lord Northumberland.[13] Although the opportunity passed, it is arguable that a marker had been set down. It was not until 1768 (and arguably the defeat of a money bill in 1769) that different ministers chose to act on this policy decision. By then the changing needs of the British government (given imperial demands) and the unwillingness or inability of the Irish undertakers to deliver the required increases in men and money, made reform of parliamentary management unavoidable.

The third point is that the Money Bill crisis did, as Charlemont insisted, make constitutional issues topical once more. The size of the civil list, the frequency of elections and the use of Poynings' Law began to come to the fore in a way that the Irish executive was uneasy about. There was not only a consistency about the issues but also about the Patriot MPs who raised them in the Commons and about the extra-parliamentary echoes they raised. By the later 1760s, as in Britain, Irish opposition politics had changed from what they had been in 1753. Over issues like the Septennial Bills the Patriot tail had the potential to wag the Commons dog long before 1779–82.

Much of the shifting historiography on mid-eighteenth century Irish politics (especially the Money Bill crisis) comes down, of course, to a matter of sources. One can trace the changing views through the availability of papers, from Falkiner and the Stone, Sackville and Pery collections, through to McCracken and his use of British Library materials. Much of the revision, rather than revisionism, from the 1970s is due to the collecting of private papers by the Public Record Office of Northern Ireland, under the guidance of A.P.W. Malcomson. This service deserves recognition as does the important sorting and calendaring done since then. By these efforts a massive amount of eighteenth-century correspondence, from the huge Foster-Masserene and Abercorn archives to the smaller, but crucial, collections of Sir Robert Wilmot, Pery, Charles O'Hara and others, was made available to the Irish historian. Suddenly the reliance on the official State Papers and the lamenting of all that was destroyed in the 1922 Four Courts shelling could be partially escaped from. There may still be papers awaiting discovery (for instance the Ponsonbys lack a substantial archive from this period) but by the 1980s most of the relevant manuscripts were known about.

Having said all of that, a reliance on private papers causes a book to see mid-eighteenth century Ireland in a particularly partial way. Wide use of newspapers (Dublin and regional), parliamentary records and pamphlets overcomes this to some extent. However, the world of local politics is largely missing in favour of Dublin and its institutions and the reconstruction of public opinion is only partially achieved. Moreover, and, most importantly, Catholic opinion being

13 Cabinet minutes for 1 Feb. 1765, in J.R.G. Tomlinson (ed.), *Additional Grenville Papers, 1763–1765* (Manchester, 1962), pp. 335–6.

absent for the most part from the sources used is, of necessity, missing from the study. 'Hidden Ireland' thereby remains hidden. However, these points stand less as an apology and more an appeal for further research in what is still a largely untilled area of Irish history.

I

Undertakers and parliamentary management in the years before 1750

Throughout the period 1692–1800, when the Irish parliament was at its most active, undertakers or managers were indispensable for Dublin Castle. In reality it was only on rare occasions that government control was challenged during the eighteenth century and, rarer still, that any challenge was successful. Despite this, no viceroy was under the illusion that he could do without managers, especially for the Commons. This was even truer in the years before 1767 when the viceroy and chief secretary were usually non-resident. The fleeting presence of lord lieutenants, some of whom stayed in office for only one session, created a reliance on Castle officials and Irish politicians to provide both political and administrative continuity. This, in essence, was the 'Age of the Undertakers'.

UNDERTAKERS AND PARLIAMENTARY MANAGEMENT

The story of the rise of the undertakers in the Williamite parliament is by now well-known having been excellently described by Hayton and McGuire.[1] After the fiasco of the 1692 parliament, when the Commons opposition threatened to overwhelm Dublin Castle, the ministry in London sought to calm matters by ensuring safe management of at least the next parliamentary session. The strategy of viceroys like Lord Capel was to include opposition leaders in the Castle administration and worked in the sense that Money Bills were not rejected as they had been in 1692. However, political peace was not guaranteed. Queen Anne's reign saw bitter party strife between Whigs and Tories, while the House of Lords was a restive chamber with the bishops bench, in particular, leaning towards Tory and Patriot politics, sometimes simultaneously.[2]

1 D. Hayton, 'The beginnings of the undertaker system', in T. Bartlett & D.W. Hayton (eds), *Penal Age and Golden Era* (Belfast, 1979, hereafter *Penal Age*), pp. 32–54; J. McGuire, 'The Irish parliament of 1692', in *Penal Age*, pp. 1–31. 2 For this see P. McNally, *Parties, Patriots and Undertakers: Parliamentary Politics in early Hanoverian Ireland* (Dublin, 1997, hereafter McNally, *Parties*); D. Hayton and D. Szechi, 'John Bull's other kingdoms: the English government of Scotland and Ireland', in C. Jones (ed.), *Britain in the First Age of Party, 1680–1750* (London 1987), pp. 241–80.

The House of Commons was even more unreliable, primarily because the government returned very few of the 300 MPs through their own electoral interest. Government officials, including the law officers, usually owed their seats to other electoral patrons and this could sometimes place their loyalty in question. The viceroys could rarely afford complacency, particularly if constitutional or economic issues arose. Dublin Castle rarely saw its first choice elected as Speaker of the Commons and on one occasion, in 1713, its candidate was defeated. All of this proved the need for close management of the Irish parliament. The key to the relationship between government and its managers was the successful way in which undertakers acted as a channel of communication between the parliament and Dublin Castle. A sign of how seriously this was taken was that the leading undertaker was made one of the three lord justices in the absence of the viceroy. In this way the gap between the Irish executive and legislature could be bridged.

Government had to choose its undertakers wisely. Primarily they had to bring to the Castle a substantial following within the House of Commons. This came from electoral interests, solidified, rather than built, through patronage. As shall be shown, patronage on its own was not enough and a candidate needed a reputation for political judgement, honour and a certain independence from the administration of the day. Patronage has often been seen as the motor force for political behaviour in eighteenth century Ireland. Lecky was clear about the corruptibility of Hanoverian politics, though he erred in believing that Irish patronage was primarily used by ministers to purchase English politicians rather than Irish ones. Johnson and Beckett concentrated more on the use of patronage to buy a majority within the Irish parliament, a picture that was modified more recently by Hayton and Dickson. Other historians, especially Malcomson and Connolly, are keen to point out that patronage has to be placed alongside ideas of honour and reputation in understanding political behaviour at this time.[3]

The viceroys never delegated their control over Irish patronage. They were either well aware, or made so, of Marmaduke Coghill's belief that patronage was essential 'to unite and keep the people together', to stop them wandering 'as sheep without a shepherd' or getting into 'factions that may make the administration uneasy'.[4] The senior posts, especially in the judiciary and the church, remained in the gift of the ministry and the king. The same was largely true for the army. It is true that recommendations from the lords justices, including undertakers like Connolly, Boyle and John Ponsonby, carried some weight with ministers. However, from the 1690s there was what could be called a conscious policy to ensure that an 'English interest' existed on the bishops' bench, in the judiciary and also on the Revenue Board. Archbishop Hugh Boulter has sometimes been seen as the

3 The best survey of the literature and most skilful analysis of patronage can be found in McNally, *Parties*, chapter 5.   4 Coghill to Southwell, 14 Jan. 1735 (BL Add. Mss.21, 123, ff.84–6).

architect of this policy, though it preceded him and remained in force after his death.[5] Pensions were not distributed in quite the same manner as places. Ministers were keen to make sure a pool of pensions were available for English, Hanoverian and Scottish rewardees. Despite this most pensions, in terms of numbers if not amounts, were made available to the viceroy to reward loyal followers of the government in Ireland. The same was true for Irish peerages, most going to Irish MPs and also borough patrons already in the House of Lords.

The distribution of patronage in the revenue service was delegated, more than most, to the undertakers. Conolly, Boyle and then the Ponsonby family were all keen to dominate this department. In 1709 Conolly paid £3,000 for a revenue commissionership and then, in 1714, sought the Speaker's place as a way of ensuring his dominance of the Board. He was First Commissioner until his death in 1729 and control of patronage over the thousand or more junior posts, as much as public service, meant that he rigorously attended business at the Board. As Katherine Conolly complained:

> He is everyday at least six hours at the Customs House ... I wish some of the commissioners were ordered to their business – for I think it is hard he should always have the labouring over him.[6]

Henry Boyle was just as aware of the importance of revenue patron-age as he demanded the place of First Commissioner in 1733 as a support for the Speaker's position.[7] What happened later, in 1739, when Boyle gave up this place, in return for the Chancellor of the Exchequer sinecure, is hard to explain. Either he believed that his supporters on the Revenue Board would give him enough influence there or that his power in other places was secure or even that the hours worked by Conolly were incompatible with Boyle's wish to spend his summers in County Cork. In any case the Ponsonbys, by taking over control of the revenue service, were able to build up a formidable patronage network that continued well into the 1760s.

Evidence of some measure of control over patronage was essential to the reputation of any undertaker. It was sign of one's standing within government and, also, one's ability to successfully meet the expectations of followers. McNally has shown how the ebbs and flows of the Brodrick/Conolly rivalry was seen through success in patronage requests. In 1720, when the Brodricks were out of favour, their failure to secure the solicitor general's place was taken as 'a declaration to the world in what credit [we stand] with the great ones, and ... is so understood by

---

5 P. McNally, "'Irish and English Interests": National conflict within the Church of Ireland episcopate in the reign of George I', *IHS*, 115 (1995), pp. 295–314. 6 Conolly to Delafaye, 17 June 1729, quoted in McNally, *Parties*, p. 106. 7 BL Add. Mss.21123, ff.84–6, Coghill to Southwell, 14 Jan. 1735.

everybody.' That same year the family were desperate to have their relation appointed dean of Cork. Lord Midleton was delighted at the outcome as 'it would really have been looked on as a designed and avowed honour done to one and indignity placed on those to whom Mr Davies is related, and especially when it is in a country where our estates and friends are.'[8] In the 1730s Henry Boyle was just as anxious to secure patronage to display his political elevation. In March 1734 he asked that his ally, Hugh Dickson, be given the vacant collectorship of Cork, not knowing that Walpole wanted to appoint his own person. Boyle was supported by the Revenue Board and Dorset offered to persuade Walpole, but all of this was to no avail as the Treasury's choice was appointed in June. Boyle was furious at this result as his letter to Dodington showed:

> If it is to be understood that Dickson is to be laid aside to make way for him, where's my credit, where's my influence or what business have I here? ... You, Sir, very well know the difficulties I have laboured under at my first setting out and the pains I was frequently obliged to be as from four in the afternoon till five or six in the morning, to persuade my troops to fight in a cause foreign to their own principles or natural inclinations, and now, just as they are brought into good discipline, I can expect no less than a revolt if they find their endeavours to support me have proved altogether ineffectual.[9]

It should be remembered that when patronage requests were granted by the Castle they did not guarantee loyalty, even though government office was sometimes a path to wealth.[10] The timing of grants of places or pensions was crucial as most viceroys wanted these to be rewards for services already rendered. Thus the end of sessions usually saw a list of recommendations for the king to agree. In 1731 Dorset advised against giving Thomas Carter his office too soon:

> I choose to defer any application on that account, being desirous to have some experience of the session here, in which I am informed by the king's servants, that Mr Carter's abilities may be of use in carrying on His Majesty's service.[11]

It is also true that for those persons who were gratified by patronage there were many more disappointed in their expectations. The reigns of both George I and George II were to see vicious struggles for rewards at both the central and local levels. County lieutenancies or sheriffs, as much as the places of solicitor general or bishop of Raphoe created winners and losers. Most of the time these were short-lived rows but in periods of political tension the disputes took on

8 McNally, *Parties*, pp. 108–9. 9 Boyle to Dodington [June 1734], in *HMC Various Collections*, vi, pp. 61–2. 10 For an example of this see L. Clarkson & E.M. Crawford, *Ways to Wealth* (Belfast, 1985). 11 Dorset to Newcastle, 29 Sept. 1731, quoted in McNally, *Parties*, p. 97.

more significance, as when William Yorke was made chancellor of the exchequer in the place of the dismissed Malone in 1761. Soon afterwards Yorke wrote with a mixture of trepidation and optimism about his post:

> Under all circumstances I must expect the little low effect of envy, such as slander, libels, etc., not knowing what other vents that passion can have, but I shall endeavour to despise them ... I have had no intimation, and hope I shall have none that it is expected I shall be in parliament; and, if so, the office will be very easy indeed.

In the event he had to go into the Commons and his position was far from easy.[12]

Whilst undertakers sought patronage to show their strength, they were just as keen to avoid being seen as taking responsibility for government legislation. In 1714 both Whig leaders were anxious to avoid the title as, according to Alan Brodrick:

> [it is said] that there are undertakers for a land tax, and augmentation of [army] forces, and indeed for everything: you know how odious a term that is, and that nothing is so likely to disappoint a reasonable thing as possessing men with an opinion that it is stipulated for.[13]

When he became heir to the Brodrick interest in 1725, Boyle, refused even to discuss with Lord Carteret what might make that political clan more amenable to the Castle.[14] Every manager or undertaker prided themselves on appearing solely as an advisor to the viceroy and a channel for his favour or patronage. On the other side the government were keen to have a choice of undertaker, though this was something which was rare in practice and, indeed, did not guarantee quieter parliamentary sessions. During the 'age of party' the viceroys were limited by the on-going Whig/Tory strife. Mixed administrations and management of the Commons were attempted by Shrewsbury in 1708 and 1710 but proved unsuccessful on each occasion. After 1715 viceroys had the choice between the two leading Whigs, William Conolly and Alan Brodrick, though, as McNally has shown, this rivalry did not automatically pave the way to stable management.[15]

One aspect of management that was often less agreeable to Dublin Castle was the frequent practice of 'buying off' opposition leaders. After the 1692 session the next viceroy, Lord Capel, was extremely active in detaching the 'sole right men', especially the Brodricks, from opposition. This method of securing both a majority in the Commons and also managers of it continued

12 Yorke to Hardwicke, 26 Mar., 28 Apr. 1761 (BL Add. Mss.35596, ff.289 & 310).
13 Brodrick to Brodrick, 14 Dec. 1714 (Guildford Record Office, Midleton Mss., iii, ff.205–7).
14 Brodrick to Brodrick, 17 Nov. 1725 (ibid., vi, ff.336–341).　　15 McNally, *Parties*, chapter 6.

during Anne's reign. In 1707 the Lord Chancellor, Sir Richard Cox, warned about bring Whigs into the administration and this would not only disoblige loyal supporters but also 'the very men whilst they personate Patriots delude many and seem to have great interest, the minute they turn courtiers (as they call it) lose all their popularity and signify little'.[16] Other officials worried that such tactics did not ensure peace but perhaps the opposite:

> No new encouragement [should be] given to such doings by buying off discontented persons here; for if anybody is bought off, there will always arise a succession of people to make a disturbance each session.[17]

However, viceroys were not keen to follow this advice and chose either to believe in the corruptibility of Irish politicians or to secure easy parliamentary management at whatever the cost.

The latter motive was even stronger when it came to possible dismissals. There were no major purges after the one which saw the Tories dismissed in 1715. On two occasions when William Conolly and his followers refused to support government, in 1719–20 and 1724–6, no action was taken. That is despite, in 1725, the urgings of Boulter for action to be taken, especially in the Irish privy council. He told Carteret that 'the next sessions will be made more easy and successful', but the viceroy chose to ignore such promises. In 1733, when almost his entire administration refused to follow Walpole's wishes and repeal the Test Act, Dorset also refused to act. Coghill was scathing about his excuse:

> He had done all that was proper for him to do, unless he should tell those in employment that they should be turned out unless they complied, which he thought not proper, having no directions to do so.[18]

There can be no doubt then that parliamentary management had many different sides to its working. The powers of recommendation, appointment and dismissal were all important ones to be used or not. And yet these were not all as reputation, honour and standing also had to be considered. The career of Henry Boyle seems to sum up much about the age of the undertakers.

---

16 Cox to Southwell, 22 Apr. 1707 (BL Add. Mss.38,155, f.21).   17 Boulter to Newcastle, 16 Nov. 1725, in Boulter Letters (*Letters Written by His Excellency Hugh Boulter, Lord Primate of all Ireland* (2 vols, Dublin, 1770, hereafter *Boulter Letters*), i, pp. 43–5; Coghill to Southwell, 21 June 1733 (BL Add. Mss.21,123, ff.41–2).   18 Boulter to Newcastle, 16 Nov. 1725, 22 Mar. 1726, in Boulter Letters, i, pp. 44–5 & 54–6; Coghill to Southwell, 13 Dec. 1733 (BL Add. Mss.21123, ff.76–7).

THE RISE OF AN UNDERTAKER

At a time when it seemed inevitable that Henry Boyle would become the next Speaker of the Irish Commons he was disparagingly described by a fellow MP:

> His friends as well as those who oppose him think him very unfit for that situation, by reason of his natural modesty and his little application to the knowledge of parliamentary proceedings. He is a country gentleman of great good nature and probity, well-beloved, but not of extraordinary abilities or much used to public business, and for these many reasons many do apprehend it will be a very uneasy chair when he gets into it.[19]

The author of this letter, Marmaduke Coghill, was no friend to Boyle and had some potential to be a rival for the Speaker's chair in 1733 but his opinion has often wrongly been taken at face value. His idea that the new Speaker would have an uneasy time in Commons proved to be true, though this was less to do with Boyle's ability and more to do with distrust marking his relationship with the viceroy, Dorset. In time Boyle was to become perhaps the most effective and certainly the longest-lasting undertaker of the eighteenth century.

The rise of Boyle in 1733 and his poor relations with Dublin Castle raises questions about why an undertaker was chosen and how they survived in that lofty position. The first point to be recognised is that in 1733 Boyle did not really have anything like a serious rival for the speakership and the role of leading undertaker. When William Conolly died in 1729 Boyle had, even then, high hopes of replacing him as Speaker and undertaker. However, Lord Carteret was able to regroup the forces marshalled by Conolly under the joint management of Sir Ralph Gore and Coghill. By 1733, after the death of Gore and the further decline of Conolly's party, there was little that the government could do to oppose Boyle. In retrospect the years 1729–33 can be seen as an interregnum between the reign of one leading undertaker and that of another. Though Gore and Coghill proved effective managers of government business for the 1731–2 session, Boyle was able to maintain the strength of the Brodrick party and to add the support of Arthur Hill's Ulster supporters to this.[20] In this way Boyle had gathered a core support of sixty MPs, enough to make him the favourite to succeed Gore and his campaign between February and June 1733 made him irresistible.[21] Coghill may have believed

---

19 Coghill to Southwell, 15 Mar. 1733 (BL Add. Mss.21123, f.26).   20 Hill to Boyle, 15 Apr. 1733; Coote to Boyle, 16 Apr. 1733 (PRONI Shannon papers, D/2707/A1/2/39–40). Boyle's success was in contradiction of Coghill's belief during the 1729 session that the Brodrick party was breaking up: Coghill to Southwell, 25 Dec. 1729 (BL Add. Mss.21122, f.102).   21 See the letters to Boyle between February and June 1733 for evidence of this successful campaign: PRONI D/2707/A1/2/54–90.

Boyle 'unfit for that position', but he was in a minority and his pique-filled letters reflect that knowledge. The only likely 'country' rival of Boyle, Thomas Carter, quickly accepted having to play second fiddle, and Coghill withdrew from the race early on.[22]

The only remaining threat to Boyle's succession into the Speaker's chair came from Henry Singleton, the prime serjeant, but his Tory past and his pride made him unattractive to most unattached country gentlemen. In addition the primate, Archbishop Boulter, would never support Singleton's candidacy as he was a key ally of the former's greatest enemy, Archbishop Bolton of Cashel. Indeed Boulter rapidly threw his weight behind Henry Boyle in late February, even hinting that he be appointed a lord justice to fill Gore's vacancy.[23] Though this did not happen Boulter quickly persuaded Lord Chancellor Wyndham to his way of thinking and on 6 March they told the duke of Newcastle:

> ... in our present circumstances it will be most for His Majecty's service and for the good of the common interest of England and Ireland that he [Boyle] should be supported by the government in this affair.[24]

Boulter told the viceroy, Dorset, that Boyle's 'pretensions' to the speakership 'could not without difficulty be opposed'. After this date the lords justices repeatedly advised ministers to support Boyle's campaign so as to avoid later conflict.[25]

Meanwhile Boyle was active in soliciting support and offers of support flooded in from Ulster and parts of Leinster to add to his 'Munster squadron'. At the start of April Boyle visited the lords justices to make public his intentions and ask for their support. Singleton did the same, appearing as the heir to Gore and the Conolly interest, but this had declined so much from the 1720s that government officials, like Luke Gardiner and Walter Cary (the chief secretary) did not hesitate to declare for Boyle.[26] By June 1733 Coghill's belief in Singleton was more the triumph of hope over expectation. When Dorset arrived in Dublin in September, he gave his public backing to Boyle and persuaded Singleton to give up his ambitions with dignity. Thus on 5 October 1733 Henry Boyle was unanimously elected as Speaker of the Commons and his twenty–three year reign began.[27]

According to his greatest critic, Coghill, Boyle had a undistinguished start in the chair:

22 Coghill to Southwell, 22 Feb., 8 Mar. 1733 (BL Add. Mss.21123, ff.20 & 24).   23 Boulter to Newcastle, 24 Feb. 1733, in *Boulter Letters*, ii, p. 91.   24 Lords Justices to Newcastle, 6 Mar. 1733 (PRO S[tate].P[apers].63/396/15).   25 Boulter to Dorset, 15 Mar. 1733 , in *Boulter Letters*, ii, p. 95.   26 Lords Justices to Dorset, 9 Apr. 1733 (PRONI Wilmot papers, T/3019/121); Coghill to Southwell, 19 Apr., 21 June 1733 (BL Add. Mss.21123, ff.37 & 42).   27 Coghill to Southwell, 20 Sept. 1733 (BL Add. Mss.21123, ff.54–9); *CJI*, vii, p. 135.

His speech on being first elected was spoke or rather read, with as much indifference and as little concern as if it had been at a tavern amongst a few of his friends. However, later when he attended my lord lieutenant with the Address, he read audibly and distinctly and in a very proper and decent manner.[28]

This description may be true, though it could be argued that, over the following decades, part of Boyle's attraction was his (perhaps exaggerated) country gentleman's ways. Like Sir Robert Walpole, Boyle never assumed any pretensions to grandeur though his marriage into the Burlington family made his entrèe onto the national political stage possible. His renowned hospitality, drinking habits, preference for Castlemartyr over Henrietta Street in Dublin and his virulent anti-catholicism were all to recommend him to the gentry of the House of Commons. Coming from a background in the Brodrick 'country' opposition Boyle was to prove a master in manipulating his relationship with the Commons.

However, in late 1733, the Speaker was more concerned about the nature of his relationship with the duke of Dorset. The viceroy did offer Boyle the choice of either chancellor of the exchequer or a revenue commissionership as a mark of his elevation. He also promised to use his influence to get a lord justice's place for the new Speaker despite his doubts about whether these two posts should be twinned.[29] Whether Boyle was unhappy with these offers is not clear but the widespread belief was that he was angry that Dorset had been slow to support his campaign for the chair. Lord Egmont referred to these attitudes in his diary noting that, according to Boyle, 'the government were not for him until they saw his interest would carry without the government'.[30] Worse than that for the future of the relationship between viceroy and undertaker was the accusation that Dorset was guilty of 'private and reserved behaviour, ... not communicating his pleasure to any and keeping those who are most ready to serve him at a distance from his councils'.[31] There seems to have been some truth in these accusations as Coghill and Singleton were still being consulted on the likely attitudes of MPs to several pieces of legislation. Boyle may also have been suffering from some acute sensitivity to any perceived slights and taking his time to acclimatise to the new heights. Whatever the cause the 1733–4 session was an uncomfortable one for both viceroy and undertaker and did not hint at great things ahead for Boyle.

The difficulties which arose during the 1733–4 session over the attempt to repeal the Test and the communication dispute between the Lords and Commons were caused almost totally by the lack of trust between undertaker and the government. This was not altogether new. In 1719 the duke of Bolton had his doubts about the far more reliable and experienced Conolly. Dorset should also be allowed the doubts which must have existed at the time about the inte-

28 Coghill to Southwell, 18 Oct. 1733 (BL Add. Mss.21123, ff.58–61).   29 Dorset to Newcastle, 22 Feb. 1734 (PRO S.P.63/397/53).   30 *HMC Egmont Mss.*, i, p. 462.

gration into government of the leader of the Brodrician country opposition since 1728. There should be little surprise if Dorset was not at least a little influenced by these attitudes, even if he accepted that Boyle's interest was too powerful to defy within parliament.

Dorset's position was worsened by his instructions from Walpole to repeal the Test Act. This had everything to do with Walpole's domestic politics after his administration was shaken by the Excise Crisis and faced a general election in which the opposition was expected to make gains. The need to placate English Dissenters thus became a priority. The Test barred Dissenters in Ireland from holding local or central government office and, though no hardship to the vast majority of presbyterians, it riled as an injustice.[32] Dorset, himself, seems to have had little appetite for repeal but followed his instructions and found even less enthusiasm among his officials. Boyle was consulted on this issue and offered no assistance to Dorset. To have undertaken for repeal was seen as suicidal and, thus the money bill was scrutinised closely in the Commons and Boyle did not oppose the many votes of adjournment which kept the house full, in anticipation of repeal being brought on.[33] There were rumours circulating in early December that Boyle had abused Cary at a dinner party. The Speaker reminded Cary that he was elected 'on the foot of the country party', not with the support of government. As for the current political situation:

> ... what the court suffered was by their own mismanagement, having no confidence or intimacy with anybody, and by throwing amongst us a bone of contention about the test, which has raised animosities and divisions not easily to be quieted.[34]

Whether Coghill's account is a verbatim one or not, the sense of frustration is clear. So when it was one of Boyle's supporters, Sir Richard Meade, who challenged the government to introduce repeal or let it drop (they did the latter) it can have come as little surprise. In the same month, December 1733, Boyle allowed the Commons to go its own way on another issue which embarrassed Dorset, the question of whether the Lords and Commons should communicate each piece of legislation before it went to the privy council. It is debatable whether, like the Test issue, Boyle could have greatly influenced MPs, though a successful viceroy/ undertaker relationship would have prevented the matter going to the lengths it

---

31 Ibid., i, p. 463   32 For Walpole and the Test see D. Hayton, 'Walpole and Ireland', in J. Black (ed.), *Britain in the Age of Walpole* (London, 1984, hereafter Hayton, 'Walpole'), pp. 95–119; idem, 'Exclusion, conformity and representation: The impact of the sacramental test on Irish dissenting politics', in K. Herlihy (ed.), *The Politics of Irish Dissent* (Dublin, 1997), pp. 52–73.   33 Boulter to Newcastle, 18 Dec. 1733, in *Boulter Letters*, ii, pp. 108–9. 34 Coghill to Southwell, 4 Dec. 1733 (BL Add. Mss.21123, ff.64–8).

did. In early December, the House of Lords, fearing a surprise attempt to introduce repeal of the Test there, passed a resolution which meant that all legislation would be communicated between the two houses of parliament. This was based on precedents from 1716 and was taken up with enthusiasm by MPs to the anger of ministers in London. In Dublin the viceroy and his officials tried to make the best of the resolutions arguing that they would soon be dropped. In early January Dorset was proved right as MPs voted by 102 votes to 27 to abandon the communication scheme after the Lords had snubbed their bill to limit tithes. The whole affair was a four week wonder but, again, Dorset's management of Irish affairs was placed in question. According to Newcastle the consensus among ministers was that the communication scheme 'was a material innovation and not to be admitted'. Even the viceroy's friend, Dodington, greatly exaggerated the threat arguing that the measure was ' a total dissolution of the dependence of Ireland on England.'[35]

After the problems surrounding the repeal of the test and the communication scheme, the priority for the Castle was now to mend its bridges with its chief undertaker. One sign of this détente was Dorset's recommendation of Boyle as a lord justice:

> The Whigs are more united in the country than they ever have been since the death of the late Mr Conolly ... the leaving of Mr Boyle in the government may contribute to keep them so.[36]

Boyle seemed to believe that this was no more than was expected given the fact that both Conolly and Gore had held that position. A clearer sign of his new elevated position was to have a hand in the disposal of patronage. The affair of the Cork collectorship, where Walpole's choice was successful despite Boyle's position as First Commissioner on the Revenue Board, did little to assuage his doubts. As Boyle asked Dodington, 'where's my credit, where's my influence or what business have I here?' A quiet interregnum, where his fellow lords justices Boulter and Wyndham greeted him as an equal and where his patronage recommendations were largely successful, may have answered this question more favourably than Boyle had expected in the spring of 1734.

THE ELEMENTS OF AN ASCENDANCY

There were three key elements to the successful undertaker: effective management of his electoral interest; smooth relationships with various viceroys; and

---

35 *HMC Egmont Mss.*, ii, p. 19; Dorset to Dodington, 5 Jan. 1734, Dodington to Dorset, 31 Jan. 1734, both in *HMC Stopford-Sackville Mss.*, i, pp. 149 & 152; Newcastle to Dorset, 5 Feb. 1734 (PRO S.P.63/397/45).   36 Dorset to Newcastle, 22 Feb. 1734 (PRO S.P.63/ 397/54).

peaceful sessions of parliament. If an undertaker could not ensure the first then the very basis of his power was rapidly eroded, as the decline of the Conolly connection after his death meant that the Gore/Coghill years could not survive beyond the former's demise. Boyle's beginning with Dorset showed that he had to revert to a position where, as Coghill put it, 'the servants make a sorry figure in all the divisions for they are almost left to stand by themselves'.[37] However, the Brodricks' experience had shown that there was more to be gained by cooperation rather than confrontation: opposition was no way to remain a successful undertaker as Boyle was to show even after the Money Bill crisis of 1753–4. Thus he spent the two decades between his election and that crisis ensuring both the success of the government finances in parliament and giving the Commons some latitude in challenging the Castle, but within strict limits. The barracks, military expenditure, coinage and the woollens trade were all allowed to come under investigation but this was no free hand for patriotism. Boyle's relationship with parliament was as much defined by outlawing opposition for its own sake as by encouraging a measure of autonomy between the executive and the legislature.

The maintenance of electoral support was absolutely crucial. Boyle's interest in the Commons was based on marriage into the Burlington Boyle family in 1726, which allowed him as head agent to 'look upon as his own' six boroughs in counties Cork and Waterford. Added to that was his own personal borough of Castlemartyr (to which he added one of the Burlington boroughs of Clonakilty) and also the direction of the Brodrick interests in Midleton and a half interest in Charleville. The Shannon papers show how closely he attended to the details of the corporation affairs in all of them. Such close scrutiny made him the dominant patron in Cork (he and his son became successive county MPs between 1715 and 1764) and gave him some say in electoral matters in the surrounding county seats of Limerick, Tipperary and Kerry. The greatest threat to this power was the marriage of one of the 3rd earl of Burlington's daughters to Lord Hartington in 1748, which had been preceded by the Ponsonby/Cavendish marriage alliances of 1739 and 1743. As Lord Burlington's heir had seemed likely to be his sister, Boyle's wife, the Cavendish marriage quickly put paid to any plans to pass on this electoral interest.

All that, however, was in the future. In the 1740s the immediate danger was the Ponsonby attempts to gain any electoral advantage in Cork and Waterford that they could. The purchase of an estate at Inchiquin in 1738 and the *pater familias*, Lord Bessborough's, desire to have a hand in the disposal of the Burlington seats all threatened to disturb the political calm as pamphleteers recognised in 1752. The Ponsonbys were very keen to build their own electoral interest by a combination of marriage, land purchases and control of revenue patronage. They, too, had to keep a close eye on their tenuous interests and had to revert, in

---

37 Coghill to Southwell, 20 Nov. 1733, quoted in McNally, *Parties*, p. 145.

1748, to legislation to secure control of the borough of Newtown[ards].³⁸ Other borough patrons, like the Gores in north-west Ulster and Lord Kildare, also kept a close watch on their electoral interests ensuring their influence in parliament. This meant that Boyle was pre-eminent among other patrons, something which Lord Chesterfield quickly came to understand in September 1745:

> For though here are no parties of Whigs and Tories, no formed opposition, yet every connection, nay almost every family, expects to govern, or means to distress if they cannot govern, the Lord Lieutenant. Anything proposed by one is for that reason opposed by twenty.³⁹

The maintaining of one's electoral strength was, therefore, the key to a share of political power in the Irish parliament.⁴⁰

As shown above Boyle's relationship with the duke of Dorset did not have an easy start. What remained consistent in this undertaker's attitude was his belief that he had set out based on the 'country', not the government interest. This did not meant that Boyle opposed the government but he did keep his independence. What was important for the reputation of the lord lieutenant was how easily he was able to deliver the government's needs, namely enough money to pay for the civil and military establishments. In this the four men between 1733 and 1750 (Dorset, Devonshire, Chesterfield and Harrington) all succeeded as government income and expenditure rose slowly in 1735–1750.⁴¹ As an indice of Boyle's effectiveness in the service of the Castle there can be no stronger one than the fact that there was no serious threat to any money bill in nearly two decades. As his nephew put it eight years after Boyle's election:

> ... since you have been in the chair, you have not been foiled in anything you made a point of, nor has there been a division about the public accounts.⁴²

Given the crises that had punctuated Conolly's years of service (especially that over the position of the Irish House of Lords in 1719–20 and Wood's Halfpence in 1724–6) this record was certainly one that supported Walpole and the Pelhams in their views of leaving viceroys largely to their own devices.⁴³

---

38 A.P.W. Malcomson, 'The Newtown Act: Revision and Reconstruction', *IHS*, xviii (1973), pp. 313–44. 39 Chesterfield to Newcastle, 12 Sept. 1745, in *Chesterfield Correspondence*, iii, p. 665. 40 The information in the previous two paragraphs owes much to the work of A.P.W. Malcomson, formerly deputy keeper of PRONI. See especially the skilful analysis in [A.P.W. Malcomson], 'Introduction: Part Three', in E. Hewitt (ed.), *Lord Shannon's Letters to his Son* (Belfast, 1982), pp. xxiii–lxxix. 41 NLI Ms.694, 'Some observations on the taxes paid by Ireland to support the government', [*c.*1730]; PRONI D2707/A1/12/3, 'Observations on the Irish economy', [*c.*1747–8]. 42 Boyle to Boyle, 16 June 1741 (PRONI D/2707/A1/4/16). 43 For this period see the differing views in Hayton, 'Walpole', *passim*; F.G. James, *Ireland in the Empire, 1688–1770* (Cambridge, Mass., 1973, hereafter James, *Empire*), chapter vii.

Money bills were an important part of building trust between undertaker and viceroy but so were the personal relationships. The quality of such relationships are difficult to assess, though it is probably true to say that Boyle commanded respect rather than gained friendships. Dorset, until his leaving office in 1737, established a lavish Castle on his visits but showed little interest in doing likewise for an active viceroyalty. He was quite popular in Dublin and it appears that he and Boyle treated one another with a wary respect.[44] Dorset's successor, the duke of Devonshire, was another successful courtier in London, a confidante of Walpole's and George II's. He proved less active in patronage disposal than Dorset had and proved anxious not to alienate Boyle, allowing him a hand in filling commissions for a new foot regiment in 1739.[45]

One potential problem between the two men, though it never emerged as an obstacle to government business, was Devonshire's favouring of the Ponsonbys. The head of that family, Lord Bessborough, gained Boyle's place on the Revenue Board in 1737 in what may well have been a concession by the latter to avoid strife. Nor does Boyle seem to have taken offence at Devonshire marrying his two daughters to Bessborough's sons, which may reflect both an absence of rancour in the viceroy/undertaker relationship and also the Speaker's easy attitude to the need for Anglo-Irish political connections. The importance of such marriages, revenue places and connections lay in the future when Bessborough and George Stone sought to utilise them. It is a sign of the largely easy relationship between Boyle and Devonshire that such things seem to meant little in the early 1740s.[46]

The appointment as viceroy of the active earl of Chesterfield in January 1745 seemed to herald different days ahead for relationships with Boyle and other Irish politicians. Historians have looked at this viceroyalty as quite different from most others in George II's reign because of the desire for independence on the part of Chesterfield.[47] It is true that great things were hoped for from the new viceroy, addressed as 'the land's desire' by an Irish pamphleteer because of his Patriot politics in England.[48] However, apart from altering the patent for appointing persons to the Barracks Board, Chesterfield did little to alter the government of Ireland and nothing to disturb any relationship with Boyle. There is little to suggest tension between the undertaker and viceroy, especially given the background of war, Jacobite rebellion and Chesterfield's support of various forms of patriotic endeavour in Ireland. Indeed in his patronage, Chesterfield acceded to many of the Speaker's requests, including to the clerkship of the Commons, Dr Edward Barry

44 For one source which suggests Dorset was a lavish and popular viceroy in the 1730s, if not the 1750s, see Dublin Public Library, Gilbert Ms. 199; [Sir Richard Cox], *Dedication on a dedication to his Grace, the Duke of Dorset* (Dublin, 1753). 45 Devonshire to [Newcastle], 29 Sept. 1739 (PRO S.P.63/402/25). 46 See PRONI, Chatsworth papers, T/3158/22–300. 47 For examples of this see Burns, *Irish Parliamentary Politics*, ii, chapter 3 and James, *Empire*, pp. 187–8. 48 *Ierne's Answer to Albion* (RIA Haliday tracts, Dublin, 1745); *An Account of Ireland, the Mad Woman* (Dublin, 1745).

as Physician General and Lord Ikerrin as a privy councillor.[49] There was to be no revolution in the Castle I 1745–6, nor any real attempt to risk the relationship with Boyle for any Irish version of 'broad-bottom' administration.

Chesterfield's successor, the earl of Harrington, was bedevilled by George II's loathing of him and his own impetuous nature. The combination of these meant that he was not to be the viceroy to threaten a relationship with his leading under-taker. Indeed he was later accused of conceding more than was suitable to Boyle, though there is little evidence of more than the usual patronage going to the Speaker. What Thomas Waite did bemoan was:

> There is a disposition to ask and to recommend everything that is vacant, and if my Lord Lieutenant gives way to it, he may never have it in his power to serve any one of his dependents.[50]

What Harrington did do was clash with the other emergent undertaker, Bess-borough over an important revenue appointment in 1750. Boyle did not request that Sir Richard Cox be made collector of Cork in the place of the man whose promotion had irked him so much in 1734. However, the Ponsonby connection on the Revenue Board (led by William Bristow and Sir Henry Cavendish) opposed the choice of Cox and Harrington furiously had to appeal to Henry Pelham for his intervention. This had less to do with Boyle's relationship with the viceroy and more to do with the Ponsonby control of revenue patronage and their wish to use this to assist electoral interests in Cork city.[51] In the event Harrington was success-ful but at the expense of an increasing perception in London of his weakness after difficulties over the money bill and the embarrassing exiling of Charles Lucas. The Ponsonbys' desire to assert their claim to Boyle's succession was, by the late 1740s, beginning to threaten the undertaker's relationship with the Castle. Herein lay one of the causes of the crisis of the 1750s: the disappearance of the main channel of communication between legislature and executive.

When an undertaker like Boyle undertook to communicate the wishes and needs of Dublin Castle to the Irish parliament he had to be at his most skilful. There was a balancing act to be performed between committing all his interest for the government in all their demands and opposing these and threatening any rela-tionship with the viceroy. It is apparent that Boyle consulted with his 'Munster squadron' in Cork each summer before a parliamentary session. He also prided

---

49 For these see Boyle to Liddell, 25 May 1745, Chesterfield to Wilmot, 30 Mar. 1745 (PRONI T3019/637, 618); Chesterfield to Newcastle, 8 Mar. 1746, in *Chesterfield Correspondence*, iii, pp. 742–4. **50** Waite to Weston, 4 Mar. 1749 (PRONI T3019/1284). **51** Harrington to Pelham, 10 Apr., Weston to Wilmot, 10 Apr., Waite to Weston, 5, 24 May 1750 (PRONI T3019/1537, 1539, 1568, 1583); Cavendish to Hartington, 7 Apr. 1750 (PRONI T3158/392); Bristow to Pelham, 17 May 1750 (PRONI Pelham papers, T/2863/1/36).

himself on constantly remaining in touch with this squadron and also trusted fellow MPs, like Thomas Carter and Anthony Malone, who were crucial to Commons proceedings. On occasions, such as the proposed augmentation of the Irish army at the end of the War of the Spanish Succession (1748), Boyle refused to commit himself until he had had time to consult his followers.[52] This behaviour, added to his support for the requests for patronage on behalf of the likes of the Gores, ensured that the Speaker's ascendancy would not be undermined claims of complacency from the 'country' gentlemen.

Avoiding placing demands on parliament was not the only way of avoiding problems with the Commons. An undertaker, like Boyle, also had to be forward in supporting popular legislation such as penal laws or bills that protected and encouraged Irish trade. With regard to penal legislation Boyle had little problem as his defence of the established church was reflexive. With regard to the Dissenters his refusal to undertake for the repeal of the Test Act established credentials that were bitterly remembered two decades later.[53] Anti-catholicism came even easier, given both his Munster background (then the centre of 'red-hot' ultras) and his family traditions of sacrifice in the protestant cause, including the death of his father in Flanders in 1693. The 1730s and 1740s saw repeated 'scares' which encouraged such attitudes. In 1732–3 there was an ongoing 'crisis' in Cork, Clare and Kerry over the presence of Irish officers in the French army, who were enlisting for that service under the cover of desertion. Thomas Tickell identified this as a 'great grievance' to local protestant gentry, a similar phrase to one the one used in the following year when the lords justices warned ministers against intervening in the case of a catholic peer, Lord Gormanstown, accused of wearing a sword in contravention of the penal laws.[54]

Right from the start of the war with Spain in 1738 there were invasion scares and Jacobite rumours in Ireland. The 1739–40 session saw Commons demands for new arms for the militia, though its effectiveness was doubted by the general officers. Devonshire reluctantly acceded to these demands, disliking further tampering with the penal laws, and during the interregnum the lords justices kept up the pressure.[55] When France declared war on Britain in 1744, there were immediate concerns about Ireland's ability to defend herself if the expected invasion fleet from Brest arrived. Part of such worries was the attitude of the catholic majority. Chesterfield was confident about their quietism if not loyalty, something which the lack of any response to the rebellion in Scotland bears out. However, there was

52 Boyle to Harrington, 19 Jan. 1749 (PRONI T/3019/1244). 53 For this see *Remarks on a late pamphlet entitled 'Advice to the Patriot Club of Antrim'* (Dublin 1756), p. 9. 54 Tickell to Cary, 25 Nov. 1732; Lords Justices, 13, 20 July 1733 (PRONI T/3019/107, 139–40). 55 Devonshire to Newcastle, 12 Oct. 1739 (PRO S.P.63/402/52); Devonshire to Legge, 14 Mar.; Printed address of the House of Commons to Devonshire [15 Mar]; Lords Justices to Devonshire, 22 Oct. 1740 (PRONI T/3019/237–8, 256).

undoubtedly Jacobite enthusiasm and some in the Castle were angry at government complacency in 1745.[56] The Commons, under the leadership of Boyle, was busy passing fresh legislation to prevent catholics from travelling abroad and to stop denominational intermarriage. Outside parliament the 1740s saw great commemorative activity on the usual calendar dates to mark the Boyne, Aughrim and the 1641 rebellion but also other demonstrations to mark the victory at Culloden and the birthday of the new 'deliverer', the duke of Cumberland. The militia were to the fore in all popular expressions of loyalty so much so that Chesterfield worried about 'improper ebulliations of zeal in well-meaning people.'[57] It is hard to believe that these 'well-meaning people' did not include Henry Boyle, though this would have done him little harm in the eyes of most MPs.

When Boyle told Walter Cary in December 1733 that he had 'set up on the foot of the country party' he did not mean that he would pursue opposition politics for their own sake. If the career of his late patron, Alan Brodrick, told Boyle anything it was that opposition to government, whether opportunistic or principled, had to have a specific target and timescale.[58] After the Money Bill crisis Boyle, now the leader of a sustained Patriot opposition, mused:

> Violent opposition to be avoided where not absolutely necessary. Temper and moderation on all accounts more advantageous, and give less room for misrepresentations and will add force to a representation to His Majesty.[59]

This sense of avoiding opposition politics, especially those which brought him to the notice of George II, marked his period as Speaker and chief undertaker. An example of this can be found in the 1739–40 session when Devonshire sought to tighten up enforcement of the regulations preventing the 'running' of woollens to France. Though war did bring a reflexive anti-catholicism in the Irish Commons there was also resistance to further attempts to restrict the woollens trade. The smuggling of wool was especially prevalent in Munster, making Boyle even less likely to undertake such legislation. At a Castle meeting in December 1739, Boyle was supposedly in agreement with the decision that a Commons committee be the one to draw up a bill but this motion was not moved. When the committee met

---

56 Chesterfield to Newcastle, 4 Oct. 1745, in *Chesterfield Correspondence*, iii, p. 678; 'Humble Address of the Roman Catholics of Ireland', Oct. 1739 (PRO S.P.63/402/26); Bishop Ryder to Ryder, 17, 19 Dec. 1745 (PRONI Harrowby papers, T/3228/1/18–9).   57 *CJI*, vii, pp. 101, 112, 116, 125, 193, 475, 483, 690, 694 & 823; *Dublin Courant*, 3 July 1744, 8 Apr., 4 July 1747; Chesterfield to Newcastle, 26 Oct. 1745, in *Chesterfield Correspondence*, iii, p. 691.   58 There is no full biography of Brodrick but see McNally, *Parties*, passim and D.W. Hayton, 'British Whig Ministers and the Irish Question 1714–1725', in S. Taylor, J. Connors & C. Jones (eds), *Hanoverian Britain and Empire: Essays in Memory of Philip Lawson* (Woodbridge, 1998), pp. 37–64.   59 'Notes by Henry Boyle on the attitudes to the new administration after the death of Henry Pelham' [mid-1754] (PRONI D/2707/A1/12/10).

after Christmas the results were far from what the Castle wanted. Boyle's friends opposed adjournments and added amendments to the scheme, 'in order to throw it out' and eventually the scheme was dropped. A bill was passed but one that was toothless, causing John Potter to lament that 'the conduct of some who ought to assist and said they would assist is monstrous.'[60] This lack of cooperation, like that in 1733 over Test repeal, was not designed to oppose the government but showed the limits of Boyle's willingness to undertake legislation.[61]

On occasions Boyle had to be wary of other sources of Patriot opposition. The main sources in the early period of his Speakership are usually overlooked by historians anxious to move on to the period of Charles Lucas. However, Thomas Carter, Anthony Malone and Sir Richard Cox were all formidable Commons orators and all three quickly became skilled in financial matters and parliamentary procedures. Any of this would have made them potential thorns in Boyle's side but only in the latter case did the Speaker need to defend himself. All three MPs were keen to get into government for profit or for power and sometimes both as privy councillors.

Carter, the oldest of the three, quickly assented to Boyle's leadership of the Commons and seems to have operated as a trusted, though sometimes independent, lieutenant. This loyalty to Boyle included Carter endangering his own relationship with Dorset in 1733 after the viceroy had assisted him becoming master of the rolls (worth £800 per annum) and a privy councillor the previous year.[62] Boyle rarely found fault with Carter and protected him in 1741 as the architect of an expensive loan of £125,000. Again, in 1749, Boyle stood alongside Carter, though with some doubts, after the latter had clashed violently with Stone over a patronage request. Throughout his ascendancy Boyle was careful never to make an enemy of this very prickly and proud man.[63]

Anthony Malone had to be handled even more carefully as he was not a colleague from the Brodrick days but a newcomer to parliament in 1727 and associated by marriage to the Gore family. He established credentials as 'our chief Patriot' by 1737, during that session's opposition to the reduction of coinage and the extent of military expenditure. Boyle did not favour Malone's appointment as prime serjeant in 1740, where support for this came from Lord Bessborough, but he accepted it and, by the next parliamentary session, Malone and Carter were the principal com-

60 Potter to Legge, 16, 18, 23 Dec. 1739, 6, 12 Feb., 6 Mar. 1740; Devonshire to Legge, 14 Feb. 1740 (PRONI T/3019/210, 212–13, 223, 226, 236,231).   61 It should be noted that the Irish economy was in dire straits in the early 1740s with war and famine decimating both trade and the population, and that this was something that Boyle was acutely aware of. See his 'Observations on the Irish economy' [c.1747–8] (PRONI D/2707/A1/12/3).   62 Coghill to Southwell, 8 Mar. 1733 (BL Add. Mss.21123, f.24); *HMC Egmont Mss.*, i, p. 450.   63 Devonshire to Newcastle, 11, 24 Nov. 1741 (PRO S.P.63/404/224, 239); Waite to Weston, 26 Jan. 1749 (PRONI T/3019/1246); Dobbs to Ward, 31 Oct. 1756 (PRONI Castleward papers, D/2092/1/8, f.58).

mittee chairmen in the Commons.[64] Cox proved more difficult to construct a working alliance with though he, like Carter and Boyle, came from a Brodrician background. Malone was always seen 'by his abilities the most considerable man here, and the most useful to government; at the same time ... the most independent and least importunate for favours', while Cox was more like Carter, quick to abuse and slow to forgive.[65] Cox, like Malone, earned his Patriot spurs in the 1737–8 session over the government proclamation lowering the value of foreign gold coins. This had resulted in Swift taking up the standard of Irish coinage in Dublin, while Cox seems to have been at the back of a Cork petition against the proclamation which asked the Commons to 'get their money back upon the old footing'.[66]

Boulter and other officials were angry at such talk and their moods were hardly improved when Boyle did not reject the Cork petition when it was brought before MPs. The Speaker negotiated a path between crushing the Patriots, thereby alienating voters in Cork city, and giving full support to the government. Thus he postponed further discussion of the petition and, when Cox and Malone proposed a resolution alleging that military payments or contingencies were responsible for the national debt, this was allowed to pass but the money bill's passage was not disturbed. Sackville wrote that Boyle 'behaved with great indifference and I believe was pleased with what was done.' [67]

However, the Speaker was more embarrassed than pleased and it may have been this that caused him to complain to Bishop Clayton of Cork about Cox and Malone. In any case the bishop was soon saying in Cork that Cox was to have been used by Boyle to betray the Patriots, specifically over the coinage issue. This sparked a severe row, reflected in an intemperate three-way correspondence which ended with Cox dismissing any chance of rapprochment with the Speaker and writing that 'the public shall be my *dernier* resort'.[68] Cox took much longer than Malone to come under the influence of Boyle's connection – this may not have happened until the 1750s and arguably even then only in a partial way. Though he did not publish a manuscript, entitled 'Irish Politics Displayed' after the 1737–8 session he dismissed the Irish parliament as a 'shadow of a senate' in 1741 and found little worth relating beyond the 'jobbery' over the militia arms while the economy was ignored despite the 1740–1 famine. Little wonder that this self-con-

---

64 Devonshire to Newcastle, 21 Dec. 1737 (BL Add. Mss.32690, f.455); Boyle to Devonshire, 7 Oct. 1742, Bessborough to Devonshire, 2 Feb. 1743 (PRONI T/3158/232, 235). 65 Stone to Weston, 19 Mar. 1747 (PRONI T/3019/6455/85); Sackville to Dorset, 27 Oct. 1737, in *HMC Stopford-Sackville*, i, p. 167. 66 Sackville to Dorset, 6 Oct. 1737, in ibid., i, p. 166; *Dublin Evening Post*, 16 Apr. 1733; *Dublin Daily Advertiser*, 21 Mar., 15 Nov. 1737. 67 Boulter to Newcastle, 29 Sep. 1737, (PRO S.P.63/400/8); Sackville to Dorset, 27 Oct. 1737, in HMC Stopford-Sackville, I, p. 167. 68 Cox to [Boyle], 3 Apr., Cox to Clayton, 3 Apr., Boyle to Cox, 11 Apr., Clayton to Cox, 7 Apr., Cox to Boyle, 20 Apr., Cox to Clayton, 20 Apr., Boyle to Cox, 2 May, Cox to Boyle [May] 1738 (RIA Ms.12/W/35).

fessed Patriot who acted 'on general utility and moderation, not on self-interest and angry resentment' remained a potential opponent of Boyle's for a few years longer.[69]

Indeed it was the 'Lucas Affair' which brought Cox into the mainstream and gave Dublin politics a Patriot voice that it had lacked since the decline of Swift. As the 1750s were to show, the coalescence of Dublin opinion, especially among the lower corporation and the crowd, with Patriot politics caused more problems for an undertaker than a handful of opposition MPs could on their own. The efforts of Lucas and others to reform Dublin Corporation, which climaxed in the 1748–9 by-election campaign in the city, has been well-documented by historians recently as has its importance to the development of Patriot politics in Ireland.[70] What has had perhaps less attention is the way in which Cox, thoughout the 1740s the most vocal exponent of patriotism, both economic and political, in the Irish Commons, turned on Lucas. What was at stake was not only the attitude of Irish protestants towards catholics but also, perhaps more importantly, Lucas' claim that Ireland was a dependent colony and treated as such by Britain.[71] This was a step too far for Cox who accused Lucas of disloyalty to the Hanoverians and of dangerous constitutional meddling:

> How self-sufficent, how ignorant, how mischievous in his nature must that incendiary be, who forces us at this time, to enter upon a subject that can bring no good to either kingdom, merely to raise up a popularity, among unthinking people.

Cox mentioned William Molyneux's work only to warn that it had damaged Irish interests in 1698, though it, at least, had been founded upon reason not popularity. The mantle of patriotism was to be placed on those who act in deeds for the utility and good of their country and not to be placed on the shoulders of constitutional speculators.[72]

In the longer term Cox's brand of 'country' patriotism was replaced by Lucas' more radical one but the 1749–50 session showed which one Boyle and the majority of MPs gave their allegiance to. Lucas compounded his alienation of Cox and the lords justices by insulting the viceroy, Harrington, after the latter had had him

69 [Cox], *Irish Politics Displayed* [c.1738] (PRONI Armagh Diocesan papers, D.I.O.4/5/8); Cox to Southwell, 3 Sept. 1741, 6 May 1742 (RIA Ms.12/W/35).   **70** See J.R. Hill, *From Patriots to Unionists: Dublin Civic Politics and Irish Protestant Patriotism, 1660–1840* (Oxford, 1997), chapter 3, passim.   **71** On the question of Lucas and Catholics see S. Murphy, 'Charles Lucas: A forgotten Patriot?', *History Ireland*, ii (1994), pp. 26–9; E. Magennis, 'A 'Beleaguered Protestant'?: Walter Harris and the writing of *Fiction Unmasked*', *ECI*, 13 (1998), pp. 86–111.   **72** [Cox], *The Cork Surgeon's Antidote, Number 2* (Dublin, 1749), p. 5. For these themes developed see *Cork Surgeon's Antidote, Numbers 3–4* (Dublin, 1749) and *The Tickler*, 19 July, 20 Oct. 1749.

removed from a levee.[73] The Commons, under the direction of Boyle and, especially, Cox, declared Lucas a libeller, an 'enemy to the country' and ordered his arrest for breach of Commons' privileges. The apothecary wisely fled into exile and attention turned to his printer, James Esdall. In seeking to eradicate all 'Lucasian' elements the victorious radical in the Dublin by-election, La Touche, was unseated in a show of 'despotic power' which disgusted one independent MP.[74]

Such strong action against Lucas and his followers did not mean that Harrington was protected against the more polite forms of 'country' patriotism. The end of the war and a trade surplus left the Irish treasury in the position where the Lords justices had suggested not asking for new taxes in the 1749–50 session. Harrington agreed to only ask for the usual supplies and, on 17 November Weston wrote that the surplus would be used to pay off some of the national debt. He knew that there would be no problem in London as to this intention but that the manner of it might be controversial. What had happened was that the viceroy had conceded the principle of the 'prior consent' of the king being needed to dispose of Irish revenue for a phrase which said that the money was spent 'agreeably to your Majesty's most gracious intentions.'[76] The Castle officials were undoubtedly aware that they had been forced into a corner by a revival of the Commons' claim to deal with Irish finances. With Harrington a weak viceroy and MPs anxious to defend their privileges, against either Lucas or government, the ministry in London conceded the matter after further pleas from Dublin.[77]

By the end of the 1749 session Boyle's ascendancy looked, on the surface, to be more secure than ever. None of the Commons orators, Carter, Malone or Cox, were opposing him while his relationship with Harrington had been a profitable one in terms of patronage. However, there was a growing challenge to his position. By 1750, Boyle was sixty-six years of age, older than Conolly had been at his death. Though he was showing no signs of illness the question of his retirement was surely in the air by this date. The battle for the succession was in reality between Sir Arthur Gore and John Ponsonby as Boyle's eldest son, Richard, had only entered parliament in 1749. The Ponsonbys, with control of the revenue service and their ambitions to increase electoral strength believed themselves to have the advantage, especially after the marriage of a Cavendish brother-in-law to the heiress to the Burlington electoral interest in 1748. All of this seemed to point to the need for Boyle to gracefully retire from the speakership after nearly three decades.

73 Waite to Wilmot, 17 June 1747 (PRONI T/3019/1346); Harrington to Bedford, 12 Oct. 1749 (PRO S.P.63/411/49–54). 74 Weston to Wilmot, 17 Oct., Cope to Wilmot, 21 Oct. 1749 (PRONI T/3019/1418, 1421); Pakenham to Fitzgerald, 10 Feb. 1749 (PRONI Fitzgerald papers, T/3075/1/11). 75 Stone to Harrington, 1 Aug. 1749 (PRONI T/30191393). 76 Weston to Wilmot, 17 Nov. 1749 (PRONI T/3019/1437). 77 Harrington to Bedford, 17 Nov. 1749 (PRO S.P.63/411/214); Weston to Wilmot, 2 Dec. 1749 (PRONI T/3019/1444).

A further challenge and perhaps the one which destabilised the situation into crisis in the early 1750s came from the ambitions of George Stone. He had a rapid rise through the ranks of the Irish church after his arrival as Dorset's chaplain in 1730. By 1747, when he was made archbishop of Armagh, Stone had collected two deaneries (Ferns and Derry) and three bishoprics (Ferns, Kildare and Derry) along the way. This made him the only candidate within Ireland and with Newcastle and Dorset supporting his candidature in London, Stone was always favourite to become primate. Even before his appointment he made clear his ambitions in an analysis of Irish politics which described how Chesterfield's vice-royalty had left government in high standing but 'tame indeed'. The reason for this was Boyle, who 'of course on some occasions [is] driven to make requests for favours which cannot and ought not to be granted'. Due to his service and influence but also his rivalry with Lord Chancellor Newport, Boyle 'should be principally, not solely considered'. The heir-apparent to the primacy was making an offer to assist Harrington as the neutral Castle voice, a kind of reincarnated Archbishop Boulter.[78] Within a month of appointment Stone made it clear that he would offer advice to the viceroy not only on the existing political scene but also on how to alter it. In the case in question there was an opportunity to use patronage powers to impose 'an equilibrium on the other's [Boyle's] pretensions' for the governorship of Galway.[79]

Edmund Sexton Pery claimed later that Stone had been active in the late 1740s courting younger, independent MPs, like himself, with the promise of reform (and personal gain). The means, of course, were the curbing of Boyle's influence.[80] This was hidden behind the mask of 'courtesy, affability and [a] hospitable table', according to Pery and the private correspondence does bear out that Stone was criticising and trying out his strength against Boyle and his 'soporific cabal'. For instance, chief secretary Weston, was advised from where he should take his Commons seat to avoid even indirect obligations to Boyle, who was 'able to be useful or troublesome to his superiors.'[81] Yet Stone's ambitions were dented by the unwillingness of Harrington to tamper greatly with the system of management that Boyle had offered for the previous fourteen years. With the exception of the clash with Carter, when he refused to recommend a patronage request, Stone avoided conflict in Dublin.

However, his actions with regard to patronage, in the spring of 1749, hinted at the primate's real ambitions. Boyle was furious at how easily Stone assumed the right to speak for Harrington over an unsuccessful commission request for the

78 Stone to Wilmot, 19 Dec. 1746 (PRONI T/3019/823). 79 Stone to Weston, 7 Mar. 1747 (PRONI T/3019/840). 80 [E.S. Pery], *A Letter to the Duke of Bedford* (Dublin, 1757), pp. 4–6. 81 Weston to Stone, pre-31 Mar., Stone to Weston, 2 Apr. 1747 (PRONI T/3019/850, 853).

Speaker's son. He was quick to ask the viceroy how he could serve government if he stood 'suspected by them [his friends] of being at the disposal of any other who shall take upon him to answer for me.' Harrington was quick to placate Boyle and assure him that Stone had only praise for him and the viceroy also applauded the primate on a quiet and somewhat humble return to Dublin that summer.[82] But these tensions did not disappear. When Harrington was replaced by Dorset in late 1750 they soared. Thus, it was little wonder that Stone's ambitions played such a key role in the crisis of the 1750s and the simultaneous ending of Boyle's ascendancy.

---

82 Boyle to Harrington, 7 May, Harrington to Boyle, 1 June, Stone to Harrington, 1 Aug., Harrington to Stone, 15 Aug. 1749 (PRONI T/3019/1331, 1337, 1393, 1395).

2

The structures and needs of government, *c*.1745–*c*.1770

The eighteenth-century Irish administration has long suffered from a harsh historical assessment. In the judgements of Lecky and later historians, Dublin Castle was a byword for corrupt officials, a repressive army and ineficency in all departments. These elements of government were seen by nineteenth-century nationalist historians as being in sharp contrast to the virtues of 'Grattan's Parliament' – a form of Home Rule. More recent surveys of Irish government generally refer to 'restricted powers' and, especially before the beginning of resident viceroys in 1767, ineffective links between Dublin officials and British ministers.[1] This chapter will not overturn these modern assessments of the Castle administration, but it aims to reveal the actual structures of the Irish government and how these met the needs of both the elite within that country and also, as importantly, those of ministers in London.

In the eighteenth century the restriction of powers, referred to by Professor Johnston, had much to do with the definition of what government was expected to do.[2] The Castle was concerned to dispense justice, to collect revenues, to regulate the economy, to defend Ireland from external (and internal) enemies, to pay officials and to protect the established religion. Some of these areas have been well covered in other places with, possibly, the exception of the implementation of the penal laws against Catholics and, therefore, need not detain us here.[3] The concerns of the metropolitan power were, to put it simply, men and money and it is these which provide the focus of this chapter. These needs were usually uncontentious, especially as ministers and the Irish elite avoided constitutional innovation (certainly between the Declaratory Act of 1720 and the 'revolution' of 1782). The

---

1 For examples of this see R.F. Foster, *Modern Ireland, 1600–1972* (London, 1988), p. 226; E.M. Johnston, *Great Britain and Ireland, 1760–1800* (Edinburgh, 1963, hereafter Johnston, *Ireland*), p. 18. 2 P.J. Jupp, 'The landed elite and political authority in Britain, c.1760–1850', *Journal of British Studies*, 29 (1990), pp. 53–79. 3 N. Garnham, *The courts, crime and the criminal law in Ireland, 1692–1760* (Dublin, 1996); T.C. Barnard, 'The government and Irish Dissent, 1704–1780', in K. Herlihy (ed.), *The Politics of Irish Dissent* (Dublin, 1997), pp. 9–27; P. McNally, 'Patronage and politics in Ireland, 1714–1727' (PhD thesis, Queen's University, Belfast, 1993).

metropolitan demands were also largely static, even in wartime, until the end of the Seven Years War. The change of the later 1760s was driven by new imperial needs, especially the desire of Britain to station a large army in North America. This resulted in the drive for an army augmentation in 1767–9. That decision ended an era, not only in Irish politics, but also led to fundamental changes in the Castle administration which shaped the government until the Act of Union.

THE STRUCTURES OF THE CASTLE ADMINISTRATION

The administration in Dublin Castle was quite unlike anything that would be recognised as modern bureaucracy. There were no legions of civil servants, little in the way of training, or promotion on the basis of seniority (or merit) and pay scales (and the methods of remuneration itself) were certainly informal. The Secretary's Office is the place to start and is crucial to any survey of the executive. It was headed by the chief cecretary, who was supported by a small number of undersecretaries and clerks. His effectiveness was limited more by his usual disinterest in all but political and patronage business than by non-residence in Ireland. The chief secretary between 1756 and 1760, Richard Rigby, was very frank about his dislike of any business except political management, while Henry Legge, one of Devonshire's officials in the 1730s, did not even bother to go to Dublin to oversee a parliamentary session.[4]

As there were few exceptions to this prioritising of duties by successive chief secretaries, the undersecretaries were the indispensable administrators. The priorities of the likes of Legge, Rigby or W.G. Hamilton in the early 1760s were not an innovation and, therefore, from the 1690s, there had been two undersecretaries and at least two clerks in the Castle secretariat.[5] By 1739 the increase in business and fees meant that four clerks were employed and this number remained unchanged until 1777. In the latter year, the secretariat's structures were divided into military and civil departments, with an undersecretary responsible for each. Until then the two undersecretaries had been distinguished by their appointment by nominal patrons, either the lords justices or the Ulster secretary.[6] The secretary to the lord justices was the more important post, and was held between 1740 and 1747 by John Potter and then for over thirty years by Thomas Waite.[7] Waite came highly recommended and proved to be an excellent choice. He quickly

4 PRONI Wilmot papers T3019/3353, Rigby to Wilmot, 28 Mar. 1758; J.L.T. Hughes, 'The chief secretaries, 1561–1921', *IHS*, viii (1952–3). 5 J.C. Sainty, 'The secretariat of the chief governors of Ireland, 1690–1800', *Proceedings of the Royal Irish Academy*, series C, lxxvii (1977, hereafter Sainty, 'Secretariat'), pp. 1–33, p. 26. 6 PRONI T3019/2533, Waite to Wilmot, 18 Mar. 1755. 7 One historian has noted how a 'striking new efficiency' entered the Castle in the 1740s: Burns, *Irish parliamentary politics*, ii, p. 95.

gained a clear grasp of detail and protocol, and was described, in 1772, as 'one of the few experts on administrative precedents, political personalities and patronage in the government of Ireland.'[8] The secretary to the Ulster secretary was junior to the other undersecretary and responsible mainly for the collection of fees and the accounting for these.[9]

One important element in the relative efficiency of the Castle secretariat in the middle decades of the century was the rapport established between Waite and the Resident Secretary (in London), Sir Robert Wilmot. The latter had been appointed in 1740 and his role was to act as a clearing house for all Irish business sent to the viceroy, when resident in England, and between the viceroy and ministers, when the former was in Ireland. This gave him extensive access to different viceroys, so much so that one claimant, in the early 1750s, appealed to Wilmot as the best channel of recommendation to the duke of Dorset.[10] This influence came from familiarity with Irish business but also access to a wide circle of political contacts in London due to his family connections and his service for successive dukes of Devonshire. Most importantly his continuity in office between 1740 and 1772 and his adeptness for the government business made the non-residence of the chief secretary much less important.

Non-residency of the viceroy is often regarded by historians as a cause of administrative slackness in Ireland prior to 1767. With regard to this, Johnston has commented 'it is not surprising that [administration] always generated a certain amount of friction, but it is surprising that this system worked as well and lasted as long as it did.'[11] It is important to remember that administratively, if not on crucial political decisions, power was delegated to experienced lords justices who were guided by the same Castle officials as the viceroy was, when he was resident. Non-residency did place a great importance on the speed of communications between Ireland and England and there can be no doubt that the passage of business was sometimes delayed. This was usually because of dependence on the postal systems on both sides of the channel and on the post-boats that crossed from Dun Laoighaire to Holyhead or Chester. Barring unforeseen delays, the average time for return post from Dublin to London was ten days and perhaps two more if outside either capital. This length of time by the mid-century was a marked improvement on earlier in the 1700s and was due to the mid-eighteenth century turnpike craze. This was shown, in Ireland, by the road network which spread northwards and westwards from Dublin after the 1730s, while, in England,

8 PRONI T3019/890, Weston to the Lords Justices, 4 June 1747; Johnston, *Ireland*, p. 47. 9 PRONI T3019/600, Lingen to Wilmot, 17 Jan. 1745. 10 Charles Delafaye was desperate to get a favourable decision in a legal battle he had over fees owed by some Dublin merchants and told Wilmot that 'the necessity every Lord Lieutenant must be under of your assistance, especially in his first entrance upon administration, must give you a very free access'; PRONI T3019/1669, Delafaye to Wilmot, 17 Dec, 1750. 11 Johnston, *Ireland*, p. 103.

the 1750s and 1760s saw a rapid expansion in the numbers of turnpike trusts.[12] However, despite this improvement, delays still happened and were usually associated with the sea crossing. In the winter of 1748, storms made the Irish Sea uncrossable for six weeks and meant that instructions concerning a proposed augmentation of the army did not reach Dublin. There, officials pointed out that the delays had allowed opposition to the scheme to arise, which meant the failure of augmentation before it had had a chance.[13]

Residency of the viceroy in Dublin actually increased the need for speedy communications with England. For those six months out of twenty-four, the lord lieutenant was often in need of rapid advice over political management and desired the speedy passage of Irish bills. Prior to the office of resident secretary being created in 1724, successive viceroys used undersecretaries in the Secretary of State's office to act as agents in London. Their job was essentially to deal with the necessary stages Irish bills had to go through under Poyning's Law. While resident secretary, Wilmot never recorded the details of this work, but we know it centred on his lobbying for the success of several Irish government bills and, more generally, his attempts to satisfy the viceroy's desire to have the Dublin parliamentary session closed as quickly as possible.[14] A study of American colonial agents in this period shows that they managed their business through a mixture of establishing contacts and following this up with gifts and bribery.[15] It is unlikely that Wilmot's work was very different and it obviously incurred the same monetary costs. He was paid £1,200 by the Irish parliament at the end of each session for dealing with the bills. Wilmot took £200 for himself and the same amount for the secretary to the English privy council, with the other £800 probably used for the fees and bribes paid to undersecretaries, clerks and doorkeepers.[16] Recognition of Wilmot's skills as an agent came in 1754, when the Irish revenue board appointed him their solicitor in London.[17]

As well as the need for an agent in London to deal with routine business, a viceroy occasionally needed someone to undertake political missions. The necessity of such agents was much greater when a viceroy was permanently resident in Ireland. Therefore, Lord Townshend employed, at different times between 1767 and 1772, his Ulster secretary, Richard Jackson, his chief secretary, Sir George

---

12 L.M. Cullen, *An Economic History of Ireland since 1660* (2nd edn, London, 1986), pp. 87–8; P. Langford, *A Polite and Commercial People: England 1727–83* (Oxford, 1992), p. 391. 13 PRONI T3019/1185, 1229, Waite to Wilmot, 5 Nov., 27 Dec. 1748. 14 For lobbying by Wilmot and earlier officials see A.P.W. Malcomson, 'The Newtown Act of 1748: Revision and reconstruction', *IHS*, xxviii (1973), pp. 313–44; PRONI T3019/3740, Rigby to Wilmot, 6 Mar. 1760; F.G. James, 'The Irish lobby in the early eighteenth century', *EHR*, lxxxi (1966), pp. 543–77. 15 M.G. Kammen, *A Rope of Sand: Colonial Agents, British Politics and the American Revolution* (New York, 1968), pp. 11–15. 16 PRONI T3019/1899, Waite to Wilmot, 21 May 1752. 17 PRONI Chatsworth papers T3158/417, 424, 425, Ponsonby to Hartington, 29 July, Devonshire to Hartington, 21 Aug. 1754, Hartington to Devonshire, 3 Sept. 1754.

Macartney, and, crucially for business, Thomas Allan.[18] However, it would be wrong to see this practice of using agents as an innovation since different viceroys between 1740 and 1767 resorted to these methods. For example, during the Dorset viceroyalty of 1750 to 1755, Robert Maxwell, a Cavan MP, was sent to London on several occasions to advise ministers of developments in Ireland. In the wake of the Money Bill rejection of December 1753, he went to lobby for the dismissal of leading Patriot office-holders.[19] Then, as Lord Hartington sought to resolve the problems left by Dorset, he sent his chief secretary, Henry Conway, to persuade ministers of the need to sacrifice George Stone.[20] The use of political agents and of administrators, like Wilmot, was a well-established practice to avoid the obstacles of separating viceroys from their ministerial colleagues, long before the era of resident viceroys.

The final part of the Castle executive was the one most intimately linked to the viceroy, and commonly called the 'household'. In 1772 Wilmot described this to the new chief secretary, Sir John Blacquiere, as having at least thirty-five officials responsible directly to the lord lieutenant. The household was primarily a political body and used to please both British and Irish claimants, though there were administrative duties attached to the offices. The household officers had to prepare for the viceroy's arrival by overseeing the readying of the Castle apartments and various other tasks, from the provision of horses to the filling of the wine cellar. Some of the household salaries came from viceregal profits, for example on bills sent to the privy council in London, but much of its budget was provided by the equipage money given to each lord lieutenant. In the 1740s and 1750s the equipage provided £2,000 per annum and was expected to deliver little or no profits on the first two years of a viceroyalty. The one-off costs to a viceroy of cloths, plate and furniture for his household always amounted to more than £4,000, but the equipage would bring large profits if a viceroy stayed in office for more than two years. This situation changed after 1767, as viceroys were expected to reside permanently in Dublin and their expenses rose until, by 1782, £20,000 per annum was not enough to cover expenditures.[21]

REMUNERATION

The question of salaries was, of course, an important one for any government official. The Castle secretariat reveals much about how office-holders were remu-

18 For different missions during Townshend's viceroyalty see two important collections of letters: Beinecke Library, Osborn Collection, Waite-Macartney letters and NAI M.734, Allan-Townshend letters. See also E.M. Johnston, 'The career and correspondence of Thomas Allan', *IHS*, x (1956–7), pp. 23–47.　19 BL Add. Mss.32,734, f.3, Hardwicke to Newcastle, 1 Jan. 1754. 20 PRONI Chatsworth papers, T3158/763, 767, Conway to Hartington, 15, 16 July 1755. 21 Johnston, *Ireland*, pp. 19–21.

nerated. In the early nineteenth century, when commentators condemned the government with the name 'Old Corruption', they reserved their greatest outrage for what was seen as venality within the administration. This view has since been revised, particularly by John Brewer, to give a softer picture of eighteenth-century government in England. However, Brewer does not deny that every office-holder, whether in Ireland or Britain, believed that their office was the same as a landed estate, carrying with it property rights. Remuneration for public service came in different forms: sinecures, salaries and fees. In addition, offices were often sought because of the influence with government this revealed. Did these characteristics mean, ipso facto, that the administration was ineffective or corrupt?

Sinecures, or offices which had no duties attached to them, have been described by one Irish historian as a burden 'which were granted to English and Irish politicians in return for their parliamentary services'.[22] Sinecures were not as prevalent in the most active departments, but they did exist in the Castle secretariat and the revenue service. In both of these departments they were sometimes used to 'top up' the salaries of active officials. For example, the Castle secretariat office-holders held a range of sinecures, including the Chamberlain of the Exchequer and the First Pursuivant at Arms. Most of these offices had small salaries which were the reward for loyal clerks, largely dependent upon the goodwill of their superiors for a fair share of office fees.[23]

Sinecures could also be extended to take in those offices which did have duties attached, but which had a holder with no intention of fulfilling the workload. This was usually, though not always, due to the appointee being English or Scottish and having no plan to come to Ireland to take up the place. These men and, very occasionally, women, had the name sinecurists and their common practice was to appoint a deputy who was expected to do the duties of office in return for a share of the remuneration. Deputies were often lower officials seeking an additional income, or sons of other placemen seeking a first job. When a sinecurist was appointed, the priority of officials in Dublin was to ensure that the business of the office did not suffer because of a delay. For example, in 1748, when the son of the viceroy, Lord Harrington, was appointed revenue collector for Dublin, Chief Baron Bowes and Waite argued for a speedy appointment of a deputy, as no legal judgements could be made in the meantime. Their concern to continue the existing and experienced deputy in place shows that sinecurists did not automatically mean inefficency.[24]

---

22 J.L. McCracken, 'The Central and Local Administration under George II, 1727–60' (PhD thesis, Queen's University Belfast, 1948), p. 62.   23 The First Clerk, James Belcher, was the First Pursivant from 1723 until his death in 1764, while another clerk, William Roseingrave, was the Chamberlain from 1748 until his death: Sainty, 'Secretariat', pp. 31–3.   24 PRONI T3019/1036, 1038, Bowes to Weston, 21 May, Waite to Weston, 21 May 1748.

Fee-taking was another common form of remuneration which drew opprobrium from later reformers. There was less comment in the eighteenth century
unless abuses became apparent and serious. Brewer has commented, in respect of
fees, that it would be wrong to use them for 'writing off the eighteenth century
executive as yet another ramshackle ancien régime'.[25] However, they did represent
a huge sum of money. In Britain, by the 1780s, fees amounted to *c.*£300,000 per
year for twelve government departments. In an inquiry of 1783, Irish MPs found
that revenue officials sometimes received ninety-nine per cent of their remuneration through fees.[26] There had been some reform of the fees system in 1758, when
military fees paid to the secretariat were abolished and replaced by fixed salaries.
The salary compensation package of £4,000 a year paid to the secretariat shows
the estimated level of those fees. Civil fees, paid for example on the passing of
patents for pensions, were just as profitable. The papers of successive undersecretaries, John Potter and Thomas Tickell, show the amounts of remuneration
involved. Between 1737 and 1739 the civil fees earned by the Castle secretariat
came to £4,665, while, in the first six months of 1746, a further £1,780 was
earned.[27]

Despite the sums involved, there was little complaint about office-holders
requesting fees for the passage of business. Where problems did arise was when
fee-taking led to either internal battles within the administration or to embarrassing abuses. William Lingen, the secretary to the Ulster secretary between 1704
to 1749, spent much of his career waging war to uphold or extend his collection
rights. This led to repeated complaints about his behaviour and caused occasional
breakdowns in the administration of the Secretary's Office.[28] Fees could also
bring the government into disrepute in the wider political world. Barrack
masters were notorious for their demands on the government and regiments
under their care and were often condemned in the House of Commons
committees for their abuses.[29] Much more famous was the case of the chief
secretary, Lord George Sackville, who, in 1755, was publicly accused in handbills
of taking £708 in military fees that did not belong to him. Although he was not
technically guilty, Sackville was openly profiteering from an augmentation in the
size of the army during wartime. No-one in government questioned his collection
rights, but Waite questioned his wisdom and the handbills of the Free Citizens

---

25 John Brewer, *The Sinews of Power: War, Money and the English State, 1688–1783* (London,
1989, hereafter Brewer, *Sinews*), p. 72.   26 Ibid., p. 73; Kiernan, *Financial Administration*, p.
267.   27 These figures are from House of Lords Record Office, Tickell Papers, volume iv, f.98
and Northumberland Record Office, Potter papers, N.R.O.650/C/22, ff.1–25.   28 In two
separate examples between 1742 and 1743 Lingen's attmpts to monopolise fees in the
secretariat caused almost complete breakdowns in relationships there; PRONI T3019/391,
458, 463, Lingen to Wilmot, 15 May 1742, Belcher to Wilmot, 15 Mar., Potter to Wilmot, 21
Apr. 1743.   29 *CJI*, vii, pp. 759–88; viii, pp. 745–8.

questioned his honesty.[30] In this case, the combination of open venality and an unpopular official made government the butt of lampoons. This showed how thin the line was between proprietary rights and greed, and how carefully officials had to tread in their search for remuneration.

MEETING THE FINANCIAL NEEDS

One crucial part of the civil administration was the revenue service. The collectors, searchers, gaugers and so on were dispersed throughout the country, supervised by the seven revenue commissioners who made up the Revenue Board. The revenue service was to grow gradually through the eighteenth century, from 1,100 office-holders in the 1720s to at least 1,600 officials in the late 1750s. The number of senior posts, alone, trebled to 350 between 1733 and 1765. An obvious consequence of this was an upward trend in the salaries bill, which rose from £59,042 in 1748 to £62,936 in 1758 to c.£73,000 in 1763, despite the fact that most officials gained more from fees than they ever did from salaries.[31]

The revenue of the government was provided by the combination of hereditary revenue and additional duties. The first was financially much more important than the second, accounting for two-thirds of the total. However, the levels of £3–400,000 per annum collected in additional supplies in the 1750s meant that the Castle could not do without this subsidy from parliament. Yet it has to be said that the hereditary revenue remained the major contributor to government income, comprising of the hearth tax, which remained largely stagnant in mid-century at £100,000 per annum, and the other customs and excise duties of over £500,000 in annual yields.

Any shortfall between this collectable revenue and government expenditure was inevitably linked to war. In the 1750s and 1760s this meant the Seven Years War (1756–63) which involved Britain and France and was fought mainly in North America and Europe. The cost of Ireland's contribution to the war effort rose steadily after 1754, when conflict was first mooted. As the military establishment rose first to 12,000 men and then to almost 16,000 after 1761, expenditure soared. Unfortunately for the Castle the period also saw a growing civil list, increasing steadily from £183,648 in 1755–7 to £262,480 in 1761–3. The wartime costs of recruitment and subsistence of regiments, the encampments for training and

---

30 Wilmot did urge the Castle to investigate the incident, otherwise 'it might have the appearance as if he [Sackville] was capable of exacting what was not his right and as if government was willing to connive in what they ought to censure'; PRONI T3019/2530, Waite to Wilmot, 14 Mar., Wilmot to the Lords Justices, 15 March 1755.   31 These figures are from McNally, *Parties*, chapter 5; *CJI*, x, pp. 767–801, 744–5; ibid., xiii, pp. 41–147; T. Bartlett, 'Townshend and the Irish Revenue Board, 1769–1772', *Proceedings of the Royal Irish Academy*, lxxix (1979), pp. 153–76.

defence, the new artillery regiment and an increasing ordnance bill meant that military expenditure climbed steadily from £874,588 in 1753–5 to £988,928 in 1759–61 and £1,149,631 in 1761–3.

War was often expected to cause problems with trade, but the revenue yields also rose in the later 1750s, due to the demand for Irish provisions from the British navy and the growing market for linen. This increase can be seen in the customs and excise duties received annually by the government, which soared by almost a quarter of a million pounds between the 1755 figures and the 1764 ones. After the dearth of 1756–7, the overall hereditary revenue rose gradually from £989,937 in 1757–9 to £1,053,939 in 1759–61 and £1,363,059 in 1761–3.[32] When the Revenue Board advised the government that expected yields would not match expenditures, the other option, as a land tax was unacceptable, was a loan. Three times in the parliamentary sessions of 1759–60 and 1761–2, MPs voted for loans, which finally totalled £550,000 by the end of the war.[33] These were successfully raised and, consequently, the national debt rose from £223,438 in October 1761 to £433,000 two years later. Some duties were appropriated specifically for the interest charges, at least 5 per cent per annum, due on the loans. The size of Ireland's revenues, loans and debts can be seen in her total military expenditure between 1755 and 1763 of £4 million being less than the lowest annual revenue in England in the same period. Consequently, their comparative debts in 1764 were just over half a million and £25 million.

Despite the apparent success (in terms of increasing yields year on year during the war) of customs and excise collection, the revenue service was never popular. In part this was the usual feeling of unease or dislike for taxation and its collectors. Ensuring that the collection of duties went smoothly meant that revenue officials were ready to use the army against smugglers and illegal distillers.[34] However, it was widely believed that the Revenue Board was much less harsh in its treatment of errant officers. Complaints against revenue officers concentrated upon their arbitrariness and corruption. One pamphlet, published in 1755 and then reprinted in 1758 with additional queries, castigated the service for the creation of unnecessary officers; the gratuities known as 'incident charges'; the Board's abuse of the Charity Fund, intended for the widows of officers; the sums kept in hand by collectors and surveyors; the level of fees; the practice of making seizures so that bribes could be demanded; and the unaccountability of the service due to the number of holidays taken.[35]

32 All of the above revenue figures are taken from the public accounts found in *CJI*, ix, pp. 269–306; x, pp. 29–101; xi, pp. 33–123; xii, pp. 47–152; xiii, pp. 41–147.   33 Ibid., xii, p. 729.
34 F.G. James, 'Irish Smuggling in the eighteenth century', *IHS*, xii (1960–1), pp. 299–317.
35 *The Management of the Revenue with Queries* (2nd edition, Dublin, 1758); Clarkson & Crawford, *Ways to Wealth*, pp. 20–35.

If these allegations had been proven, they could have had a detrimental effect on the Irish war effort in the 1750s. The accusations soon found a wider audience when, in November 1757, they formed the basis of a Commons inquiry into the revenue service. The chief motive for the inquiry was a wish to embarrass the Speaker and first commissioner, John Ponsonby, and though it did not get too far, the committee's report still upheld some of the complaints.[36] In the next session the Castle, itself, sponsored a bill to reform the service and to make revenue collection easier, which incorporated some of the findings of the inquiry of 1757–8 while studiously avoiding any hint of criticism with regard to the Revenue Board.[37] The feeling that the Board had escaped lightly and that arbitrary practices were still rife emerged in a later episode in the 1759–60 session, when Patriot MPs brought in a petition from Cork city containing the merchants' grievances. Allegations about illegal siezures of tea, the interpretation of an export prohibition and the fact that every disputed case had to be referred to Dublin were accompanied by an attack on the city's collector, Sir Richard Cox. The latter believed that this was all part of an attempt by Cork's Patriots to court popularity and smear him.[38] The petition came to nothing but the Revenue Board was left in no doubt how politicians, anxious to make a name for themselves, could do so, even during wartime, by utilising the issue of taxation.

MEETING THE NEED FOR MEN: THE MILITARY ESTABLISHMENT

Another key part of the government was the military establishment, which was responsible for the army, barracks, internal defences and anything concerning these. The Castle secretariat was again the hub of this 'department' as the channel of communication between the military's General Board, the viceroy and the Secretary of War in London. There was a certain amount of autonomy, with orders coming from the Castle and not the War Office and this extended to disciplinary matters, as Henry Boyle told the powerful duke of Cumberland in 1755.[39] The military establishment, itself, comprised the General Board, the ordnance establishment and the Barracks Board which all were marked by indifference and chronic absenteeism.[40] The General Board was particularly notorious for the

---

36 PRONI T3019/3282, Waite to Wilmot, 10 Dec. 1757; PRONI T3158/1566, Cavendish to Devonshire, 10 December 1757; *CJI*, x, pp. 750–815.　37 *CJI*, xi, pp. 439, 527–8.　38 PRONI Donoughmore papers T3459/C/2/5, Hutchinson to [　], 29 Nov. 1760; *CJI*, xi, pp. 160–9; PRONI Shannon papers D2707/A1/5/44, Cox to Shannon, 1 August 1761.　39 PRONI T3019/1745, Sackville to Wilmot, 3 July 1751; J.H. Houlding, *Fit for Service: The Training of the British Army, 1715–1790* (Oxford, 1981, hereafter Houlding, *Fit*), p. 41.　40 The history of the eighteenth-century Irish army has been clinically told by Alan Guy in two articles: A. Guy, 'An Whole Army Absolutely Ruined in Ireland', *Annual Report of the National Army*

absenteeism of the generals, who looked on Irish duty as a chore or punishment.[41] More opprobrium fell on the Muster Master General (often a civilian) and his six commissaries who delegated their duties to deputies, gained handsome profits from office and constantly bought and sold these for £2,000 or more from the 1740s.[42] The Irish commissariat did not undertake review circuits and, thus, the task of checking the state of regiments passed to the generals.[43] In turn, the generals chafed at having to come to Ireland, in rotation, to do the basic duty of checking the fitness of regiments.

The system of appointing to commissions and the remuneration of officers was modelled on the British establishment. With regard to commissions, a purchase system operated, which officially meant that every commission that had been bought could be sold by its holder to the next in line, in terms of seniority. This system was supervised by the viceroy and in many cases military needs, so stressed by Cumberland in England, were ignored in favour of patronage. The papers of Sir Robert Wilmot are full of details concerning the working of the purchase system and the impression given is that political and not military logic often applied to the granting of commissions. Recommendations from commanding officers of regiments were factors in the success of a prospective candidate, but the interventions of lords justices or other Irish politicians were just as important. In the case of new regiments, especially those 'raised for rank' during the Seven Years War, the commissioned officers were largely left in the control of the undertakers in consultation with successive viceroys.[44]

This working of the purchase system verifies the argument of Alan Guy that the Irish establishment suffered from the lack of control by the War Office in London. Few viceroys or chief secretaries had any military experience and most would have replicated Rigby's lack of interest in such matters, apart from the profits military business brought.[45] A notorious example of this mismanagement was the Barracks Board, which in 1760 consisted of seven members (all Irish peers and MPs), a secretary and twenty-seven barrack masters.[46] This establishment was created in 1704 with an annual budget of £13,336 to pay for the upkeep and repair of over one hundred barracks. In November 1745 a Commons committee found that these costs had risen to £20,000 annually, although many

Museum (1978–9), pp. 33–49; idem., 'The Irish military establishment, 1660–1776', in T. Bartlett & K. Jeffrey (eds), *A Military History of Ireland* (Cambridge, 1995), pp. 211–30. **41** BL Add. Mss.35,357, f.201, Col Yorke to Hardwicke, 4 Mar. 1757; J. Caldwell, *Debates Relative to the Affairs of Ireland in the Years 1763–4* (2 vols, London, 1766), i, p. 302. **42** PRONI T3019/1208–9, 1271, Waite to Wilmot, 3 Dec. 1748; Clements to Wilmot, 21 Feb. 1749. **43** A. Guy, *Economy and Discipline: Training of the British Army, 1715–95* (Manchester, 1985), p. 28; BL Add. Mss. 35919, f.267, Waite's administrative survey for Charles Yorke in 1747. **44** For such discussions see NLI Ms.8064, Halifax's journal entries of 24, 25 November 1761. **45** PRONI T3019/3353, Rigby to Wilmot, 28 Mar. 1758. **46** *Gentleman and Citizen's Almanac* (Dublin, 1760), p. 59.

barracks had either been closed or were in a hopeless state of disrepair. A major factor in this increase was that barrack masters were supposed to earn £50 a year, but earned up to six times as much.[47] Despite Waite's claim, in 1747, that the barracks were seen in Ireland as a boon, the administration of them continued to be a source of heated parliamentary discussion for decades to come.[48] Between 1745 and 1752 three Commons committees delivered damning reports about the Board and the competence of the surveyor general, Arthur Jones Nevill. Nevill was granted £24,000 in 1752 for further building and, only after he had mismanaged these funds and attempted to use the unpopular Archbishop Stone as a shield, was he finally dismissed by furious MPs in December 1753.[49]

This sacking led one historian to see the barracks as a sign of that 'inefficiency [which] seems to have been an almost permanent feature of Dublin Castle's administration of the army.'[50] This argument is supported by the lack of reform in the 1750s, despite the parliamentary findings. The fact that the Barracks Board was a fund of substantial patronage for the government protected it from overhaul and it continued to swallow up the vast majority of defence building funds. This was not so much because the barracks were a key to defence against possible insurrection but because they housed soldiers and thus allowed the Irish political elite to avoid the unpopular decision to quarter the army on civilians.[51] Attempts to reform the administration of the barracks, as in 1758 when the new surveyor general, Thomas Eyre, drafted a plan to make the viceroy sole authority for all appointments and to ensure greater supervision of spending, crashed on the rocks of government indifference and opposition from the undertakers.[52] The running of the barracks was, thus, the most obvious sign of a ruinous military administration.

MEETING THE NEED FOR MEN: RECRUITMENT

The state of Irish regiments reflected this poor administrative performance. The standing army had been established in Ireland in the years after the Williamite victory. A British act of 1699 fixed the maximum level of soldiers at 12,000 during peacetime. The composition of the establishment was shaped by the Castle and the General Board, though other forces, as in the 1755 augmentation, sometimes had an input. In those discussions, the British commander-in-chief, the duke of

---

47 K.P. Ferguson, 'The Army in Eighteenth Century Ireland' (PhD thesis, TCD, 1980), p. 77; *CJI*, vii, p. 765. 48 BL Add. Mss. 35919, f.268, Waite's administrative survey of 1747. 49 *CJI*, vii, pp. 759–88 for the 1746 report; ibid. viii, pp. 82–3 & pp. 457–748; PRONI T3019/1848, Waite to Wilmot, 20 Feb. 1752 for discussions in 1749–50 and the 1751–2 report and resolutions. 50 Houlding, *Fit*, p. 52. 51 Bartlett, 'Army', pp. 180–2. 52 For the 1760 papers see *CJI*, xi, pp. 530–807; for the 1764 debates and vote (102 votes against 29 on a resolution to make the board accountable to the Commons) see ibid., xiii, pp. 866–7 and pp. 877–8.

Cumberland, was able to force his 'very expensive and very useless' scheme of additional heavy cavalry on the Irish executive.[53]

The 1755 augmentation revealed that the recruitment, disposition and training of Irish soldiers were supposed to be driven by their role as a resource pool for British demands. This had been clear from the 1690s and, with expensive wars in 1689–97, 1702–13, 1739–48 and 1756–63, Ireland's tasks were always set by metropolitan needs. The priority of Irish Protestants to secure their defence against invasion or rebellion was superseded by the British campaigns against France in Europe or North America. It would not be correct to see these priorities as polar opposites, since Irish Protestants connected the French threat to their own concerns about Jacobitism. However, as the 1740s and 1750s wore on, Jacobitism seemed more of a phantom, at least to ministers in London, and thus Irish concerns were largely ignored.[54] Political problems were to result from this approach, especially as Britain sought augmentation of the Irish establishment in the 1760s.

The state of the Irish army was not helped by the decision to have 324 men per infantry regiment in Ireland. This contrasted with the figure of 500 in Britain and therefore a shortfall had to be made up if an Irish regiment was to serve abroad. This composition had been decided upon because more regiments, however officer-heavy, could then be placed on the Irish establishment in peacetime and, thus, the numbers of officers languishing on the half-pay lists would be less. In theory, this allowed regiments to be filled out more quickly in wartime, because the basic structure was in place, and, during peacetime, basic training could continue under the officers. The reality was somewhat different. The Irish regiments were bedevilled by absenteeism among officers, so basic training was poor, and the need for completion, from peacetime vacancy levels of 30 per cent, increased the pressure for recruits on a small pool of resources. That this pressure led to other standards slipping, is revealed in the gradual reduction of minimum height regulations from five feet, six inches in March 1756 to five feet, four inches in January 1760.[55] Whatever problems this may have caused, in terms of the fitness of recruits, it was judged a success for completing regiments.

The mechanics of completing the Irish army to its full strength of 12,000 men were quite complex because of the rule that recruitment was only allowed in Britain. This regulation had been ordered in the 1690s, for fear of Irish Catholics flooding into the army, and was rarely flouted. However, during wartime much of this logic was ignored as recruits became much harder to find. The 12,000 limit was broken, the army increasing to 13,822 in July 1748 and to over 14,000 men by January 1760 and to almost 24,000 by 1762, 8,000 of these serving abroad.[56] The

53 PRONI T3019/2796, Devonshire to Wilmot, 3 Apr. 1756; PRONI T3158/1198, Fox to Devonshire, 8 Apr. 1756. 54 For British demands see Brewer, *Sinews*, pp. 29–50 and Langford, *Polite People*, p. 629. 55 NLI Ms.681, ff.1, 82–8, 95 & 216, 8 Mar. 1756, 28 Nov. 1758, 10 Apr. 1759 and 26 Jan. 1760. 56 PRONI T3019/1085, Waite to Weston, 26 July 1748;

methods used to provide these numbers were well-tested, though not altogether successful. One was to bring regiments from Britain or overseas to Ireland, though these had invariably been depleted either by battles or disease, or were new, unfit forces. A second was more successful, that of 'raising for rank', which was widely used during the late 1750s. This was where a peer or senior officer would be permitted to raise a regiment in return for the rank of at least Lieutenant-Colonel. Although this method was disliked by George II and many generals, because it rewarded birth instead of service, it was used. Apart from providing possibly 2,000 men in 1762–3, when Britain was facing both France and Spain, the method was also politically useful, providing fresh sources of patronage. The third method used during wartime was recruitment in Ireland itself. This did not mean that Catholic recruits were acceptable, at least not until the American War of Independence, but that Irish regiments could beat for recruits in Ulster. This method was first used in 1745 when the Jacobite rebellion made recruitment in England impossible.[57] This was clearly an extraordinary situation but, although the end of the emergency saw the ban put back in place, the precedent of lifting it had been established and had proved successful in terms of recruits. Thus it was an easier argument for the Castle to win in 1755. Then, the chief secretary, Colonel Conway, found a total of 10,200 (with possibly 2,500 unfit for service) on the establishment and felt it could be raised to 15,000, with four regiments serving abroad, by recruiting in Ireland.[58] Cumberland agreed, 'provided you can be sure, with every precaution used, to prevent Papists entering among the new levies', and a plan was devised to persuade him.[59] The chosen solution was to send regulations to each of the recruiting parties working in Ulster, allotting each a district, which they had to keep to, and ordering that every recruit was to have his religion sworn to by the local clergyman and JP. Ultimate responsibility lay with the commanding officer, who had to attest to the records kept by his recruiting parties.[60] Problems arose almost immediately, as the earl of Abercorn alleged that half the new recruits were Catholics and that the certificates used by recruiters were not working, partly because of their own laziness and partly because of the maliciousness of Presbyterian ministers.[61] A tightening up of regulations followed, with recruiting parties ordered to send the names of the

CJI, xi, pp. 524–8; ibid., xii, pp. 862–6. **57** In 1739 Devonshire had allowed a regiment to recruit in Ulster with the logic that it was going to Gibraltar and any Catholics in it would be a negligible factor there; PRONI T3019/119, Legge to Devonshire, 11 December 1739. For 1745 see PRONI Transcripts of the State Papers, T1060/1, Newcastle to Chesterfield, 5 Sept., Chesterfield to Newcastle, 7 Sept. 1745. **58** The figures are calculated from RIA Ms.12/B1/8, State of the Army, Mar. 1755; PRONI T3158/1052, 1062, Newcastle to Devonshire, 2 Jan., Fox to Devonshire, 8 Jan. 1756. **59** PRONI T3158/976, Fox to Hartington, 12 Nov. 1755. **60** The regulations are taken from NLI Adjutant General's Order Book, M.681, ff.2–12, April–June 1756. **61** PRONI T3158/1240, 1246, 1243, Abercorn to Devonshire, 29 April, 6 May, Devonshire to Abercorn, 6 May 1756.

clergymen and JPs used to Dublin.[62] However, despite these problems, this method and the regulations accompanying it were used continuously during the Seven Years War.[63]

The question of the recruitment of Catholics did not disappear.[64] Most, if not all, Irish Protestants were opposed to it, but one viceroy, Lord Halifax in 1762, thought the question merited further discussion. Spain had entered the war on the French side and a Catholic peer, Lord Trimleston, offered the Irish government the prospect of raising 5,000 recruits, who would fight the Spanish in Portugal. Halifax was enthusiastic, although he was aware of the sensitivity of Catholic recruitment. However, he believed that, by sending the recruits to Portugal under strict regulations, any suspicions would be allayed.[65] Knowing just how desperate for recruits ministers were, Halifax sent Trimleston to London with the regulations.[66] However, the Whiteboy disturbances reached a new pitch in Munster and this caused a backlash against the proposal among both Irish Protestants and British ministers. In this climate, the proposal to raise Catholic recruits was quietly dropped. In the longer term, the growing demand for soldiers meant that 'raising for rank' or free recruitment in Ulster was never going to compete with the use of Irish Catholics.[67] That decision lies outside our period but, given the pressures, was an inevitable one.

MEETING THE NEED FOR MEN: FITNESS FOR SERVICE

With the pressure to bend, break and rewrite recruiting regulations to complete the establishment, the next problem was to make regiments fit for service. With a high numbers of recruits and the dilution of the conditions of service, the need for training increased. An example of the potential unfitness can be seen in 1755, when five regiments, including two of the longest standing, Folliott's and Loudon's, were sent from Ireland to Britain. All were understrength and spent most of the spring recruiting.[68] By May 1755, Folliott's had recruited to 64 per cent of 500 men, but its ranks contained almost 50 per cent new recruits, figures which were comparable to Loudon's. With the training that new recruits required, neither regiment was declared fit for service until mid-1756.[69] This

62 NLI Ms.681, f.10, 3 May 1756.   63 Devonshire remained suspicious that Catholics had entered the army and wanted to ensure that they were not sent to America to desert to the French: PRONI T3019/2894, 2926, Devonshire to Wilmot, 7 Aug., Devonshire to the Lords Justices, 10 Sep. 1756.   64 In 1755 one Cork newspaper had called for the use of the 'unhappy natives in the service of king and country': *Cork Journal*, 3 Nov. 1755.   65 Halifax to Egremont, [6–12?] Feb. 1762, *CHOP*, i, pp. 154–5.   66 For the conditions see PRONI T1060/8, Halifax to Egremont, 14 Mar. 1762.   67 *CJI*, xii, p. 865.   68 PRONI T3019/2524, Sackville to Waite, 12 Mar. 1755.   69 Houlding, *Fit*, p. 127.

problem of the high ratio of recruits to seasoned soldiers was a constant one for Irish regiments, making them a particular example of 'the manpower problem – too few recruits to complete the establishments, too many recruits among the men already with the corps'.[70]

In addition to this problem, training in Ireland remained haphazard. There was some progress, as Conway finally got the General Board to adopt Cumberland's 1748 regulations on firings and manoeuvres in 1756. Also the new artillery company, though notoriously top-heavy, did provide specialised garrison and field training in Dublin after 1756. Furthermore, there is evidence that the officer corps were certainly interested in training theory (if not practice) as many of them were subscribers to the latest manuals, which were regularly reprinted in Dublin.[71] However, the decision taken in the 1690s to house 12,000 men in over 100 dispersed barracks militated against concentrated regimental training. Though more isolated barracks had been closed by 1755, each still only held four to five companies. In addition, the troops had law and order duties, including assisting revenue officers against smugglers or illegal distillers, which meant that detachments were regularly called away. All of this made the provision of coordinated training a virtually impossible task.

Some efforts were made, however occasional, to bring large numbers of troops together for training, either at annual reviews or in Dublin's barracks or else in the wartime encampments. All regiments gathered together once a year for their review and were able to exercise in regimental manoeuvres for a week beforehand. As well as annual reviews, regiments were rotated, so that every two to three years they would get to spend time in larger barracks, the best being in Dublin, where regiments used the training ground at Phoenix Park for full-scale manoeuvres and mock battles using artillery.[72] In addition, there were eight summer encampments held in the Seven Years War, usually lasting 12 to 18 weeks each and including up to 13 regiments in the largest one of 1759.[73] These were designed to improve the basic and advanced skills of regiments and those with the highest percentages of recruits were always selected for this duty. Despite the expense in stores of hay and ammunition the administration persevered with this method.[74] Yet, even with all these efforts, the Irish army retained a reputation for being poorly trained and ill-prepared for war until the Act of Union.

---

70 Houlding estimates that, in the period 1750–73, Britain had an average completion rate of 93% for its regiments and percentages of recruits stood at an average of 18.5%, while the figures for Irish regiments in the same period stand at 87.5% and 22.5%; ibid., pp. 128–32.   **71** Ibid., pp. 200 & 70.   **72** For these details see ibid., pp. 51–3.   **73** NLI Ms.681, ff.105–8, 2 June 1759.   **74** The cost of the hay magazines was usually around £4,000 per camp, while the ordnance costs (outside that of the new artillery company) rose during the war from £12,494 in 1754–5 to £77,725 in 1760–1: *CJI*, ix, pp. 277–8 and xii, pp. 250–76.

THE DEFENCE OF IRELAND

One test of the effectiveness of the military establishment lay in its ability to deal with internal defence.[75] This raises the question of how much of a threat Catholics posed to the Protestant landed elite. The answer to this lies more in the realm of perceptions than in realities, given the crushing military defeat of Irish Catholics in the 1690s. In Britain, the elite lost much of their hostility to Catholicism or, more accurately, their fear of it, after 1745. The ideas of the Enlightenment, the entry of Catholic subjects into the empire (in Quebec) and the journey of the Young Pretender to London in 1750, to take the Anglican communion, all contributed to this. This change in attitudes should not be exaggerated, as hatred of 'popish France' or fear of Irish Catholics could stoke up the flames at any time.[76]

Any change in attitude was much slower and less steady among Ireland's Protestant elite during the mid-eighteenth century. The numbers game was crucial to the perceptions of local Protestants, though at government level some shift in opinions can be assumed. During the 1740s, local Protestant demands for action had resulted in the 1744 Disarming Act and in the orders to close mass houses and arrest regular clergy.[77] Perhaps because there was no Irish rebellion in 1745 and the fact that later viceroys were not as strongly anti-catholic as was the third duke of Devonshire (1737–1744), attitudes in the Castle and among some Irish Protestants showed a thaw. In April 1756 therefore, when Lord Limerick arrested Archbishop Michael O'Reilly of Armagh on suspicion of plotting with the French, the evidence shows that both the peer and Lord Chancellor Newport acted from routine, rather than conviction.[78] The government went further, to its cost, in 1762 when officials refused to believe the reports from Munster Protestants that the Whiteboy disturbances were really a cover for a Jacobite insurgency.

At the same time this behaviour should not be interpreted as complacency as, in 1756 and 1757, two viceroys, Devonshire and Bedford, supported bills to register the Catholic clergy. Although less harsh than the 1704 Registry Act, these bills were intended to get the addresses of all Catholic clergy and force them to take an oath of allegiance to the crown. In other words the Catholic church was still seen as both a religious institution and a defence problem.[79] Also the government lost no time in 1755–6 in taking security measures to deal with alleged French engineers and enlisters.[80] Although Irish Catholics lacked military leaders

75 For an overview see S.J. Connolly, 'The defence of Protestant Ireland, 1660–1760', in Bartlett & Jeffrey (eds), *Military History*, pp. 231–46.   76 C. Haydon, *Anti-Catholicism in eighteenth century England* (Manchester, 1993), pp. 164–79.   77 D. Dickson, *New Foundations: Ireland, 1690–1800* (Dublin, 1987, hereafter Dickson, *New Foundations*), p. 85.   78 PRONI Roden papers, Mic.147/9, pp. 104, 147–8, Devonshire to Limerick, c.23 Apr., Newport to Limerick, 1 May 1756.   79 J. Brady, 'The proposal to register Irish priests, 1756–7', *Irish Ecclesiastical Record*, xcvii (1961), pp. 209–22.   80 For French engineers and enlistment see NAI M.1A/52/166, p. 302, Newport to Maunsell, 14 Aug. 1755; NA Ms.1A/52/63,

in this period, wartime meant that the French or Spanish threat had to be taken seriously.

There were signs that Irish military commanders shared successive viceroys' opinions about Catholics posing little military threat on their own. In 1751, Lord Molesworth accepted that the army was a 'frontier garrison', the majority of the population being Catholic, but he argued that they posed a negligible threat, except as a possible adjunct to an invasion. Molesworth wanted to see more spending on forts such as Galway or Limerick, to produce entrenchments supported by an expanded ordnance, capable of withstanding or obstructing any invasion attempt.[81] This assessment was not acted upon and, in 1756, Lord Rothes and his generals carried out fresh defence surveys. Rothes, too, stressed the need for forts to be like entrenchments and he emphasised the lack of artillery and skilled engineers. Again, they placed the blame on government parsimony and the false prioritising of the barracks.[82] In both reports the threat posed by Irish Catholics was regarded as a minor one, assuming they remained unsupported.

One sign that the Castle agreed with their generals, at least in part, was the repeated decision to rely on regular forces and not the home-grown militia. Among many Irish Protestants there was a long-standing affection for such a force, going back to the exploits of 1689–91. This tradition was boosted by a successful array in 1756 and the 1757 Act passed for England.[83] However, Castle officials were always dubious about the utility of such forces and cautious about issuing weapons to them. Despite the huge array of 1756, most of the militia arms remained in their stores and, when Thurot landed in February 1760, the 5,000 militia men who came to Belfast were almost all unarmed.[84] Once the news of this broke in the *Belfast News-Letter*, there was a storm of criticism both outside and inside parliament about ignoring the militia in preparations to meet this landing.[85] There was much truth in this claim as 28,000 new firelocks lay in storage in

Wilmot to Waite, 4 Sept. 1756.   81 PRONI T3019/1740, 'Extract of Lord Molesworth's Letter to a Friend', 20 June 1751.   82 PRONI T3158/1283, Rothes to Devonshire, 13 July 1756; PRONI T3019/2851, 'General Folliott's report on the defences of Connacht', 29 June 1756; BL Add. Mss. 30196, ff.11–13, Rothes to the Lords Justices, 27 Aug. 1756, Rothes to Folliott, 9 Sept. 1756.   83 J. O'Donovan, 'The Militia in Munster, 1715–78' in G. O'Brien (ed.), *Parliament, Politics and People* (Dublin, 1989), pp. 31–48; P.D.H. Smyth, 'The Volunteer Movement in Ulster' (PhD. thesis, QUB, 1974); H. McAnally, 'The Militia Array of 1756', *Irish Sword*, i (1950), pp. 94–104; E.H. Gould, 'To Strengthen the King's Hands: Dynastic Legitimacy, Militia Reform and Ideas of National Unity in England, 1745–60', *Historical Journal*, xxxiv (1991), pp. 329–48; J. Robertson, *The Scottish Enlightenment and the Militia Issue* (Edinburgh, 1985), chapter 4; *The Necessity of a well-disciplined militia in Ireland* (Dublin, 1746). 84 PRONI T3019/3710, Strode to Bedford, 22 Feb. 1760.   85 The story of the landing and the following storm can be followed in *BNL*, 26 Feb. 1760; *FDJ*, 26 Feb. 1760; PRONI T3459/A, General Ligonier's papers, Feb.-Mar. 1760; PRONI T1180, reports on Thurot's landing; PRONI T3019/3740, Rigby to Wilmot, 6 Mar. 1760; *CJI*, xi, pp. 907–9, 918 & 927–8.

Dublin and only 1,200 weapons had been issued to Lord Charlemont.[86] The propaganda continued, as the grand juries of Down and Antrim were critical of the lack of arms and Bedford was criticised, to his fury, by the corporation of Belfast.[87] Despite all of this, the militia remained the last resort of the military establishment.

One difficulty for internal defence was to reconcile a reliance on the regular army with the wartime British demand for troops to be sent overseas. In February 1760, when Thurot landed, the two weakest regiments on the establishment, Strode's and Browne's, were the ones based in north-east Ulster. This is explained by the fact that only 8,500 men were available to the government and the majority of them were stationed in Munster and Connacht where any invasion attempt was expected.[88] Throughout the Seven Years War, the problems the establishment had in completing regiments and the drafting of troops abroad meant that Devonshire and Bedford constantly complained about the demands of ministers, Pitt in particular. Though the clashes of Bedford and Pitt are usually commented upon, the struggles between the Castle and the ministry began in September 1755, when Devonshire warned Hartington:

> [G]ive early notice [to the ministry] how improper it would be to draw any troops from Ireland. What will be a trifle here would be a dangerous weakening of Ireland.[89]

In October 1756 a draft of 3,200 men was ordered and Bedford wrote later that such a draft 'must necessarily have weakened the army and reduced it below the standard which the parliament thought necessary to keep up, in this time of danger.'[90] Even before setting foot in Ireland, Bedford was aware of both the military and political dangers of leaving Ireland under-manned, a point he was to forcefully make several times between 1756 and 1760. These grievances seem justified when the total of 16,242 men sent to serve in Germany, North America, the West Indies and West Africa is noted. This, surely, confirms Ireland's role as a manpower pool for the British army.[91]

The drafting of regular troops for service abroad was only one problem with the securing of Ireland's defences. Thurot's landing showed that at least one aspect of Rothes' and Molesworth's advice, that of the need to build up fortifica-

---

86 *BNL*, 18 Mar. 1760; *CJI*, xi, pp. 876–8. Bedford had actually made plans the previous winter to sent 1,200 arms to Armagh, 1,400 to Down and 1,000 to Cavan: PRONI T1060/5, Bedford to Pitt, 26 Dec. 1759. 87 *BNL*, 1 Apr. 1760; Bedford to Pitt, 24 Mar. 1760 in *Bedford Correspondence*, ii, p. 411. 88 Soon after Thurot's landing a letter from Mallow reported that 20,000 French were said to have landed in County Clare: PRONI T3019/3742, Brereton to [ ], 6 Mar. 1760. 89 PRONI T3158/857, Devonshire to Hartington, 6 Sept. 1755. 90 PRONI T3158/1442, Bedford to Devonshire, 19 Nov. 1756. 91 *CJI*, xi, pp. 476 and 482–3 and xiii, pp. 684–5.

tions, had not been acted upon. Despite a lengthy defence of Carrickfergus Castle, it was surrendered to the French. Although neither Molesworth nor Rothes had visited Carrickfergus, a letter from County Down, in the aftermath of the landing, blamed the town's fall on the 'disordered and defenceless state of that garrison.'[92] However, the building of coastal entrenchments, beyond minor repairs to forts in Connacht and Munster, did not excite either government officials or MPs. Much more energy and money were expended on the expansion of the ordnance establishment after the April 1756 decision to form an artillery company. This was to consist of 125 men and added £1,000 per annum to the ordnance bill, following the 1751 and 1756 reports. Under Lord Kildare's stewardship, the company concentrated on providing field training for the infantry and the establishment was further expanded in 1760 to a regiment of four companies.[93] In terms of defence needs, this was certainly an expensive extravagance and, like the barracks, the wasteful expansion reached the point where the surveyor general advised a halt.[94] Throughout the mid-eighteenth century, the defence of Ireland lay in the hands of the British navy and not, thankfully in the opinion of those who worried about it, in the Irish administration.

MEETING IMPERIAL NEEDS AFTER THE SEVEN YEARS WAR

The reality that the defence of Ireland was intricately connected to the British military effort was not lost on London. Thus, the priority placed on the Irish establishment, of providing men for the wider imperial pool, was revealed once more in 1762. As the Seven Years War drew to a close, ministers in London assessed their massive debts and the need to provide defence in North America and the West Indies.[95] When the discussion turned to what Ireland could do, an augmentation of the country's army to 18 or 20,000 men was suggested. This was intended to provide the bulk of the men to be stationed in North America.[96] It was at this point that politics intervened, and the Irish adjutant general, Robert Cuninghame (a favourite of Archbishop Stone), travelled to London to discuss

92 *FDJ*, 26 Feb. 1760. 93 F. Forde, 'The Royal Irish Artillery, 1755–1801', *Irish Sword*, xi (1973), pp. 1–15; for training see NLI Ms.681, f.16, Cuninghame to the garrison commanders, 26 June 1756. 94 PRONI T1060/9, Report on the ordnance by the surveyor general, 30 Aug. 1765. 95 J.L. Bullion, *A Great and Necessary Measure: George Grenville and the genesis of the Stamp Act, 1763–5* (Missouri, 1982), pp. 23–4; idem., 'The Ten Thousand in America: More Light on the Decision on the American Army, 1762–3', *William and Mary Quarterly*, xliii (1986), pp. 646–57; idem., 'Security and Economy: The Bute Administration's Plans for the American Army and Revenue, 1762–3', ibid., xlv (1988), pp. 499–507; P.D.G. Thomas, 'New Light on the Commons Debate of 1763 on the American Army', ibid., xxxviii (1981), pp. 110–12. 96 J. Shy, *Towards Lexington: The role of the British army in the coming of the American Revolution* (Princeton, 1965), pp. 69–74.

the details of the Irish augmentation with ministers. He was keen for more top-heavy regiments, with more commissions for patronage, but he also insisted that the 6–8,000 extra men should stay in Ireland. This made a mockery of the whole proposal, but was a sign of how Cuninghame and his political masters in Dublin would seek to make augmentation acceptable to the Irish parliament.[97] Thus, ministers chose instead to tax the American colonists for the 10,000 men stationed among them and out of this decision came the fateful Stamp Act.

The violent response of the American colonists to this taxation and the unchanging need for more troops was to bring the size of the Irish establishment back into the spotlight in 1765 and 1767. In all of these discussions, the ascendancy of imperial necessities and political concerns over Irish defence was a constant. This is hardly surprising when the British needs are considered. By the end of the Seven Years War the average annual personnel in the British army was over 90,000 men, equal to the numbers used during the War of the Spanish Succession. That does not show the real increase, as troops were now needed in all corners of the globe and, especially, in the huge North American expanse, to meet the French and Indian threats. As the British debt had almost doubled to over £132,000,000 by 1763, the demand on the Irish establishment can be easily understood.[98]

As the attempt to raise a Stamp Tax in North America had patently failed by 1765, ministerial eyes turned to Ireland once more. One of the Secretaries of State, General Conway, looked to his brother, the Irish viceroy, Lord Hertford, to see whether the Irish parliament would agree to an army augmentation. Political management, as ever, was to the forefront of the viceroy's mind as he told Conway that if ministers agreed to pass unnamed popular Irish bills (perhaps including the corn bounty and a Septennial Act) then:

> [M]y brother is of opinion, by passing [the bills] here, [that] might make that measure [augmentation to 20,000 men] practicable before the end of this session of parliament.[99]

Given that Conway had been a chief secretary with the Hartington administration of 1755–6, he was acutely aware of the need to placate Irish opinion. Therefore he insisted on the need to pass the desired bills and also to get George III to declare that 12,000 troops would always remain in Ireland for defence purposes.

This scheme never got off the drawing board but the need remained and Lord Townshend was sent to Ireland in 1767 with directions to secure an army aug-

---

97 PRONI T3019/4378, Stone to Halifax, 13 Oct. 1762; Hamilton to Hutchinson, 4 Dec. 1762 in *HMC Donoughmore Papers*, 12th Report, Appendix vi (London, 1891, hereafter *Donoughmore Papers*), pp. 241–3.   98 Brewer, *Sinews of Power*, p. 30.   99 PRONI Grafton papers, T2959/2/2, Conway to Grafton, 7 Apr. 1766.

mentation. Despite the fact that successive ministries and administrations in Dublin Castle had come up against the need to match military realities against the management of Irish politics, it was believed in London that Townshend should meet with few difficulties so long as a very few 'popular' concessions were made.[100] This misconception meant that Townshend was not given extra patronage powers to secure the measure and thus faced strong resistance on the grounds of finances and, most importantly, the lack of a guarantee that 12,000 men would stay in Ireland. Townshend met with repeated refusals in London to budge on the latter point, despite his argument that MPs were agreeable to augmentation with a 'security clause' and the scheme was defeated in the Commons in May 1768. The augmentation to over 18,000 men was finally passed in November 1769 with a 'security clause' enshrined in the act.[101] This episode reveals how the Irish administration could, with proper management of Irish politicians, meet imperial needs. Repeated failures to do so in the American and Revolutionary Wars made ministers look at different methods of governing Ireland.

CONCLUSIONS

The politicisation of the issue of the army, in the aftermath of the Seven Years War, came as a surprise to ministers who believed that Ireland's needs (in terms of men and money) were exactly the same as growing imperial ones. The government of Ireland was a largely uncontroversial area from 1720 to the late 1760s and this goes some way to explaining the political peace which predominated in the same period. The augmentation of the army in Townshend's years was followed by budgetary problems, growing difficulties with trade regulation and, of course, the 'Catholic Question' (or questions). What might be called the politicising of the routine of government from the 1770s onwards was one important reason why that later period was a much more contentious one.[102]

100 George III to Grafton, 1 Sep. 1767, in Sir John Fortescue (ed.), *Correspondence of George III from 1760 to December 1783* (6 vols, London, 1928), i, pp. 503–4; Shelburne to Townshend, 29 Oct. 1767, *CHOP*, ii, pp. 195–7. 101 T. Bartlett, 'The augmentation of the army in Ireland, 1767–69', *English Historical Review*, 96 (1981), pp. 540–73. 102 For the military context of the 1790s see A. Blackstock, *An Ascendancy Army: The Irish Yeomanry, 1796–1834* (Dublin, 1998).

3

The making of a political crisis,
1750–1754

The Money Bill Crisis is one of the best-known events in the 'long peace' period of 1730 to 1770. In the later eighteenth century, both government and Patriot politicians looked back to the early 1750s as a watershed. Some, like Lord Charlemont, believed that the political events of these years taught the Irish public to think of constitutional change, while others, like Lord Clare, argued that 'independency' and radicalism were born in 1753. Ever since the eighteenth century, historians, too, have argued over the significance of the early 1750s. Thus, the genesis of the celebrated Money Bill Crisis is worthy of study.

THE APPOINTMENT OF DORSET

The immediate origins of the political crisis lie with the appointment of the Duke of Dorset as viceroy in the autumn of 1750. The reasons for this had nothing to do with Irish politics. The Harrington viceroyalty was certainly far from a triumph for the government and there were plenty of unsolved problems. The replacement of Harrington by Dorset was significantly to change political affairs, but this was not apparent at the time. Harrington's dismissal was the result of manouevres in London. He had been living on borrowed time since the dramatic events of 1746, when he threatened George II with resignation unless the royal favourite (Lord Carteret) was dismissed, and the king's dislike for him had not lessened with time. Harrington's tearful parting from Henry Pelham, who was willing, but unable, to do anything for him, marked his final humiliation.[1] After Harrington's death, his loyal servant, Edward Weston, spoke of a 'merciful release' after a period of isolation and loneliness.[2]

The appointment of Dorset was due as much to his lobbying as to Harrington's fall from grace. The duke had, since April 1750, been manouevering to get the post of viceroy, using, according to Pelham, the channel of Lady Yarmouth, George II's mistress, to get to the king. If this account is to be believed, it was money and

---

1 BL Add. Mss. 32722, ff.255, 283, Pelham to Newcastle, 31 Aug., Hardwicke to Newcastle, 31 Aug. 1750. 2 PRONI Wilmot papers, T3019/2015, Weston to Wilmot, 3 Apr. 1756.

not ambition that motivated the notoriously mean Sackville family. Pelham alleged that Dorset had suggested:

> He should hold over the [Lord] President's place with the lieutenancy till the king thought of a proper person to make president, not with a view to the keeping of both but to be ready to surrender at an hours warning when called for.[3]

Another reason for Dorset's lobbying was that his son, Lord George Sackville, greatly desired to become chief secretary. In August 1750 both men had their wishes granted.

There was little apprehension over these appointments, even if the expectations of Archbishop George Stone of Armagh, Dorset's chaplain on his previous term of office in Ireland, soared. At first, Dorset's choice of who would undertake his business in the Irish parliament (Boyle, the Ponsonbys or Stone) was not clear. The fact that Stone, the most active of the three lords justices, would have the ear of the new viceroy with regard to patronage, took a while to become apparent. Therefore, Dorset's administration had a short honeymoon period of almost a year.

However, by the summer of 1751, there were signs that there was a new power in the Castle. This became apparent in several ways. With regard to Boyle, he was soon to hear rumours that he had decided to retire from the Speaker's chair, in return for a peerage and a pension. It is difficult from this distance to pinpoint exactly where these rumours began. However, the fact that Stone and John Ponsonby felt it necessary to visit Boyle and assure him that they had nothing to do with the rumours suggests that they were attempting to deflect contemporary observers, who believed them to be the culprits.[4] Boyle had no doubts and called a meeting of his allies to deny the stories and to blame Stone and the Ponsonbys for them. This version of events was so widely believed that Edward Barry told Lord Orrery that Ponsonby had been actively canvassing support among MPs to become Boyle's successor since early 1751.[5] Whatever the truth was, there is no doubt that the effect of such rumours was to place a question mark over the ageing Boyle's future. His desire, to retire when he wanted and to nominate both his reward and his successor, was to create great problems for the government in the three parliamentary sessions which followed.

Boyle was not alone in being targeted for retirement, as rumours, some founded on truth, swept Dublin in 1751 about other governmental changes. Many of the rumoured changes were connected to the seriousness with which both Sackville

---

3 BL Add. Mss.32723, ff.7, 48, Pelham to Newcastle, 23, 28 Sept. 1750.   4 [Edmund Sexton Pery], *A Letter to the Duke of Bedford* (Dublin, 1757), p. 9.   5 Stone later unconvincingly denied any involvement in such rumour mongering, PRONI Sackville papers, T2860/1, Stone to Newcastle, 2 Oct. 1754; Barry to Orrery, 4 Mar. 1752, in *Orrery Papers*, p. 101.

and Stone took the business of administration. Given Sackville's career it was natural that he would become closely involved in military affairs. First, he stream-lined the passing of information between the Irish General Board, the Castle and the War Office in London. Second, he took an active role in the General Board itself and, as part of this, eventually persuaded the elderly commander, Viscount Molesworth, to stand aside in May 1752 in favour of the younger earl of Rothes.[6] With regard to the revenue service, the Castle also continued to work closely with Pelham and the Irish commissioners to introduce some effective changes. More English-born commissioners were appointed, better attendance at the board was demanded and more active regulation of the conduct of inferior officers pursued. All of this was seen as a way of increasing the revenue yield and this certainly rose in the 1748–52 period.[7] These changes, like those in the army establishment, certainly did the reputation of both Sackville and the Ponsonby family, by now the dominant force in the revenue service, no harm at all with English ministers. Within the Secretary's Office itself there were moves afoot for greater effective-ness, and there the veteran first clerk, James Belcher, was replaced by his young understudy, Henry Meredyth. The judicial bench also saw change, as Richard Marlay was persuaded to retire and rumours circulated that Lord Chancellor Newport was to be pensioned off.[8] This was not true but there must have been, by mid-1751, an impression in Dublin that the Dorset administration would be much more pro-active in government business than many previous regimes.

There was no reason why these changes should have led to political problems. They did, however, as patronage seemed to be 'running in one channel' (that is, Stone's) even before his patrons had come to Dublin. The appointment of one of his favourites, Philip Tisdall, as solicitor general in August 1751, reinforced earlier fears, especially as the post was expected to go to Anthony Malone's brother. William Yorke, one of the English-born judges, wrote of his anger at Stone's machinations in this case. Removing Marlay on a pension had created a vacan-cy which made Tisdall's only dilemma a choice between the positions of lord chief justice, attorney general and solicitor general.[9] Now Anthony Malone, like Thomas Carter, had personal reasons to harrass the primate and so the admin-istrative changes and/or reforms became political issues.

The authority possessed by Dorset increased as the Pelham ministry cast out its last threatening rivals, the Bedfords, in March 1751. The new secretary of state

6 PRONI T3019/1598, Waite to Wilmot, 5 Apr. 1751; BL Add. Mss.32727, ff.45, Rothes to Newcastle, 11 May 1752.   7 For more details on this see PRO CUST.1/40–52, Irish Customs' Minutes, 1748–1751; PRONI Pelham papers, T2863/1/21, 22, Brian to Pelham, 6, 18 April 1747. Between 1748 and 1752 the English-born commissioners were Thomas Brian, Henry Cavendish and William Bristow, who were ably supported by John Bourke.   8 PRONI T3019/1786, Memorandum on Irish business, 24 Aug. 1751; PRONI Castleward papers, D2092/1/8, p. 11, Waring to Ward, 21 Sept. 1751 for the rumours about Newport.   9 BL Add. Mss.35591, f.452, Yorke to Hardwicke, 26 Dec. 1752.

with responsibility for Ireland was the earl of Holdernesse, little more than a puppet for the Pelhams. Given these developments and the grip on power possessed by George Stone, the only weapon left to Henry Boyle was his ability to manage the Irish House of Commons. Whether he could do this, maintain a relationship with the new viceroy and the Castle, and provide for himself and his allies was a question that he and others, like the Gores and Lord Kildare, wanted answered as the session of 1751 began.

THE 1751–2 PARLIAMENTARY SESSION

Even with all of these forces building up in the background there was quite a normal beginning to the second Dorset viceroyalty. As Sackville reported on his arrival, there were positive appearances: 'the Primate, Speaker and the Ponsonbys are in great harmony and friendship'.[10] Dinners at the Castle, though less magnificent than in Harrington's time, were well attended and by 'all persons of rank' then in Dublin. Dorset and Newcastle were able to discuss business as usual and the former could report that 'nothing material has happened since [my] arrival in Dublin.'[11] Dorest's chaplain was full of optimism:

> The Duke of Dorset is very acceptable to all sorts of people here; 'tis thought the business of the nation will be carried on with great unanimity and cheerfulness; the chief managers are well agreed, and they say the man [Carter] that sought to rule by dividing is not to intermeddle.[12]

There were certainly potential disputes that could affect the smoothness or otherwise of the management of parliament but these, especially contested elections, were present in all sessions and rarely affected the Castle's majority. The election for Cork city involved Boyle, through his support for Thomas Newenham, and the Ponsonbys who put up Henry Cavendish. At another level, the battle for popularity in Cork was between the new revenue collector, Sir Richard Cox, and the Revenue Board, controlled by the Ponsonbys, which had very unwillingly appointed him. In April 1751, Cavendish denied the 'artful insinuation ... that a desire of popularity at Cork has influenced me' to oppose the decision to appoint Cox. The latter was hardly loved in Cork, certainly not by the crowd or lower orders, which hated him for his harrassment of Charles Lucas in 1749.[13] However, the Ponsonbys, despite their concerted effort to use revenue patronage to build up

10 PRONI T3019/1804, Sackville to Wilmot, 3 Oct. 1751. 11 BL Add. Mss.32725, ff.203, 311, Dorset to Newcastle, 15 Oct. 1751, Newcastle to Dorset, 18 Oct. 1751. 12 PRONI Abercorn papers, T2541/IA1/2/100, Hudson to [Abercorn], 22 Oct. 1751. 13 PRONI Chatsworth papers, T3158/392, Cavendish to Hartington, 7 Apr. 1750; PRONI Gosford papers, D1606/1/1/2, Cox to Acheson, 17 Oct. 1749.

a following in the city, were unlikely 'popular' opponents. In the event, Cavendish was persuaded by the Castle not to contest the poll to prevent a damaging Commons battle, one from which the Ponsonbys were unlikely to emerge victorious. The election left a bitter legacy, in terms of hardening attitudes between Boyle and Lord Bessborough, which was to increase greatly during the 1751–2 session.[14]

Elections, although they raised the temperature in politics, were not enough to overturn management by the chief undertaker. Nor were they enough to convince the Castle and ministers in London of his indispensability. One way of doing this was through the money bill. In 1751, a surplus once more arose in the treasury and the intention, as in 1749, was to apply some of this to paying off the capital of the national debt. To avoid any problems with the issue of 'previous consent' having to be recognised, the Commons committee of supply, led by Anthony Malone, who was certainly the most forward proponent of parliament's financial powers, inserted in the preamble to the 13 November 'heads of bill', a reference to 'gracious recommendation' of the king to spend on the national debt. At the time Sackville did not mention this wording, while Dorset referred to the use of 'recommendation' in his opening address to parliament.[15] The leading historian of the early 1750s, Declan O'Donovan, is surely correct to point out that no-one, at this stage, either expected or wanted a battle over 'previous consent'.[16] Boyle seems to have chosen to quietly manage government business for Dorset.

On the other side, despite all the talk before the session and the expectations of Stone, there was no great momentum from the Castle, at this stage, to break Boyle's power. Stone himself gave the 23 October sermon to parliament, but one should be warned against reading too much novelty or particular meaning into the message he was delivering. Like most Church of Ireland clergymen of the age (and Sir Richard Cox in 1749), Stone could have preached about the dangers from popery or from Protestant disunity. He chose the latter theme on this occasion and reminded his listeners of the God who had delivered them from the land of Egypt, of their English origins and of the necessity for a happy union between the two islands. He went on to warn against internal disunity and idle theories about Ireland's state:

> Free states have less to fear from the attacks of open enemies than from distempers bred within themselves; they are generally led astray by grasping at any forms of liberty and impracticable visions of irrational unconstitutional independency.[17]

14 PRONI T3158/398, 404, Cavendish to Hartington, 18 June 1751, Ponsonby to Duncannon, 27 May 1752; for Cox's propaganda during the election see *A Dialogue between Jack Lane and Simon Curtin* (Cork, 1751). 15 PRONI Transcripts of the State Papers, T1060/4, Dorset to Holdernesse, 14 Oct. 1751. 16 O'Donovan, 'Money Bill', p. 100; Pelham to Sackville, 11 Oct. 1751, in *Stopford-Sackville Mss.*, p. 176. 17 *Sermon preached by George [Stone], Archbishop of Armagh on 23rd October 1751* (Dublin, 1751).

There are elements of the 1751 Union debate and also the continuing problems with Dissenters in Ulster over tithes and small dues in this sermon.[18] However, it is hard to escape the conclusion that Stone was primarily using the opportunity to preach loyalty and to present the Dorset administration in the best possible light, ahead of any storms.

If the battle between the Castle and their chief undertaker was not going to break out over elections or the money bill, then what would it do so over? The unlikely answer came in November, with a Commons inquiry into the affairs of the surveyor general, Arthur Jones Nevill, and his carrying out of barracks repairs and rebuilding since 1749. At first the Castle expected nothing more than a censure for Nevill, whom Stone had got elected to a Wexford borough, for care-lessness over his accounting and supervision. The omens were promising, as the committee was chaired by William Richardson, a County Armagh MP, sympa-thetic to government, whilst most people believed Nevill was basically honest, if lazy.[19] What was to become a *cause célèbre* seemed, at this stage, little more than a run-of-the-mill inquiry into administrative incompetence, or malpractice, depending on one's viewpoint.

While that inquiry rumbled on into December the money bill returned from London with the word 'consent' inserted in place of 'recommendation'. Stone later told Newcastle that he was surprised at the change and went around different MPs to canvass their support. Boyle and Malone were alleged to be either opposed to the amendment or vague about their opinions. Sackville was more uneasy than Stone about the change, though he knew, as Dorset did, that the amendment had been made with the advice of the British attorney general and thus carried minis-terial weight. Sackville also conceded some collusion between the Castle and MPs over the original preamble:

> The word consent was not left out accidentally and a debate about the power of the Crown over the surplus of His Majesty's revenue would not be very eligible, especially as nobody disputes the enjoyment of that power since it has been so prudently exercised, and how far it would bear searching to the bottom in a house of Commons I know not.

This letter and Stone's later account are evidence that the Dorset administration, in late 1751, was still unsure of its abilities to engage the chief undertaker in battle.

---

18 The Union debate had been sparked by [Lord Hillsborough], *A Proposal for uniting the Kingdoms of Great Britain and Ireland* (Dublin, 1751); [Nicholas Archdall], *An Alarm to the people of Great Britain and Ireland* (Dublin, 1751); *Answer to the late proposal for uniting the kingdoms of Great Britain and Ireland* (Dublin, 1751). On Dissenters see BL Add. Mss.32725, f.499, Bishop of Derry to Newcastle, 14 Dec. 1751. 19 PRONI T3019/1822, Sackville to Wilmot, 28 Nov. 1751.

In the event they were spared the choice, as Boyle chose not to 'search to the bottom' the issue of 'previous consent' in this session.[20] The Speaker still seems to have been undertaking government business for Dorset as a way of proving his power and, thus, the money bill passed without a division on 10 December.

Given the secure passage of the amended money bill and the lack of any other contentious legislation, there were reasons for the optimism of the Castle officials during and after the Christmas adjournment. Only the fear that the vacant archbishopric of Tuam would not be filled by Dorset's nominee worried Sackville. Discussions on the new Gregorian calendar, which England had introduced and assumed that Ireland would follow, did not lead to 'disagreeable altercations' so that the signs were good for a quick end to the session.[21] This was what Pelham hoped, not because he feared political problems, but because Irish patronage business could be handled so much easier after the end of a parliamentary session. At this point no stable alternative had been found to Boyle as chief undertaker and so there was no question of him not being made a lord justice in the next interregnum.

Before the session ended, Boyle was to show his authority in the house of Commons, though in a measured and deliberate manner which could not be seen as open opposition to the government. The Nevill inquiry provided the opportunity, when it became clear that the surveyor general had worked from a different estimate of costs to the one provided by Lord Harrington's administration. Cox created a 'great noise' out of this and Boyle moved to severely censure Nevill and possibly expel him from the Commons. At this stage Sackville defiantly told Wilmot that it was better to lose this fight 'than to be thought accessory in any shape to such violent proceedings.'[22] He was less trenchant in his report to Pelham, writing that he supported Nevill in the Commons against 'violent measures, though he [Sackville] is far from intending to justify the surveyor-general in every part of his conduct.' In both letters the blame for this 'violence' was laid at the door of Cox. Sackville claimed that this MP was being used by Boyle, which 'we suppose to have been in return for our showing ourselves able to support the alteration in the money bill independent of the Speaker and his party.'[23]

However, this support for Nevill was a tactical error by the Castle. The government had not gained any extra strength in the Commons, where Boyle had been able to parade his continuing influence, by supporting both a popular inquiry and a set of resolutions which were far from extreme. In fact, there was probably never any intention to dismiss or expel Nevill, who was instructed to make good repairs

20 PRONI T3019/1822, Sackville to Wilmot, 28 Nov. 1751; PRONI T2860/1, Stone to Newcastle, 2 Oct. 1754.   21 PRONI T3019/1834, Sackville to Wilmot, 7 Jan. 1752; Pelham to Sackville, 19 Jan. 1752, in *Stopford-Sackville Mss.*, pp. 178–9.   22 PRONI T3019/1848, Sackville to Wilmot, 15 Feb. 1752.   23 PRONI T2863/1/38, Sackville to Pelham, 15 February 1752.

from his own money, while Harrington was cleared of any involvement and another two year's supplies were granted for further barracks work.[24]

Sackville compounded his error when he aimed for popularity with the Dublin crowd by opposing the building of a new bridge over the Liffey. This issue arose on the same day that the Nevill inquiry reached its reporting stage and centred on the proposal from Clements, Luke Gardiner and others, to build a new bridge across the Liffey to connect their developments in Sackville Street to College Green. It was opposed by many of Dublin's merchants, as the scheme would prevent ships from docking at the Customs House. Sackville took up their case and Boyle, caught between his support for Clements and his wish to avoid unpopularity with the Dublin crowd, attempted to play for time with a week's postponement of debate to 28 February. According to Waite, the closeness of the vote on the postponement (Sackville lost by 82 votes to 69) meant that 'neither Speaker not Prime Serjeant [Malone] looked all that elated with it.'[25] Sackville concurred, crowing at the divisions among Boyle's supporters on this issue. He was then able to adjourn further discussion to 1 June, thus shelving the bridge scheme indefinitely. While this allegedly made him 'as popular as ever was Lucas in Dublin', Sackville also noted that 'almost all the people in employment divided against me'. Though the Bishop of Derry praised Sackville's stance, he was clear about the consequences:

> I am sorry to find that there is at present a great, and I fear a growing spirit of party among us. I should judge, and I hope, by its violence it will be less lasting.[26]

The bishop was correct that the defeat of the 'Bridge affair' had been a pyrrhic victory for Sackville. The chief secretary had needlessly risked and lost a Commons vote, had alienated some of the leading office-holders (especially Clements) and had raised party strife to new heights. The Commons was far from unmanageable for the Castle, but the advantage had passed back to Boyle. The Nevill inquiry and the 'Bridge affair' had shown the immaturity of Sackville and Stone for all to see, though they were quick to deny this. The fact that they both wrote to different ministers on 10 March (the day the bridge scheme was finally dropped) is hardly a coincidence. Sackville told Pelham of his relief that the Nevill inquiry was finally over, with censure being the outcome, and he claimed that Dorset's interposition with MPs had prevented any reflections on Lord Harrington or the expulsion of Nevill. Thus the Castle had been victorious and could ignore the Commons' resolutions:

24 PRONI Foster-Masserene papers, D207/21/1–16, 'Papers on the case of Arthur Jones Nevill'. **25** PRONI T3019/1851, Waite to Wilmot, 22 Feb. 1752. **26** BL Add. Mss.32726, f.235, Bishop of Derry to Newcastle, 7 Mar. 1752; PRONI T3019/1850, 1859, Sackville to Wilmot, 22 Feb., Waite to Wilmot, 29 Feb. 1752.

The harshness of the resolutions is in great measure owing to the disputes he [Nevill] has had with several persons of great weight here, and among others with my Lord Kildare in some county matters.[27]

Stone agreed with Sackville's analysis of what lay behind the resolutions, that is, Nevill's incompetence and the actions of a 'powerful party' (Boyle's) which had been defeated on other points. The party included Lord Kildare, who 'thought it not below him to engage what influence he has on other points, on the condition that this man [Nevill] was ill-treated.' Stone developed his letter into a more general analysis of Irish politics:

It is no new thought with me (for I have expressed it in letters) that the power of the lord lieutenant had of late insensibly passed into other hands, and that it must at some time or other occasion a struggle to redeem it. The party in possession were determined to have a struggle for it; and the roughness of the barracks transaction has been with a view to persuade my lord lieutenant of the expediency of putting himself with the king's authority into their hands absolutely.[28]

According to Stone's analysis, the ministry faced the choice of supporting the resistance of the current Castle administration, which explained their backing of Nevill, or giving up the claim to govern in Ireland. In other words, back Stone and Sackville with the power to dismiss and appoint officials, or allow the Castle to be dictated to by the likes of Boyle and Kildare.

These letters drew a mixed response from ministers. Newcastle, undoubtedly egged on by Andrew Stone, praised the Castle's conduct. He was full of promises of support for whatever measures were deemed necessary, delighted that Dorset had steered government business through the Commons and had 'resisted any attempts there may have been, either to weaken the authority of the Castle or to govern by an Irish independent interest.' However, he warned Stone that London was full of rumours and criticisms of the Dorset administration, though he did not believe the stories 'of an inclination to set up a secret Irish faction'.[29] Pelham was quicker than his brother to respond and did so in a much cooler fashion. He was careful not to criticise the behaviour of either Dorset or Sackville and bitterly attacked Cox for his ingratitude to Harrington, who had made him a revenue officer. But he mentioned nothing of further actions by the Castle and on the barracks affair he wrote:

27 PRONI T2863/1/39, Sackville to Pelham, 10 Mar. 1752.   28 BL Add. Mss.32726, ff.246–8, Stone to Stone, 10 Mar. 1752.   29 BL Add. Mss.32726, f.379, Newcastle to Stone, 4 Apr. 1752.

> This affair has made some little noise here, and, in general your surveyor is much blamed. Whether he deserves so severe a censure as is contained in the resolutions of the Commons I know not, but he ought to deserve a great deal before such resolutions are come into.[30]

This implicitly hints that the Castle would have done better not to protect or screen someone so obviously incompetent if not dishonest. While management of the Commons had not been lost, the credibility of the Dorset administration had been damaged in London, never mind Dublin.

When the Commons reassembled after the Easter adjournment, the harrassment of Nevill continued to embarrass the Castle and when Sackville attempted to get a further adjournment of discussion, on 14 April, he was heavily defeated. According to Walpole's memoirs:

> ... the ladies made ball, the mob bonfires, the poets pasquinades – if Pasquin has seen wittier he himself never saw more severe or less delicate lampoons.[31]

There is no evidence to corroborate Walpole's report but the Castle was clearly not amused by the continuing parliamentary attack on Nevill. To put a stop to this the pensions of Bellingham Boyle and Cosby Nesbit (a connection of Clements) were temporarily stopped. Sackville was also active in the Commons, though once more his judgement can be questioned. To rebut rumours that the surplus in the Irish treasury was to be sent to Hanover (a precursor of the theories of 1754–5), he lectured the Commons to stop 'the old distinction of English and Irish interests [being] set on foot.' In response, the Commons passed a 'positive' address to the king, proposed by Sir Arthur Gore, which denied any intention that MPs were aiming at independency. Sackville's report of this address was a glowing one, but the omission of any compliment to Dorset and the criticism of Stone was in reality 'a very poor performance' for the Castle.[32]

Other Dublin officials were careful not to refer to the snubs contained in the Commons' address to George II. Waite told Wilmot that Sackville had emerged from the session with his reputation enhanced, while Boyle and his allies had 'crests considerably fallen and I fancy they will be lower before the next session.' The new archbishop of Tuam, John Ryder, claimed that 'the Castle stood their ground and must prevail in the end.'[33] Others sang from the same hymn-sheet.

30 Pelham to Sackville, 16 Mar. 1752, in *Stopford-Sackville Mss.*, p. 182. 31 Walpole, *George II*, i, p. 283. 32 PRONI T2863/1/40–2, Sackville to Pelham, 2 May [with enclosed address], 7 May 1752. 33 PRONI T3019/1898, 1895, 1893, Waite to Wilmot, 17 May, Ryder to Wilmot, 9 May, Sackville to Wilmot, 7 May 1752. Sackville told Wilmot to say in London that the chief secretary had 'no intention to be governed by those whose great object has been cowering the office of lord lieutenant, setting him up for a pageant and exercising the real power in his name.'

John Bowes wrote that the only difference about Dorset as viceroy was that his connections in London were much stronger than either Chesterfield or Harrington's had been. This meant that Dorset was in a better position to negotiate with the chief undertaker:

> Thus circumstanced, it was reasonable to think the administration would be brought back to the Castle, ... but I know of no act done or intended, to lessen the Speaker's influence or power as one of the king's first servants.[34]

TO BUILD A COMMONS MAJORITY, PART ONE

Pelham and other ministers were not deceived by attempts to put a positive gloss on the Castle's management of the session. The problem was not that an attempt to 'bring government back to the Castle' had been made; it was the bungling of this that infuriated ministers and cast some doubt over Dorset's return. Pelham, in particular, was scathing about the conduct of the administration:

> What does Dorset think and what has he been doing? By Lord George's letters one would think they were infatuated or quite asleep at the Castle ... they have quarreled with the Speaker; were beat in the House of Commons; and have contrived to have almost all the men of business against them.[35]

Newcastle amended his earlier support for the Castle, despite Stone's fresh demands for dismissals.[36] Instead Newcastle told Pelham that Stone had 'taken my letter-in-aid a little too nicely' and he avowed that he had never authorised the Castle to create opposition or stop pensions. From other letters coming out of London at this time there was a definite reserve about the wisdom of the course that Dorset's administration had taken in Ireland. The only thing in Dorset's favour, was that his potential replacement, Bedford or the 'fat friend', was hated by the Pelham Whigs.[37]

For the rest of the interregnum, almost directly contradictory courses were taken by the leading figures in the Irish government. Dorset and Sackville met Pelham in early June and conceded some ground from their earlier positions,

34 [Bowes] to Dodington, 26 May 1752, in *Stopford-Sackville Mss.*, pp. 182–4; BL Add. Mss. 35591, f.371, [Yorke] to Hardwicke, 2 July 1752.   35 BL Add. Mss. 32727, f.230, Pelham to Newcastle, 21 May 1752.   36 Stone was direct in his demand for sackings after the session had ended: BL Add. Mss. 32727, f.110, Stone to Newcastle, 7 May 1752; PRONI T2863/1/48, Stone to Pelham, 26 May 1752.   37 BL Add. Mss.32727, f.365, Newcastle to Pelham, 10 June 1752; Dodington to [Bowes?], 30 June 1752, in *Stopford-Sackville Mss.*, p. 184.

though Lord George only 'partly so'. Pelham accepted the need for some reform but demanded 'a little more phlegm and cooler conduct' with regard to Boyle. Sackville reported that Cox was disliked, but that the Castle was not allowed to sack him, that Pelham believed all the differences were personal and had asked Sackville if he had any plans to remove Boyle as Speaker. When the chief secretary mentioned the possible involvement of Henry Fox, through his brother-in-law Kildare, Pelham laughed at the suggestion 'and said he fancied the politics here was little understood in Ireland'.[38] With Sackville chastened by Pelham, the interest of the ministry turned to the accusations that Andrew Stone and William Murray were, or had been, Jacobites. In these circumstances there was little room for much interest in Irish affairs.[39]

Despite the responses of Pelham and Newcastle, Stone rejected the idea of reconciliation with Boyle in order to rebuild the previous management system, and suggested other ways of building a government majority. Before Dorset left Dublin, 'he had not the least private intercourse with the Speaker or any of his friends since the end of the session', even though Boyle was made one of the lords justices.[40] Stone continued with this approach of non-cooperation, and told Pelham in July:

> I would willingly have supposed the Speaker's extraordinary conduct to have proceeded from the advice of men worse than himself … but his own part has been such, and so many astonishing facts are lately come to my knowledge, that it will be impossible for me hereafter to have the least reliance on him.[41]

Sackville agreed with this approach, despite his chastising by Pelham, and told Wilmot that he believed Boyle 'sees he has a bad game to play … [and] may wish to withdraw before it is too late'. His engagements to Malone and others would make this difficult but Sackville would welcome Boyle's retirement as it 'might be the means of shaking those who are out looking for protection.'[42] This was far from the 'phlegm' that Pelham wanted to see and more of an attempt to construct a majority independent of Boyle; in other words trying to follow the strategy of 1751–2 in a more successful manner.

The key to building such a government majority was to shake Boyle's support in different ways: seeking signs of popularity; detaching further interests, includ-

38 For quite different reports of these discussions see PRONI T3019/1914, Sackville to Stone, 10 June 1752; BL Add. Mss.32727, ff.408–11, Stone to Newcastle, 12 June 1752; BL Add. Mss. 32728, f.68, 106, Pelham to Newcastle, 19 June, Newcastle to Stone, 26 June 1752. 39 The 'Fawcett affair' was followed closely in Ireland where the Patriot press drew comparisons between Andrew and George Stone's politics: U[niversal] A[dvertiser], 5, 12 Mar. 1753. 40 PRONI Roden papers, Mic147/9, ff.77–8, Foster to [Limerick], 16 May 1752. 41 Stone to Pelham, 25 July 1752, in *Stopford-Sackville Mss.*, pp. 184–6. 42 PRONI T3019/1961, Sackville to Wilmot, 31 Aug. 1752.

ing Kildare, through patronage; and seeking to win any by-elections that might occur. The first of these three is often ignored, as it is believed the Dorset administration was irredeemably unpopular. However, the Castle used all the traditional means of highlighting public support, such as plaudits from the crowd, freedoms from corporations and friendly addresses, in the newspapers. When the viceroy left Dublin, there was a concerted effort, through the medium of friendly aldermen, to gather a crowd for the send-off. This was made easier because of the popular stance taken by Sackville over the Liffey Bridge.[43] The Ponsonbys were also active in the search for popular acclaim and got the grand jury of County Kilkenny and the corporation of Cork city to award gold boxes to Sackville and Lord Bessborough.[44] The propagation of such news was of vital importance and here, the cooperation of George Faulkner, owner of the *Dublin Journal*, was vitally important to the government. It would be wrong to believe that the Castle, either in the interregnum or after the Money Bill was rejected in December 1753, neglected to fight their corner in the press or the popular arena.

However, government patronage was always a more important weapon and it was in this area that Stone's progress in 1752-3 seemed inexorable. It was made quite clear that the primate was the key person in the regency. When looking for a minor post, Lord Orrery was told: 'All places and preferments flow from that channel.'[45] This was problematic for Boyle, as his allies were being approached by the Castle and he was unable to help them. Robert Fitzgerald, an MP for County Kerry, became disillusioned with Boyle in this period:

> The Speaker [is] single against all the men in power and utterly unable and, I wish I could not add, unwilling to serve his truest friends. His hopes are that the duke will not come over ever more, an imagination that has little basis ... I have long lived in hopes; I cannot subsist upon such diet.[46]

Confirming Fitzgerald's fears and perhaps influencing him to support the government in 1753-4, was the fact that, in February 1752, Boyle was unable even to fill a vacancy in the deanery of Cloyne. His days as a chief undertaker with the disposal of some patronage seemed to be numbered.[47]

Whether the intention was to isolate Boyle, or to make it look like he was abandoned by his friends, strong efforts were made in 1752-3 to destroy his influence. Rumours began to circulate in the summer of 1752 that Lord Kildare

---

43 It was almost as important to contradict the perception in England that Dorset was deeply unpopular through inserting reports in the London newspapers of the duke's send-off; PRONI T3019/1903, 1905, 1907, Waite to Wilmot, 24, 26, 28 May 1752.   **44** PRONI T3019/2145, Sackville to Wilmot, 12 Aug. 1753.   **45** Barry to Orrery, 28 Nov. 1752, in *Orrery Papers*, p. 117.   **46** NLI Talbot-Crosbie papers, Ms.8054, Fitzgerald to Crosbie, 30 Dec. 1752.   **47** Stone to Sackville, 10 Feb. 1753, in *Stopford-Sackville Mss.*, p. 190.

had been offered a share in patronage, in return for supporting the Castle. Stone denied that he had sent anyone to make this offer to Kildare, who made it public, either to expose the 'plot' or to rebut rumours that he was abandoning Boyle.[48] Following this, stories began to circulate, in September 1752, that Sir Arthur Gore was canvassing in Cork to replace a retiring Boyle as Speaker. Sackville was delighted at this:

> Surely Sir Arthur would not think of staying in that country without permission upon such an errand, and if he has permission it is not very prudent in the Speaker to give anybody reason to suspect he has any thoughts of retiring. A report of that sort must surely lessen his following.[49]

In July 1753 the Castle turned its attention to another likely ally of Boyle's, Nathaniel Clements. Clements went to London to pledge his loyalty to the administration and, by September, Sackville hoped that he would influence a number of MPs in Ulster to support the government.[50] With these developments, Stone was confidently telling Sackville in April 1753:

> The more judicious say it is amazing to see so strong a party broke in so short a time and they acknowledge that it could not have been under any other government.[51]

With this ongoing use of patronage and government influence, there is little doubt that the Castle was clearly intent on building a government majority in the Commons without the assistance or involvement of Boyle.

The Speaker was never likely to give up without a fight and he was far from quiet during the interregnum. His approach was to rally support, against Stone in particular, while at the same time denying any intention of breaking with government. To spread the latter message, in June 1752, he sent his son-in-law, Lord Carrick, to London with a letter for Pelham. The letter denied that Irish Protestants were 'aiming at independency', a claim that had been made in the previous session and was to be repeated over the next decade and beyond. Furthermore, Boyle defended his own conduct in the late session and stated that Lord Carrick could furnish details to convince Pelham of his support for government. He finally reminded Pelham that the Irish MPs:

> have honoured me with their confidence, who I can in great truth say have at all times where His Majesty's service has been concerned shown themselves to be most zealous in the support of it.[52]

48 Kildare to Stone, 5 Oct, Stone to Kildare, [Oct. 1752], in ibid., p. 187. 49 PRONI T3019/1966, Sackville to Wilmot, 14 Sept. 1752. 50 PRONI T3019/1975, Sackville to Wilmot, 21 Sept. 1752. 51 Stone to Sackville, 16 Apr. 1753, in *Stopford-Sackville Mss.*, pp. 194–6. 52 PRONI T2863/1/50, Boyle to Pelham, 13 June 1752.

This mission to Pelham shows that the Speaker was not going to ignore any possible channel to the king, bar Newcastle (the closest ally of Stone). It also shows that Boyle and some of the other Patriots may have believed that Pelham would rein in, if not replace, Dorset. This was supported by rumours in the winter of 1752–3 that Boyle had been called to London to meet not only ministers but perhaps even George II, but in the event he did not. Instead, he sent another letter to Pelham, one that Stone described as 'very extraordinary'. In this, he wrote that the Castle/parliament relations were as bad as they had been during the Wood's Halfpence quarrel of the 1720s. He also implied that Dorset had ignored him from early on and that political peace in Ireland was 'now in danger of being interrupted and disturbed to answer the private views of a very few'.[53] Like Irish Patriots before and after him, Boyle would use every opportunity to persuade British ministers that it was bad government and not patriotism that threatened the Anglo-Irish nexus.

Of course Boyle could not afford to rely on the good offices of Henry Pelham alone. To rally his supporters, he continued in the way that he had done for the previous two decades and 'declare[d] in the country that the life of a country gentleman is what he like[d] best'.[54] This was taken as a possible hint of retirement, but had more to do with a political veteran going back to his roots. Dinners were held in Dublin and the south of the country, including one, on 1 July 1752, where Lord Kildare was the special guest.[55] The emergent opposition to Dorset knew that they could not rely on a ministerial reshuffle going in their favour and, therefore, a new Dublin newspaper, the *Universal Advertiser*, began, in 1753, to challenge the pro-government line of the *Dublin Journal* with the skilful polemics of Sir Richard Cox. Then there was the publication of *The History of Roger*, which painted a positive, if not flawless, picture of the Speaker and ran to five editions in 1752. Given the important role of print, especially Jonathan Swift's *Drapier's Letters*, during the Wood's Halfpence crisis of the 1720s, the Patriots were always likely to use similar methods in the 1750s.

These activities, like the Nevill inquiry from the 1751-2 session, were meant to damage the Dorset administration, to 'wound through the sides'. But they were not an announcement of open war. The bombast of the Kildare mission to London in mid-1753 was significantly different. Lord Kildare was always a difficult character, driven more by personal honour and a sense of his importance as premier peer in Ireland rather than by any political judgement. In line with this, it is not surprising that the last straw for Kildare was opposition to his candidate for an Athy by-election in May 1753. This, he believed, was inspired directly by Stone, who denied the allegation and said that he had rejected offers from

---

53 PRONI T3019/1963, Waite to Wilmot, 1 Sept. 1752; PRONI T2863/1/51, Boyle to Pelham, 23 Jan. 1753. 54 PRONI T3019/1962, Sackville to Wilmot, 31 Aug. 1752. 55 Kildare to Kildare, 30 June 1752, in *Leinster Corr.*, i, p. 43.

discontented burgesses asking him to nominate an opponent to Kildare's man.[56] Whatever the truth, the outcome was that Kildare went to London in June 1753 and, against the advice of Henry Fox and others, delivered a memorial to George II. In it, he listed the faults of the present Irish administration, especially Stone and Sackville, and asked that Dorset be removed. In England, the effects were disastrous as Pelham and his ministers (even Fox) leapt to defend Dorset. The secretary of state, Lord Holdernesse, was instructed to write to Lord Newport, expressing royal and ministerial support for the viceroy, and Lord Hardwicke denounced the memorial in even stronger terms as an insult to the royal prerogative.[57]

Whether or not Boyle had approved of Kildare's mission, he was silent about it, while Luke Gardiner expressed his surprise and it was alleged that Sir Arthur Gore was 'horrified'.[58] When even Anthony Malone seemed to equivocate about Kildare's performance, it seemed that there was nothing to be salvaged from the affair. However, Dublin public opinion believed that Kildare had defended the liberties of Ireland. In the wake of the earl's visit to London, Patriot feeling, whipped up by the *Universal Advertiser*, was certainly on the increase. Waite made the point that, though the 'best persons' were opposed to Kildare's actions, the opposition would stop at little to avenge themselves on Stone.[59]

The snubbing of Kildare by ministers had closed the door of conciliation, but it had also revived Patriot politics. In this context, the possibly accidental, but definitely damaging, loss of the Linen Bill of 1751, became a focus of national pride and anti-English feeling. Members of the Linen Board, like Bishop Synge, suggested appointing an agent to ensure the success of the next bill, while the Patriot press thundered:

> Contrary to the usual practice … this bill was returned to us from England, so mangled and mutilated, that it became absolutely unavoidable to suffer it to drop.[60]

William Bruce, a Dissenting minister in Dublin, wrote a pamphlet on the same subject, even though he was worried about the 'licentious and ungentlemanly' newspaper comment. Yet, he concluded, 'the spirit of the parties is so sharpened against one another that even such gross abuse is not altogether without its advocates'.[61]

56 PRONI T2863/1/66, Stone to Pelham, 19 May 1753. 57 Holdernesse to Newport, 29 June, Hardwicke to Newport, 29 June 1752, in C. Yorke, *The Life and Correspondence of Philip Yorke, Lord Chancellor Hardwicke* (3 vols, Cambridge, 1913), ii, pp. 124–6. 58 Gardiner to Dorset, 3 July 1753, in Stopford-Sackville Mss., p. 195; PRONI T3019/2157, Sackville to Wilmot, 1 Aug. 1753. 59 *UA*, 3, 10 July 1753; PRONI T3019/2156, Waite to Wilmot, 31 July 1753. 60 PRONI Mic149/9, pp. 88–97, Synge to Limerick, 25, 29 May, 2, 7 June 1753; *UA*, 4 Aug. 1753. 61 [William Bruce], *Some Facts and Observations Relative to the Fate of the Late Linen Bill* (Dublin, 1753); PRONI D2092/1/8/, p. 30, Bruce to Ward, 24 July 1753.

As the 1753 session approached, the main interests had not shifted sides during the interregnum. Boyle could still be assured of Kildare's support and, probably, that of the Gores. Where he may have lost ground was among some of the smaller groups and the independent country gentlemen, though their views would not really be known until parliament assembled. The Castle had got over the same period without creating any new enemies, even if the ones it had from 1751-2 were more hardened than before. In fact, late attempts at winning over some converts, like Cox, or conciliating Boyle through Luke Gardiner, proved costly as they created even more rancour.[62] Under these circumstances, one can understand Stone's nervousness whether the government would have a majority and whether contested elections or a fresh Nevill inquiry could shake this.[63]

A SHORT, SHARP SESSION, 1753–4

Neither side went into the session of 1753-4 assured of victory, nor did either side seem to expect that the crisis would reach the proportions that it did. Some of Boyle's supporters believed, right up to the start of the session, that a quarrel could be avoided. The Castle crowed as the Patriots avoided a showdown over the opening Commons' address and its usual compliments to the viceroy.[64] William Yorke believed after this damp squib that:

> ... tho' restless and unquiet spirits may, and certainly are, still subsisting, yet the abovementioned circumstances have so dampened them, that they'll not be able, in this House, to give the same uneasiness, as was at first apprehended.[65]

Yorke was worried about the continuing arguments over the 1751 Linen Bill, but it appeared that even this might not ruin the present calm, despite the earlier warning signs.[66] The elections for County Armagh and County Galway had raised

---

62 *Letter from a Kilkenny Clergyman [Bishop Michael Cox] to Sir Richard Cox* (Dublin, 1753); PRONI T3019/2179, Sackville to Wilmot, 27 Sept. 1753.   **63** PRONI T2863/1/67, Stone to Pelham, 30 Aug. 1753; PRONI Abercorn papers, T2541/IA1/2/159, Hudson to Abercorn, 29 Sept. 1753.   **64** PRONI Anglesey papers D619/21/B/63, Rooney to Bayly, 13 Oct. 1753; RIA Charlemont papers, Ms.12/R/9, no. 28, Adderley to Charlemont, 9 Feb. 1755; PRONI T2863/1/55, Sackville to Pelham, 12 Oct. 1753.   **65** BL Add. Mss.35592, f.169, Yorke to Hardwicke, 11 Oct. 1753.   **66** PRONI Mussenden papers D354/1029, Richardson to Mussenden, 13 Oct. 1753. Richardson was a firm government supporter and had been ready to move a new Linen Bill with Anthony Foster (also a government supporter) when the Patriot Nicholas Archdall leapt up in the Commons to move the bill. This caused great fury among Linen Board members, or at least the Castle nominees, but Richardson also alleged that these tactics had not helped the Patriots.

party spirits, as national politics intervened in local matters, but in both cases government candidates were returned and the Patriots seemed to be losing ground.[67]

With all this vacillation on the Patriot side and the successes of the Castle, the renewed Nevill inquiry (into the conduct of the official responsible for the upkeep of barracks) took on a new significance. As far as the government was concerned, it looked like an unwinnable case. Nevill had actually asked, in July 1752, for instructions on the repairs he was to make but then, in the spring of 1753, he had contested two different reports on the work to be done. Though Nevill's objections were supported by his replacement as surveyor general, the quarrel had delayed work beginning until August 1753, weeks before parliament was due to sit. On top of this evidence which was to come before the Commons committee, there were other suspicions: Nevill's selling his office to Eyre and Stone's intervention over the two reports. Whatever about Nevill's honesty, his political *nous* was certainly in question.[68] Only stubbornness, or a belief that the government had a secure majority, could have persuaded Sackville to support his former official.

At the same time the money bills were passed with one, later to be the fateful one, dealing specifically with the Treasury surplus of around £328,000. Once again, the solution was to appropriate £120,000 of this to pay more of the national debt. After debates between Malone and Philip Tisdall, in the committee of six appointed to draft a bill, both sides had avoided the issue of whose consent was needed for this application of funds. Most observers knew, however, that the 'previous consent' of the king would be insisted upon in London. The debates on the main money bill centred on a battle over Lord Kildare's attempt to introduce an absentee tax of four shillings in the pound. Malone was persuaded to abandon Kildare and his spokesperson, Thomas Pakenham, and so the measure fell, leading to increasing government confidence in their control of the Commons. Given this, Sackville denounced the failure to insert 'previous consent' and called for the sacking of Boyle, Malone and Carter, to make the point that vacillation would not save inveterate opponents of government.[69] Stone agreed, saying that Boyle was merely trying to keep his popularity and urged ministers to amend the bill and dismiss any recalcitrant officials. In his reply, Newcastle urged the Castle and all king's servants in Ireland to 'use your utmost endeavours to get the bills passed on their return', while also conceding that dismissals might now be inevitable.[70]

Although Newcastle was growing more impatient with the Patriots, he was horrified at the next move of Stone and Sackville, when they attempted once more

67 Both elections are important in the local and national spheres but space prevents greater treatment of them here. See E. Magennis, 'Popery, Patriotism and Politics: The Armagh election of 1753', in A. Hughes & R. Weatherup (eds), *Armagh: History and Politics* (Dublin, forthcoming). 68 PRONI D207/21/4, 'Papers relative to the case of Arthur Jones Nevill, 1753'. 69 PRONI T3019/2202, 2204, Sackville to Wilmot, 11 Nov., Sackville to Pelham, 16 Nov. 1753. 70 BL Add. Mss.32733, ff.289, 293, Stone to Newcastle, 21 Nov., Newcastle to Dorset, 22 Nov. 1753.

to shield Nevill from parliamentary censure. On November 17, the Castle pressed the Commons to widen the inquiry in an attempt to delay and confuse matters. They won this division by 118 votes to 115, as Sackville told Wilmot:

> ... as I wanted to know the real disposition of people, I begged my friends to push it to a decision on this trifling question, because if we lost it just by a few then be certain they could attempt no violence or injustice.

However, this interference in a Commons inquiry would not have won over any independent MPs and the government was dependent on a handful of officials, especially Clements and Gardiner (and those they influenced) for their majority. The risks taken by Sackville in pushing for confrontation became clear on 22 November, when the Commons committee resolved to censure Nevill for failing to act on their resolutions of 1752. The administration contested two resolutions and lost both (116 votes to 123 and 120 votes to 122). Sackville was brutal in his condemnation of Clements' defection to the opposition and stated that Boyle had 'declared he must quit the chair if Nevill was not expelled.' The Patriots had not wasted any time in mobilising support and thus the Commons was as full as in the last days of Queen Anne. Yet all of this did not persuade Sackville and others that they had been mistaken in making a stand over Nevill. Reflecting this viewpoint, Waite argued:

> Between you and me, my good friend, it is a most melancholy consideration to those who are in the service of government if they cannot be protected by that government whom they serve honestly and to the best of their abilities.[72]

That the Castle had failed to protect Nevill from censure and had probably ensured his expulsion from the Commons, while alienating many of those independent MPs who were crucial to any majority, was ignored in this analysis. Opinion in London was less focussed on the pride or honour of Dorset's administration. As tales of bonfires from Bandon to Charlemont, celebrating the expulsion of Nevill, the abuse of Stone and Kildare being chaired through the streets of Dublin, were printed in the *London Evening Post*, ministers hit the roof.[73] Newcastle brusquely told Stone:

> ... we are of the opinion that it was unlucky that the friends of government took upon them in any degree the defence of Mr Nevill Jones ... you have suffered yourselves to be beat upon an insignificant point; and are less able by that means to stand the great question when it comes.[74]

71 PRONI T3019/2206, Sackville to Wilmot, 17 Nov. 1753.   72 PRONI T3019/2208-9, Waite to Wilmot, 22 Nov. Sackville to Wilmot, 22 Nov. 1753.   73 PRONI T3019/2217, Waite to Wilmot, 6 Dec. 1753; Walpole to Montagu, 6 Dec. 1753, in *Walpole Corr.*, i, p. 186.   74 BL Add. Mss.32733, f.259, Newcastle to Stone, 30 Nov. 1753.

If one bears in mind that Newcastle was ordinarily very supportive of the Dorset administration, then ministerial despair at the Castle's management of Irish politics in this matter is obvious. The impression from London, once more, was that a personal quarrel was being mismanaged into a constitutional one.[75]

Sackville, meanwhile, was unrepentant about the path chosen by the government. To the question, asked by Pelham, about what the Nevill affair or support for William Brownlow in the Armagh election had to do with the king's business, he replied:

> We should have been left at the mercy of the speaker, of Lord Kildare, and the prime serjeant [Malone], and all English influence would have been at an end.

Waite also thought that, if the Armagh election was lost, then Stone might be voted an enemy of Ireland. He called, in the present situation, for the ministry in London to 'turn over a new leaf' and start backing Dorset and Sackville.[76] In such a feverish atmosphere the Castle successfully supported Brownlow, in his defence of his election, winning a division, on 8 December, by 120 votes to 119.

Again though, the question can be (and was, at the time) asked, whether the Castle was expending too much energy and increasing party strife even before the money bill's return. One sign of this was Waite's conviction that the Nevill and Armagh votes meant that already 'our friends will look for satisfaction ... they have a right to expect security and protection.'[77] Undoubtedly those MPs who supported the Castle were looking at defectors like John Macarell and Clements and expected their dismissal. Such sackings in due course would bring fresh patronage opportunities. In the meantime and with a crucial money bill vote looming, ministers must have wondered whether the Castle had sold its support and protection cheaply. The other consequence of Nevill and the Armagh election contest was that the government's strategy had reduced Boyle's ability to retreat from confrontation. If, as Sackville had stated all along, Boyle was wary of open opposition, then this challenge to his speakership, remembering that he had not lost an election vote in twenty years, was counter-productive. Throughout the session, Sackville had been saying how Boyle was always trying to distance himself from Malone and Kildare. Now he would be less able to do so, if he hoped to survive as Speaker.

The story of the money bill, which was only intended to pay off some of the national debt, rather than raise taxes, is easily told. It returned and, as expected,

---

75 Because of this impression Stone was stung into another lengthy exposition of the 'undertaker theory': BL Add. Mss.32733, f.369, Stone to Newcastle, 5 Dec. 1753.   76 PRONI T3019/2218–9, Sackville to Wilmot, 6 Dec., Waite to Wilmot, 6 Dec. 1753. Waite had the sense to ask Wilmot to burn his very critical letter.   77 PRONI T/3019/2223, Waite to Wilmot, 11 Dec. 1753.

had been amended with 'previous consent' added to the preamble. Dorset called a meeting of all his officials and, after stating the line from the English privy council and urging support for this, he was forced to endure the silent leave-taking of Boyle and his allies. There was now no going back.[78] A two-day debate followed on the rights and wrongs of this amendment and also what it meant (the Patriots saying that it was to take money out of Ireland and that it was an attack on the financial powers of the Irish parliament; the government supporters arguing that it was a normal and correct exercise of prerogative). Then, in a midnight sitting on 17 December, the bill was defeated by 123 votes to 118. Over twenty MPs, who were on either the civil or military establishment, voted with the Patriots, though Clements and Gardiner, at the last moment, supported the Castle. The immediate reports from Dublin were apocalyptic in tone, Waite noting the popular celebrations for the vote, and Sackville commenting that 'Lucas's doctrine was modest in comparison to what is now encouraged'.[79] Others, including the normally silent Newport, wrote to England, fearful of what would come next, especially with the Dublin crowd celebrating the government's defeat with great energy. In public, Sackville was said to be putting a brave face on the defeat, reportedly comparing it to 'a rubber at whist, played for amusement.'[80] This rather bizarre show of bravado or disdain for the views of MPs was hardly likely to win over any new support.

The expressions of public support for the Patriots always raises the question of 'paid' crowds, but Bishop Synge stated that 'on the utmost enquiry I cannot find they were raised or encouraged'.[81] In his detailed reconstruction of this dispute, Declan O'Donovan has pointed to the crucial role of economic hardship and the importance of this to an understanding of such crowd activities. There was no dearth, but the harvest of 1753 had been poor and prices in Dublin and other towns were rising during this winter. With high food and fuel prices and poor trade in linens and other commodities, the worries of the urban crowds were apparent, but even more striking were the problems of the landed gentry. Though they were no strangers to debt, the problem in 1753 lay in trying to get credit or specie when the Treasury funds were tightly controlled. The pressure put on the bankers, which lasted from December until the closure of Dillon and Ferrall's bank in April 1754, finally forced the Castle and leading Dublin merchants to intervene and pledge their support for bankers' notes. In these difficult economic circumstances, the rumours of Treasury money being taken out of Ireland (as the later Stuarts had done) were more easily believed.[82] Then, the usual economic

---

78 BL Add. Mss.32733, f.445, Stone to Stone, 15 Dec. 1753.   79 PRONI T3019/2226–7, Waite to Wilmot, 18 Dec., Sackville to Wilmot, 18 Dec. 1753.   80 BL Add. Mss.35592, f.223, Newport to Hardwicke, 19 Dec. 1753; PRONI T2541/IA1/2/176, Bracegirdle to [Abercorn], 18 Dec. 1753.   81 PRONI Mic149/9, pp. 108–9, Synge to Limerick, 25 Dec. 1753.   82 For this see D. O'Donovan, 'Money Bill', pp. 74–9.

Patriot calls to improve Ireland could easily become arguments that the destruction of that kingdom was being engineered by bad ministers. In this way, economic and constitutional questions merged.

RESPONSES TO THE MONEY BILL VOTE

The first task for the Castle, as most of its business was completed by the Christmas adjournment of 22 December, was to get instructions on what to do next. No risks were taken; the messenger to London, Robert Maxwell, was sent with letters from Stone and Dorset, plus division lists, all eloquently putting the case for dismissals of the leading Patriot placemen, including Clements (in Stone's view, not Dorset's), and the success that would follow this.[83] The need for unanimity and a strong response from the Castle were all the more necessary as Kildare readied himself to go on another mission to London. The tragedy of his previous trip turned this time into farce. First, he could not get a boat and then, after finally getting to London, he was refused a royal audience. Fox tried to restrain his troublesome in-law and then, after a week, got him a short and inconclusive meeting with Pelham.[84] Though Kildare had achieved nothing of what he had set out to do, the mission was seen by many in Dublin as a courageous attempt to bring the views of the Commons' majority to the king and his ministers, something which the Castle had tried to prevent.[85]

The response from secretary of state Holdernesse eventually arrived in Dublin on 9 January. As expected, Carter, Malone, General Dilkes, Bellingham Boyle were all dismissed from office or pension. However, Boyle and Clements escaped the sack and parliament was to be quickly prorogued. Holdernesse's letter was certainly fervently supportive of the Castle and of royal prerogative, so much so that Synge wrote:

> I wonder why such a letter was wrote ... I own the style choked me. Except for four years it has not been much in use since the Revolution [of 1688].[86]

However, behind the public support there were still private misgivings in London about the Castle's management of affairs. Newcastle wondered still whether the dispute was personal, asked if Boyle could still be brought back to the government

83 BL Add. Mss.32733, ff.503,541, Dorset to Newcastle, 21 Dec., Stone to Newcastle, 24 Dec. 1753. 84 BL Add. Mss.32734, f.57, Hardwicke to Newcastle, 20 Jan. 1754. 85 *UA*, 12 Feb. 1754 for reports of Kildare's reception on his return to Dublin. 86 PRONI Sackville papers, T2760/20, Holdernesse to Dorset, 28 Dec. 1753; PRONI Mic149/9, p. 114, Synge to Limerick, 24 Jan. 1754. In an earlier unsent memorandum Wilmot had urged most of these actions and may have advised ministers in London: PRONI T3019/2221, 'A plan of instructions to Lord George Sackville', 10 Dec. 1753.

side and inquired if the Castle had much support from leading political interests.[87] The claim that the administration had support from Ulster was not helped by Thomas Connolly's illness preventing him lending his important support. Such doubts explain why the news of the money bill's rejection sparked rumours in London about who would be Dorset's successor. Granville, formerly Lord Cartaret, was mentioned, possibly because it was widely believed that he had solved similar Irish problems in 1724.[88]

Though the instructions had arrived in Dublin there were still differences of opinion among government officials. Synge believed this as early as late December:

> ... those at the helm begin to blame each other and on the one side charge ill success to too sanguine conduct on the other.[89]

These differences emerged when those loyal to the Castle met on 13 January to discuss the state of Irish politics. Three reports were sent to London in the aftermath of this meeting. Newport's letter to Hardwicke was determinedly obtuse on political subjects. Dorset's missive to Newcastle was cautious about Boyle, blaming Malone for all the problems. The viceroy also accepted some blame for the crisis and refused, even with dismissals, to promise that peace would return. Stone's report for Newcastle was, as might be expected, much more truculent. He explained Dorset's cautious letter as one that would be read by many while his report was intended to be a private one for Newcastle. In this he denied any blame or personal ambition (even offering not to become a lord justice) and he also advised that Boyle and Clements should be dismissed.[90]

Hardwicke was frustrated at Newport's, while Newcastle and George II were delighted at the sparky letter of Stone. However, the instructions that came from London in response did not mention Clements and instructed another effort with Boyle.[91] Thus Dorset's administration remained short of the powers that some in it, Stone and Sackville especially, needed to deal with their enemies. Holdernesse's instructions referred again to the sackings already ordered and told Dorset to prorogue parliament with no speech. This all happened with the minimum of fuss by 5 February. The Castle levees continued to be crowded after the sacking of Malone, Carter and Dilkes, even if the Patriots refused to attend. Waite explained these developments as being due to inflated notions of popularity among those dismissed and a desire among the ambitious to fill the vacancies.[92]

87 BL Add. Mss. 32733, f.582, Newcastle to Dorset, 28 Dec. 1753.   88 Rigby to Bedford, 25 Dec. 1753, in *Bedford Corr.*, ii., p. 142. For a different view of Cartaret see P. McNally, 'Wood's Halfpence, Carteret, and the government of Ireland, 1723–6', *IHS*, xxx (1997), pp. 354–76. 89 PRONI Mic149/9, pp. 108–9, Synge to Limerick, 25 Dec. 1753.   90 BL Add. Mss. 35592, f.245, Newport to Hardwicke, 13 Jan. 1754; BL Add. Mss. 32734, ff.35–47, 49, Dorset to Newcastle, 14 Jan., Stone to Newcastle, 14 Jan. 1754.   91 BL Add. Mss. 32734, f.77, Newcastle to Stone, 24 Jan. 1754.   92 PRONI T3019/2259, Waite to Wilmot, 19 Jan. 1754.

Given this relative calm, there was a belief in government circles that they could now begin to rebuild a majority for the next session almost two years away. The first thing was to publicly defend the Castle's stance over the money bill. A pamphlet, quickly written by Justice Christopher Robinson, was printed and distributed through the Post Office, and Wilmot was instructed to have it reprinted in London. This pamphlet, known as *Considerations*, was the first of many pro-Court pamphlets which addressed the rejected money bill. Robinson's was also the clearest advocacy of the government case: that 'previous consent' posed no constitutional threat; that it was based on historical precedent; that additional supplies (not just the hereditary revenue) voted by parliament were granted in trust to the king and thus his to dispose of.[93] At the same time efforts by the government were made to replicate the Patriot celebrations that had followed the rejection of the money bill. When Lord Shelburne and Sackville came into Dublin in early February, bonfires and processions followed, while a public dinner was held for seventy Ulster MPs and peers to toast their loyalty to the king and Castle.[94]

However, the key question for Dorset and his allies was that of further dismissals, especially that of Boyle. Dorset agreed to further talks with the Speaker, whom Sackville alleged:

> ... has no mind to be out of employment, and he begins to talk of being willing to carry on the king's business [in] another session. This unexpected turn prevents any final determination, but I know he engages to stand by his old friends in other company.[95]

The chief secretary was undoubtedly frustrated that Boyle was playing both sides and, as February dragged on and there was no sign of the Speaker being sacked, it was said that government supporters were beginning to get anxious about their recent conduct.[96] By early March, Dorset was concerned enough at this turn in events to write to Newcastle demanding that action be taken against Boyle:

93 For the publication and distribution of the official Castle pamphlet see PRONI T3019/ 2264, 2266, Waite to Wilmot, 22, 24 Jan. 1754. The most coherent arguments in this lengthy and often tedious 'paper war' can be found in [Christopher Robinson], *Considerations on the late bill for payment of the remainder of the national debt* (Dublin, 1754); [William Bruce], *Remarks on a late pamphlet entitled Considerations on the late bill for paying the National Debt, etc.* (Dublin, 1754); [Sir Richard Cox], *The proceedings of the honourable House of Commons of Ireland in rejecting the altered Money Bill on December 17th 1753 Vindicated, etc.* (Dublin, 1754).
94 PRONI T3019/2272, Waite to Wilmot, 11 Feb. 1754; BL Add. Mss.32734, f.131, Sackville to Maxwell, 11 Feb. 1754. For caustic reports of these activities and those organised to counter the Ulster dinner see *UA*, 12, 16 Feb. 1754. 95 BL Add. Mss. 32734, f.131, Sackville to Maxwell, 11 Feb. 1754. 96 PRONI T3019/2279, Sackville to Wilmot, 20 Feb. 1754; BL Add. Mss. 35592, f274, Yorke to Hardwicke, 28 Feb. 1754.

> It becomes now a consideration of little importance, whether the Speaker
> is in fact the leader of the Patriot party or led by it. It is evident that if this
> party is suffered to prevail the authority of government will be manifestly
> overborn by riot and violence and the acknowledgement of a con-
> stitutional dependence of this country on England thrown very far back.

Dorset was now convinced that the Patriots, with Boyle at their head, were growing more bold by the day and that further dismissals, especially of the Speaker,
were needed. The viceroy, by this stage, also wanted Cox, John Gore and Clements
dismissed along with any revenue officers who had voted with the opposition.
He suggested several replacements, including Arthur Hill, Eaton Stannard and
Anthony Foster for Boyle, Malone and Carter. All of this would bolster government morale and cow the Patriots.[97]

As the Castle worried about their next move, the Patriots continued to mobilise
their support and this started to grow in early 1754 despite the dismissals. The
printing of Sir Richard Cox's answer to *Considerations*, called *Proceedings ... in
rejecting the money bill*, was crucial to the politicisation. This pamphlet had the
better of the argument as it stated how much financial control the Irish parliament
had built up in practice since 1692, even if not in the Castle's more theoretical
viewpoint. Cox did not deny that hereditary revenues were granted to the king but
he pointed out that, since the times of James II, there had been no permanent
revenue grants. Also, additional duties were raised separately to the hereditary
revenues (though this did not answer the question of where the surplus might have
come from and whether it could be designated as hereditary or additional). With
regard to precedents, there was one example, from the last years of Queen Anne,
of the Commons appropriating surpluses and then there was the precedent set in
1749. Then, Cox claimed, the Castle and ministers had accepted appropriation
without asserting previous consent. When the opposite happened in 1751, the
reason that MPs had not rejected the money bill was that they were busy with the
Nevill inquiry and content to assert their rights on appropriation in their closing
address to the king.[98]

Thus summarised, the Patriots did have a strong case. There were precedents,
however slight, for disposal of surpluses without previous consent. More importantly, Cox was not claiming that the Irish parliament had the sole right of
disposal, merely that it should have some say. This distinguished his pamphlet
from those that supported the government. They had to claim that 'previous consent' was an inalienable royal prerogative with which the Irish parliament had no
right to interfere. Whatever way it was expressed, this was an aggressive case denying the right of the Irish parliament to have control over the country's finances. It

---

97 BL Add. Mss. 32734, ff.188–200, Dorset to Newcastle, 9 Mar. 1754.   **98** Cox, *Proceedings*,
pp. 35–7, 42–8, 51.

was this assertion by the Castle and by ministers, however unintentionally, which made the issue a constitutional one. As Lord Chesterfield told a correspondent, 'the [factional] affair is become national, and consequently very serious'.[99] With the amendments to the money bill and the raising of Ireland's dependency on England, the government was defending all those measures which were best left unasserted. Sackville and Stone had, from the opposite end of the spectrum (Court Whig not radicalism), put themselves in exactly the same tactical position as Charles Lucas in 1749: leading an assault on the comfortable and unspoken assumptions of Irish Protestants about the Anglo-Irish relationship.

BUILDING A COMMONS MAJORITY

More than anything else, it was the failure of the Castle, after the dismissals of early 1754, to create a likely majority for the next session of parliament that destroyed Dorset's chances of returning to Ireland. Other factors, like the death of Pelham, also affected the situation but it was the ability of the Patriots to hold their ground, while the Castle failed to gain any, that ensured a final disgrace for the viceroy. This was despite the fact that, before Dorset left Ireland, he had certainly got much of what he wanted. Cox and Boyle were eventually dismissed on 19 April and the three lords justices appointed were Stone, Newport and Lord Bessborough. All of this seemed to promise fair wind to the Castle for the interregnum.

However, two factors were to frustrate this scenario. One was the death of Henry Pelham, removing the minister believed to be the main supporter of further harsh measures against the Patriots. The second was the failure to use existing patronage and to get London to create any more to attract new strength to the Castle. Pelham's death in March 1754 meant, in general political terms as Edward Weston put it, that 'the cement is now gone'.[100] In Britain the ministry was now headed by Newcastle, who was charged with the difficult task of holding together the fissiparous elements of the 'Old Corps' Whigs. In effect, this meant keeping in check the ambitions of Henry Fox, William Pitt and their rivals for power. The next parliamentary session in London saw Newcastle defying these ambitions, though he never gained the debating strength in the Commons to be of holding off Fox and his ally, the duke of Cumberland. The Irish political crisis soon became a part of these considerations. Stone and others had long suspected that Fox was guilty of conspiring with Kildare to weaken the ministry.[101] There is little evidence to support this, though there were signs in London that the opposition

99 Chesterfield to Dayrolles, 1 Jan. 1754 in *Chesterfield Correspondence*, iii, p. 2490. 100 PRONI T3019/2289, Weston to Wilmot, 12 Mar. 1754. 101 In 1752 Stone had pointed out that the Irish opposition 'would now be entirely disconcerted, did they not keep up their spirits with some real or pretended assurances of a support in England from a person [Fox] nearly allied to the first nobleman [Kildare] here'; see BL Add. Mss. 32727, f.110, Stone to Newcastle, 7 May 1752.

press supported the stand taken by the Patriot opposition in Ireland. Politics in Dublin seemed to offer a welcome respite to the quagmire of unprincipled opportunism after Pelham's death.[102]

However, back to Fox, whose real opinions were not greatly influenced by his relationship with Kildare and was more concerned to defend the reputation of English government in Ireland. Though Fox did try to protect his brother-in-law from what he saw as a self-destructive streak, Fox was actually, in 1750, an early convert to the dangers posed by Boyle. At this point, perhaps influenced by Lord Hillsborough, Fox also raised the prospect of an Act of Union and in January 1754 asserted the royal prerogative over the money bill. Yet he also despaired at the ministers' attempt to 'support Dorset, who is frightened out of his wits and cannot be supported; and to keep up the primate's power, which the Irish will not bear.'[103] In essence, this was soon to strike a chord with other ministers, including Pelham and Newcastle.

However mistaken the Patriots may have been in their hopes of Fox changing ministerial strategy, Pelham's death did remove a politician who was becoming increasingly convinced by Stone and Sackville's arguments on the necessity for deep-seated change. According to Dudley Ryder, Pelham fully approved of the Castle's requests for government actions and agreed that they were correct to have 'thought it proper to take some power out of the hands of the others [Boyle and his allies].'[104] Like Fox, Pelham was also increasingly keen on alternative means of managing Irish affairs. In line with this, Pelham, Arthur Dobbs, MP for Carrickfergus, and Lord Hillsborough discussed the idea of an Act of Union in April 1753 and concluded that it was something that could and should be introduced, perhaps at the start of the next reign.[105] For all these reasons, when the Castle received the news of Pelham's death, Stone, Dorset and Sackville were said to be shocked. On the other hand:

> The Patriots here have taken it into their heads that Mr Pelham was their great enemy, and therefore when his death is known I have no doubt but they will be indecent enough to express their joy in print.[106]

---

102 BL Add. Mss. 35356, f.583, Hardwicke to Newcastle, 27 Sept. 1754; Stone to Sackville, 27 Aug. 1754 in *Stopford-Sackville Mss.*, p. 225; BL Add. Mss. 32737, f.210, Newcastle to Hardwicke, 28 Oct. 1754; PRONI T3158/1014, Fox to Hartington, 13 May 1755; *London Magazine*, Jan. 1754. 103 On Boyle and union: Nottingham University Library, Newcastle (Clumber) papers, 1213, 1215, Fox to Pelham, 28 May 1750; on the money bill, Fox wrote that the Irish parliament had 'rejected a point of the king's prerogative that is essential and cannot be given up'; Fox to Hervey, 23 Dec. 1753 in Earl of Ilchester (ed.), *Henry Fox, First Lord Holland, His Family and Relations*, (2 volumes, London 1920), ii, p. 72–3. 104 PRONI Harrowby papers, T3228/1/63, entry in Dudley Ryder's diary, [post 13 Jan. 1754]. 105 PRONI D2092/1/8, p. 32, Dobbs to Michael Ward, 5 Apr. 1753. 106 PRONI T3019/2285, Waite to Wilmot, 10 Mar. 1754.

The Patriots were proved wrong in their expectation that Fox would become the new leader of the ministry, but political instability did follow. Newcastle's appointments showed no signs of willingness, either to reward recognised talent, or to risk much in the way of change. The new secretary of state with responsibility for Ireland was Sir Thomas Robinson, a respected diplomat but no political dynamo. This caution infused the ministry's Irish policy, if policy it can be called. For a year after Pelham's death the repeated calls from Dorset and from Dublin for Clements' removal were investigated but never acted upon. The major reason for this was that the new ministry was so keen to manage George II they had no wish to sack his mistress's paymaster. A second reason was that ministers were reluctant to act without a guarantee of success. In line with this, Newcastle and Hardwicke wanted removals to bring the opposition to heel, not exclude them from politics altogether.[107]

Therefore, the ministers were prepared to consider changes that would not rule out reconciliation with the Patriot opposition. As part of this, in April 1754, while Dorset was still in Dublin, the idea of not appointing lords justices but an English lord deputy was raised. This would avoid the difficulty of either appointing Boyle or an anti-Patriot commission. Granville was consulted, because of his experience, and advised doing nothing precipitate, while also questioning how far the ministry should support the Dorset administration. Newcastle was less cynical than Granville but did look into precedents for a lord deputy and considered Lord Hertford as a possible candidate.[108] The duke was forced, by fierce opposition from the Castle administration, to shelve the idea, which it believed would be seen as an unfavourable comment on their conduct.[109] With this scheme set aside and little sign that opposition was melting away, Newcastle remained cautious about giving Dorset any further power to sack others. By August 1754 this bcame an article of faith among ministers, as George II gave his rather frustrated opinion that the lords justices should concentrate on using their present resources to build a majority.[110] With hindsight, this was probably the point of no return for the Dorset administration.

The lords justices, especially Stone and Bessborough, were keen, obviously, that ministers would take a less cautious approach to sacking Patriot placemen. They correctly tied the continuing, if not growing, influence of the opposition to

107 Stone to Newcastle, 14 Jan. 1754 in Falkiner (ed), 'Stone/Newcastle Correspondence', pp. 735–8; BL Add.Mss. 32995, f.209, Cabinet minutes of 9 April 1754. The April meeting had decided against replacing the lords justices by a lord deputy but this discussion showed the extent of unease at the conduct and record of success for Dorset and his allies in Ireland. 108 BL Add. Mss. 32734, f.283, Granville to Newcastle, 19 Mar. 1754; BL Add. Mss. 32995, f.58, Memorandum on Irish affairs, [Jan. 1754].   109 For fierce opposition see B.L Add. Mss. 32737, f.62, 192, Dorset to Newcastle, 27 Apr., Stone to Newcastle, 27 Apr. 1754. Others in the Castle did not hold the same views, see PRONI T3019/2300, Waite to Wilmot, 10 Apr. 1754. 110 Sackville to Stone, 31 Aug. 1754 in *Stopford Sackville Mss.*, i, p. 228.

the fact that Clements had escaped any punishment at all. Time and again the Castle reminded those in London that Clements not only had influence over four MPs, all of whom opposed the government, but also had huge power through his control of Treasury funds.[111] Clements went to London in October 1754 to plead his own case with Newcastle and answer the accusations of the Dublin administration and Wilmot reports that he was penitent but again denied any influence over the Gores and others.[112] At this point Stone asked Newcastle to either sack Clements or to make him joint Teller of the Exchequer with a government supporter alongside him for security. This appeal fell on deaf ears, as did the similar ones in January 1755 from Sackville and Dorset.[113] Wilmot believed that for the Castle to retain any credibility, ministers must force surrender by the opposition over previous consent, or else proceed with further sackings. Even if ministers were unaware, the Dublin administration and its friends in London knew that the fate of Clements had become a touchstone of the money bill crisis.

The absence of further dismissals caused other problems for the lords justices. Later, in 1757, Edmund Sexton Pery argued that the sackings had not worked because the vacancies created had not been wisely filled.[114] By March, Dorset recommended Arthur Hill to have Boyle's post in the exchequer, while Lord Forbes, Eaton Stannard and Anthony Foster would replace Dilkes, Carter and Malone respectively. In the event the legal appointments were altered with the semi-retired Lord Chief Justice Henry Singleton appointed to be Master of the Rolls (later replaced himself by the English-born William Yorke) and Eaton Stannard made Prime Serjeant.[115] These changes did not add any strength to the Castle forces, which Stone had hoped to do by appointing independent gentlemen like Pery, William Richardson of County Armagh and Foster, to office. With the likelihood of further patronage diminishing, support for the Castle began to appear increasingly shaky. This situation was, as William Yorke put it, 'the cause of murmurings and discontent'. One example is Robert Fitzgerald, MP for a Kerry borough and a defector from the 'Munster squadron', who had complained in late 1752 about Boyle's inability to help him. In the spring of 1754, Stone was appealing to him to remain constant and patient, while conceding:

> I can say nothing particular, as I know not with certainty what opening may now be determined or when executed.[116]

111 PRONI T3019/2382, Lords Justices to Dorset, 29 July 1754. 112 PRONI T3019/2450, Wilmot to Waite, 23 Oct. 1754. 113 Stone to Newcastle, 7 Oct. 1754 in Falkiner, 'Stone-Newcastle Correspondence', p. 748; Sackville to Stone, 15 Jan. 1755 in *Stopford-Sackville Mss.*, p. 236; PRONI T3019/2457, 'Memorandum on removing Clements', Oct. 1754. 114 [Pery], *Duke of Bedford*, p. 32. 115 BL Add. Mss. 32734 ff.188–200, Dorset to Newcastle, 9 Mar. 1754; Burns, *Irish Parliamentary Politics*, ii, p. 178. 116 PRONI Fitzgerald papers, Mic369/1/19, Stone to Fitzgerald [15 May 1754].

In the event as these openings did not appear, those who looked to the Castle for security began to feel very vulnerable.

In a letter to Hardwicke, William Yorke explained how such feelings might arise as the Patriot wave refused to ebb:

> I think the spirit of opposition to the government, commonly known here by the name of Patriotism, far from being abated, tho' it now makes it's chief appearance in the country, [no] industry or art is wanting to keep it up, not only among the [gentry], but also the common people, by debauching and poisoning their minds with every false and inflammatory story that can be invented, and thereby making them uneasy and discontented with everyone placed above them.[117]

Right from the rejection of the money bill, the Patriot activities, like the addressing of MPs, the holding of dinners, the founding of Patriot Clubs and Independent Freeholder Societies, and the publishing of their toasts, were coordinated. By the summer of 1754, Clements' survival became a cause for opposition celebration.[118] The Patriots were certainly very active in using the press, particularly the *Universal Advertiser*, to publish the vast number of congratulatory addresses from grand juries, assizes and Patriot Clubs and essays on the behaviour of ministers and the lessons of history[119]. Rumours were deliberately circulated that the Irish administration was deeply divided and had lost the ear of the English ministry, or that Dorset was out of favour with George II.[120] Pamphlets continued to pour from the presses, especially from the vitriolic pen of Cox, all full of abuse, though some were contained thoughtful expositions of the constitution. Most, if not all, showed signs of an 'Irish interest' being championed once more along the lines of the late 1710s and the Wood's Halfpence crisis of 1724–6.

By itself this should not have caused great alarm among government ranks but, when added to the instability of the ministry, the Castle's failure to build or con- solidate its support caused it growing problems. In April 1754, Waite showed some confidence, reporting quiet in Dublin, (though the 'Mahomet riot' – when actors were attacked for not repeating Patriot lines – was not long past), and Kildare ignored at the county assizes in Naas.[121] By November, Archbishop Ryder noted the decline of such expectations of an opposition collapse:

> Our Patriots, as they call themselves, do everything that can be done with impunity to irritate the people against government, in order to prepare

117 BL Add. Mss. 35593 f.54, Yorke to Hardwicke, 12 Nov. 1754.   118 Waite to Sackville, 4 July 1754 in *Stopford-Sackville Mss.*, p. 217.   119 In late 1754 a compendium of such materials was published: *The Universal Advertiser or a collection of essays, moral political and entertaining* (Dublin, 1754).   120 Cuninghame to Sackville, 19 Aug. 1754, in *Stopford Sackville Mss.*, i, pp. 224–5;   121 PRONI T3019/2300, 2312, Waite to Wilmot, 10, 24 Apr. 1754.

them for the work of the next session of parliament. I cannot learn that any addition of strength has been gained to the court, but it is believed they will prevail in the end; and yet, I fear there will be tumults and violence.[122]

Other observers told the same tale. Yorke, reporting from his autumn Leinster circuit in County Kildare, wrote that the earl of the same name had attended the assizes with a retinue of supporters 'to keep up the spirit of party and popularity'. He later reported that in Meath, when Patriot grand jurors praised Boyle, Carter and Malone, his judicial colleague, though a government supporter:

> ... did not think himself so hurt, as I did, and therefore I had no reason to think he would join with me in showing that resentment which I think we ought to have shown by withdrawing ourselves from such company.[123]

As the Patriots appeared bolder and Castle supporters wondered about the ability of the lords justices to answer their patronage demands, a government Commons majority seemed further away as ever. It was this situation which made Dorset's position increasingly untenable.

The final nail in the viceroy's coffin was the fact that a ministry shorn of Pelham's abilities and under pressure, especially from Fox and Cumberland, needed the support of the Cavendish family. There was an even greater urgency as 1754 wore on because of the growing threat of war with France, which began with hostilities in North America.[124] The third duke of Devonshire was one of the Whig's elder statesmen, a member of the Regency Board and returned eight MPs. More importantly for Irish affairs, he was related by marriage to both the Ponsonby family and to Henry Boyle. But most crucial for the ministry was Hardwicke's belief that Devonshire could influence Fox to support the administration in the winter of 1754.[125] The courtship of the Cavendish family from December 1754 laid the ground for Devonshire's eldest son, Lord Hartington, to be appointed as Irish viceroy in March 1755. The deaths of Lords Albemarle and Gower provided openings in the king's household to relocate Dorset with some dignity. When he heard the news of Dorset's fall, Walpole commented that 'the ministry had perceived that it was unsafe to venture Ireland again under the Duke of Dorset's rule'. This neatly summed up the duke's failure and fate.[126]

---

122 PRONI T3228/1/66, Ryder to Ryder, 30 Nov. 1754.   123 BL Add. Mss. 35592, f.319, 35,593, f.54, Yorke to Hardwicke, 11 Apr., 12 Nov. 1754.   124 The Castle was increasingly concerned with the provisioning of the French fleet in Cork and Waterford; see PRONI T3019/2422, 2464, 2472, Lords Justices to Dorset, 7 Oct., 'Memorandum on the 1738 precedent for peacetime corn export bans', 23 Oct., Waite to Wilmot, 2 Nov. 1754.   125 BL Add. Mss. 32737, f.449, Hardwicke to Newcastle, 15 Dec. 1754.   126 Walpole, *George II*, ii, p. 3.

4

Patriotism unmasked?: the search for a settlement, 1755–1756

The announcement, in March 1755, that Lord Hartington was to be the new viceroy of Ireland, was seen by most observers as being due to the duke of Dorset's failure to deliver a reliable management system. In contrast, Stone was openly furious, pointing to the exclusion of the lords justices from the decision-making, and he offered to go to London to try and influence Newcastle.[1] When the lords justices demanded that Hartington should begin his period in office by sacking Nathaniel Clements, Devonshire told Lord Bessborough:

> ... it might be expected from the consideration that animosity existing or thought to exist in Ireland might easier be composed by a Lieutenant who was not in the country when they took rise.[2]

Other government supporters were not as afraid of change as the lords justices were. Chief Baron Bowes believed that the Patriots' joy at Dorset's removal was mixed with relief and hoped that they 'have resolved how to conduct themselves, I wish it may be for peace and think it probable.' An independent MP, Charles O'Hara, was pleased, though he commented 'what healing means may occur to him [Hartington] ... but the undertaking seems very delicate.'[3] All the signs were that Hartington would not be continuing with Dorset's methods.

HARTINGTON AND THE 'HEALING ARTS'

John Bowes was worried about setting the bad precedent of government changing officials, 'whenever they [the opposition] want to bend a Lieutenant to their purposes.' However, he was realistic enough to know that Dorset was

1 Stone to Stone, 4 Mar. 1755 in Falkiner, 'Stone-Newcastle Correspondence', p. 761. 2 PRONI Chatsworth papers, T3158/630, 635, Lords Justices to Hartington, 16 Mar., Devonshire to Bessborough, 25 Mar. 1755. 3 PRONI Wilmot papers, T3019/2538, Bowes to Wilmot, 22 Mar. 1755; PRONI O'Hara papers, T2812/10/3, O'Hara to O'Hara, 1 May 1755.

unable to bring peace to Ireland at a time when the threat of war was great.[4] As Walpole put it, 'Ireland was in a state of confusion, swarming with Papists, and the Whigs ... ready to burst into a civil war.'[5] Hartington chose Colonel Henry Seymour Conway, the brother of Lord Hertford, to be his chief secretary, as a nod in the direction of Cumberland, Conway's patron and Fox's ally. It soon became clear that both men had similar Whig ideas, in particular their belief that the Patriot opposition had raised constitutional issues opportunistically. This understanding of Irish politics was influenced, firstly, by a jaundiced view of patriotism, reflecting the apostasy of Pulteney in 1742 after Walpole's fall, and, secondly, by the belief that Boyle's opposition was an unexpected act of desperation.[6] One historian sums up these attitudes like so:

> English ministers feared popular agitation in Ireland, especially of constitutional issues, but at the same time found themselves hard put to take such agitation seriously.[7]

A strategy paper, written in April or May 1755 for Hartington, has these attitudes at its core. It advocated the use of 'healing arts' or conciliation, rather than sackings, to resolve the crisis. Pensions, but not restoration to office, are mentioned to compensate those turned out. Any further opposition in parliament would not be tolerated and met by another prorogation. The surplus in the Treasury would have to be applied for through the government and previous consent to its use emphasised in the viceroy's speech to parliament. Clements would remain in his office and further removals were almost entirely ruled out. At this stage, no decision was taken about the future lords justices.[8] The Whiggish view on patriotism as a buyable commodity runs all through these initial thoughts. It is interesting to note that the main proposals in the settlement, the reconciliation with the Patriots and the removal of Stone, were decided by Hartington, possibly even before he came to Ireland in May 1755.

Before he made that journey Hartington met Henry Boyle's son, Richard, in London. At the same time the viceroy also received two letters from Stone, in which he disingenuously offered to retire.[9] The letters contained a robust defence of his actions and a pointed warning that, if he was excluded:

4 PRONI Emly papers, T3087/1/10, Bowes to Pery, 18 Mar. 1755; PRONI T3019/2568, Bowes to Wilmot, 15 Apr. 1755.   5 Walpole, *George II*, ii, p. 23; *Charlemont Mss.*, i, p. 5. 6 Horace Walpole expressed the typical view of patriotism at this time, ironically on the eve of the Pitt/Newcastle ministry, that 'No mob in England would suffer itself to be the dupe of a Patriot', cited in Langford, *Polite and Commercial People*, p. 230.   7 Burns, *Irish Parliamentary Politics*, ii, p. 251.   8 PRONI T3158/639, Hartington's strategy paper [Apr./May] 1755.

> Mr Ponsonby ... would be greatly disabled from performing that
> service to government, and from distinguishing himself in giving the
> chief support to your excellency's administration here, which I must
> presume you would wish to receive from his hands.[10]

Despite this veiled threat, rumours from London pointed to a change in personnel in Dublin Castle and reported Stone's retirement.[11]

As Hartington came to Ireland in May 1755, ostensibly to view defence preparations, the initial welcome was, by his and Conway's accounts, somewhat cool.
Conway pointed out that this reception did not prevent excessive entertaining, as
'it's the great business of life [in Ireland] to stuff and be stuffed. Immoderate eat-
ing is among the prime social virtues, but immoderate drinking lifts you up to the
skies'.[12] Political business got underway quickly with the discussions at the Castle
levees focusing on the terms of restoration for Boyle and his allies.[13] The shape of
the deal seemed to be that the Speaker would become an additional lord justice or
solely Chancellor of the Exchequer, the latter being the preferred option in the
Castle. On previous consent Hartington commented:

> ... if they [the opposition] would concur thoroughly with me in carrying
> on the king's business, prevent any censure or retrospect [*sic*], and endea-
> vour to restore the tranquillity, I would not wantonly bring on a question
> which might disturb it.[14]

Rumours of such a settlement led to inflated optimism about its content with
one Patriot MP commenting:

> This is a total happy revolution, the good king himself has declared in
> our favour and he observed our conduct which has and always will
> reflect shame on others.[15]

Just as the settlement seemed within reach, it was placed in danger. The major
problem was Hartington's wish to return to London, his preliminary negotiations
completed. Stone was angry that he was unlikely to be re-appointed a lord justice

---

9 PRONI T3158/643, 650, Stone to Hartington, 5, 12 Apr. 1755. 10 Walpole, *George II*, ii, p.
19. 11 PRONI T3019/2591, Clements to Wilmot, 29 Apr. 1755. 12 BL Add. Mss. 32854,
f.422, Hartington to Newcastle, 8 May 1755; PRONI T3019/2599, Waite to Wilmot, 6 May
1755; Conway to Walpole, 8 May 1755 in *Walpole Corr.*, xxxvii, pp. 392–5. For the numerous
dinner parties see NLI Ms.1466, Hartington's list of dinner guests from May 1755 to May 1756.
13 BL Sloane Mss. 4164, f.56, Henry to Secker, [May 1755]. Henry claimed that everyone was
'joyous' at these levees, even Stone, 'a man who had been eased of a load'. 14 PRONI T3019/
2604, Hartington to Wilmot, 11 May 1755; PRONI T3158/672, Hartington to Devonshire, 16
May 1755. 15 PRONI MacCartney papers, D572/2/78, Carew to Morres, 8 May 1755. 16

and warned that his ally, Arthur Hill, was reluctant to leave the Exchequer.[16] At the same time Malone and Boyle were threatening that 'it will not be in their power to prevent disturbance and difficulties in parliament', if Hartington returned to London leaving the same regency behind him.[17] Meanwhile, Newcastle would only agree to Boyle's restoration as Chancellor of the Exchequer if Hartington returned to London, leaving the same lords justices behind him as a sign of balance. Newcastle wrote that he was opposed to the viceroy staying in Dublin,

> simply to prevent the King from continuing in a commission one of his servants [Stone], who has certainly done nothing to offend the king, however unfortunate he has been in displeasing others who have openly opposed his Majesty's measures and attacked his prerogative.

In contrast, Fox advised against a hasty return:

> ... you did not go over to get over one session *tellement quellement*, and then to look on to another, but to have the honour, I trust, of having settled on a lasting footing the peace and quiet of a nation.[18]

Despite Hartington's contempt for opposition threats, he decided to stay in Dublin and avoid provoking any further disputes by appointing a fresh lord justices' commission. He still believed that the only possible pressure on Boyle was that 'they were weary of opposition and desirous of coming back in again, but at the same time were endeavouring to make the best possible terms they could.'[19] However, the reality of Irish politics in 1755 was more complex than Hartington or Conway allowed for. The undertaker system had already begun to fragment during the challenge to Boyle and the money bill crisis, as Kildare, Stone, the Ponsonbys and the Gores had all played independent and important roles. In this context the Patriots' lack of consistent demands, beyond the exclusion of Stone, at the same time as they were unwilling to enter a parliamentary session with this question unresolved, is hardly surprising. This situation was also noted by Bowes, who identified that the opposition polemics in the *Universal Advertiser* had not lessened and 'how greatly these [papers] are read and attended thro' the country.'[20]

PRONI T3158/669, Stone to Hartington, 16 May 1755. **17** PRONI T3158/681, Hartington to Devonshire, 23 May 1755; PRONI T3019/2618, Conway to Wilmot, 23 May 1755. William Henry pointed out that Sir Richard Cox posed a threat to any settlement as he refused to go to the Castle and had reportedly stormed out of a meeting of the Patriot leaders; BL Sloane Mss. 4164, f.56, Henry to Secker, [May 1755]. **18** PRONI T3158/700, Newcastle to Hartington, 5 June 1755; Fox to Hartington, 8 June 1755 in Ilchester, *Henry Fox*, p. 76. **19** PRONI T3158/663, Hartington to Devonshire, 11 May 1755. **20** PRONI T3019/ 2624, Bowes to Wilmot, 31 May 1755.

Sir Richard Cox, who had so far refused to appear at the Castle, was said to be writing the paper, despite the denials of Boyle. The danger of Patriot apostasy was summed up when Cox was himself attacked in pamphlets for being prepared to do a deal with the government and had his previous record as the scourge of Charles Lucas cast up to him:

> Are not thy ways all noted? Thou must be a sillier fellow than even thine enemies call thee, if thou thinkest they are yet forgotten: Have men forgotten dost thou think for whom that well reputed man, poor Love [Collector of Cork replaced by Cox], was so badly treated? In what session was there a blacker or fouler jobb, than that [the exiling of Lucas] which paved thy way to his employment?[21]

Cox, like Boyle, knew that the public did not regard office-holding and patriotism as irreconcilable but would repudiate those who used treachery or apostasy to get into office. At this point, therefore, the Speaker was not in the position of being able to easily settle with Hartington without, at least, Stone's clear dismissal. Kildare was not in a much better position, despite Fox's repeated arguing that 'if he cannot distinguish between honour and popularity, between the best and worst guides, I am sorry for him'.[22]

The progress towards a settlement was hindered by distrust. Every nuance in Hartington's behaviour was interpreted in various ways. When he went into Munster, Boyle's territory, in the summer of 1755, to inspect coastal defences accompanied by John Ponsonby, this was seen by some of the opposition as provocative.[23] Relations between the viceroy and Boyle hit a low point when the Speaker retired to his country seat in County Cork, and didn't return to Dublin until August. The former chief secretary, Sackville, gloated at this situation and speculated that Boyle 'was at a loss how to proceed between my Lord Lieutenant and his old Patriot friends'.[24] He was said, by Fox, to be supported in his views by Newcastle and Hardwicke, who were also opposed to the removal of Stone and the discrediting of Dorset.[25] To break this stalemate Hartington sent Conway to

21 *Joshua Pym to Dionysius* [Cox] *the Aeropagite* (Dublin, 1754), p. 3.   22 Fox to Hartington, 1 June 1756 in Ilchester, *Henry Fox*, ii, p. 76.   23 In late May Kildare reported that party strife was on the increase because 'the primate was very much cast down, now up, at private parties in the evenings at the Castle, long whispers and conferences; nobody there but Lady Betty Ponsonby's friends'; Kildare to Kildare, 24 May 1755 in *Leinster Correspondence*, i, p. 24. Hartington was compared by one opposition newspaper to the Tory Ormond touring in Munster in 1709: *BNL*, 27 May 1755.   24 Malcomson points out that 'his [Boyle's] delicate and difficult task was to defeat his enemies without at the same time surrendering to his new "patriot" friends': A.P.W. Malcomson, 'Introduction' in E. Hewitt (ed.), *Lord Shannon*, p. xxxi.   25 PRONI, T3019/2646, Sackville to Wilmot, 11 July 1755; Fox to Hartington, 8 June 1755 in Ilchester, *Henry Fox*, pp. 75–6.

London in June 1755. He was to secure Newcastle's agreement to the restoration of Boyle and to the exclusion of Stone from government, on the basis that it was 'a step prudentially taken on the opinion of all those my Lord has conversed with of all parties' and not 'a condescension to the Speaker and his party'.[26] Newcastle suspected that the deal rewarded opposition without either promises or evidence of good behaviour and he refused to agree to Boyle's restoration, unless it was at the end of the session. This refusal was followed by lengthy negotiations, pressure on Newcastle from Devonshire, Fox and Carteret, and a sharp exchange between Hartington and the duke. By mid-July, Conway was able to tell the viceroy that Newcastle had agreed that Stone should be asked to request his own retirement and that Boyle could be restored to the exchequer before parliament opened.[27]

However, as this was happening, Hartington began to wonder about the wisdom of the settlement he was proposing. Walpole believed that this hesitation was caused by the absence of Conway's guiding hand, which allowed the viceroy to fall under the influence of the Ponsonbys. The reality was more complex, as Hartington's views were not formed just by his relationship with his in-laws, but also by his growing anger at the grinding pace of the negotiations. So far these had brought neither a secure Commons majority nor the promise of a stable regency to follow. Hartington was also angry that his decision to stay in Dublin and the likely exclusion of Stone had not convinced Boyle of his good intentions. He wrote in despair:

> the more I consider it, the more I am convinced that the speaker and Malone wish to come in, but they are afraid of the popularity that will attend it, and that their friends will have them.

This seemed to be supported as Boyle's demands were rising by late August, with the request for a parliamentary censure of Stone.[28] Also, given that Dublin was a hothouse of rumour about the negotiations, it is little wonder that Boyle chose to be cautious in his dealings with the Castle.[29]

On the other hand, Hartington's frustration with the attitudes of the Patriots seems to have made him more sympathetic to the former supporters of Dorset.

---

26 Conway to Hertford, 16 June 1755 in *Walpole Corr.*, xxxvii, p. 398.   27 Memorandum of Newcastle on Irish affairs, 3 June 1755, cited in J.C.D. Clark, 'Whig Tactics and Parliamentary Precedents: The English management of Irish politics, 1754–6', *Historical Journal*, xxi (1978), pp. 275–301, p. 287; PRONI T3158/750, 757, 767, Devonshire to Hartington, 3 July, Newcastle to Hartington, 10 July, Conway to Hartington, 16 July 1755; BL Add. Mss. 32856, f.610, Hartington to Newcastle, 4 July 1755.   28 Walpole, *George II*, ii, p. 183; BL Add. Mss. 51381, f.16, Hartington to Fox, 6 June 1755; PRONI T3158/759, Hartington to Devonshire, 11 July 1755; PRONI T3019/2660, Waite to Wilmot, 26 Aug. 1755.   29 Sackville noted that 'secrets are not kept in Dublin, either through necessity or vanity'; PRONI T3019/2648, Sackville to Wilmot, 26 July 1755.

Certainly he grew increasingly concerned that government servants, like the solicitor general, Philip Tisdall, might not support him in parliament. He told Devonshire that he had to 'leave the primate out of government, but would endeavour to qualify it in such a manner as it should not disgust his friends and those of the government and on the other hand not excite the opposition too much.' The question being asked was whether the 'king's friends' would support a treacherous administration.[30]

It was in these circumstances that Hartington and John Bowes suggested that a lord deputy should be appointed instead of lords justices. They agreed that the scheme would be difficult to implement, but claimed that it would avoid the appearance of a victory for Boyle or any sign of 'an end of English influence'. The scheme asked the fundamental question of whether ministers in London, and the administration in Dublin Castle, would construct their own party in the Irish Commons or continue to rely on the existing undertaker system of parliamentary management. The response showed an absence of the will required for the first and a lack of conviction that the present system was to blame for Dorset's problems. The treatment of Hartington's idea shows that ministers preferred the status quo to devising a new long-term strategy.

Only Newcastle gave a positive response to the argument for a lord deputy, going so far as to suggest Lord Hertford as a candidate. However, most ministers followed Fox's argument that the removal of Stone would not alienate the government supporters, as it would be the basis of ending opposition.[31] Conway spelt out the reasons for this consensus about the undesirability of change. He described a combination of age-old Whig cynicism about political opposition and a desire for an immediate solution to a management problem. Conway dismissed the idea that the Patriots would take their 'victory' as a signal to attack government. Instead, Boyle's party would be split by the cries of the disappointed and 'these notions of constitution, etc. are the arm of the party, taken up for the purpose of opposition, and your Lordship has experience enough of the world to know [they] are always laid aside when these purposes are served'. In a second letter, Conway insisted that Boyle's restoration was crucial and that, on balance, Hartington's scheme could destroy any chance of peace.[32] This picture of Conway is at odds with J.C.D. Clark's portrayal of him as a strategist devising long-term ministerial schemes to destroy the influence of Irish parties and is more true of a pragmatist seeking a quiet parliamentary session.

The major reason for the desirability of a quiet parliamentary session was the need to get supplies of money and men from the Irish parliament. In

---

30 PRONI T3158/801, Hartington to Devonshire, post 30 July 1755. 31 BL Add. Mss. 51381, f.35, Hartington to Fox, 21 Aug. 1755; PRONI T3158/787, Fox to Hartington, 23 July 1755. 32 PRONI T3158/807, Conway to Hartington, 7 Aug. 1755; PRONI T3019/2658 Conway to Hartington, 23 Aug. 1755.

March 1755, the first wartime invasion scares struck Dublin. These were occasioned by the news that the French navy was ready to sail, with Ireland as a possible target. In April, Waite wrote that Dublin was seized with 'different notions', some saying that Nova Scotia had fallen, and others that the French had landed in the west of Ireland. He believed at this stage that 'it is certain that there are a great many French officers in this kingdom' and that the 'whole [western] coast is alarmed at the appearance of French convoys.'[33] By August there were reports of Jacobite riots in Dublin and despair among the capital's Protestants at the news of General Braddock's defeat in America.[34] The prevailing pessimism was summed up by Fox who wrote, in July, that he was unhappy at the prospect of a war 'which I don't see how we can carry on or get out of.' This was not an uncommon opinion given the military strength of France, the isolation of the American colonies and the feelings of political malaise that gripped Britain at the time.[35]

Little wonder then that the lord deputy scheme was laid aside in favour of the proposals to remove Stone and restore Boyle. Welbore Ellis, a close friend of Fox, believed that Hartington now had the full power to deal with the opposition, but that should he fail, 'men will be convinced that the evil is not to be cured by gentle methods and prudence.'[36] The viceroy still needed a core for a Commons majority and turned to two groups to deliver this. With the primate excluded and the Speaker expected to be amenable, Lord Kildare's forces were seen by the government as vitally important. Although Kildare was the man who had brought Boyle and Malone back to the Castle, there were some lingering doubts about his political judgement.[37] Therefore the Ponsonbys, with their family links and their readiness to sacrifice Stone, were the other group turned to by Hartington. Having secured both political connections, the details of the deal were finalised by September 1755: Boyle restored, Stone removed, no lord deputy but new lords justices headed by Kildare and Bessborough.

MAJORITIES AND MANAGEMENT RESTORED

The parliamentary session of 1755–6 was to prove a successful one for the government. The money bill passed quietly, an augmentation of the army was

33 *FDJ*, 23 Mar. 1755; PRONI Anglesey papers, D619/21/B/126, Rooney to Bayly, 24 Apr. 1755; PRONI T3019/2596–7, Bourke to Waite, 1 May, Waite to Wilmot, 3 May 1755. 34 PRONI T3019/2660, Waite to Wilmot, 26 Aug. 1755.   35 PRONI T3158/787, Fox to Hartington, 23 July 1755. In England the mood in 1755–6 was one of deep pessimism, summed up in John Brown, *Estimate of the Manners and Principles of the Times* (London, 1757 – published in Dublin in 1758) and Kathleen Wilson, *Sense of the People: Politics, Culture and Imperialism in England, 1715–1785* (Cambridge, 1995), pp. 185–205.   36 PRONI T3158/819, Ellis to Hartington, 15 Aug. 1755.   37 PRONI T3158/844, Fox to Hartington, 29 Aug. 1755. Wilmot emphasised to Dudley Ryder the importance of the Castle secur-

agreed on for the war effort and a new Speaker, John Ponsonby, was elected unopposed. The session showed just how powerful a politician Boyle remained, but also how much his earlier ascendancy as sole undertaker had been eroded.

The opening Commons address boded well for Hartington. The administration refused to allow anything that would look like a censure of Dorset or an expression of Patriot triumphalism. After some discussion with Boyle, Kildare and John Ponsonby, Conway reported that the agreed address was to be 'less a remonstrance than an excuse.' There was to be no mention of previous consent or the prorogation of parliament. In Dublin, the reaction among government supporters was divided between those who 'don't quite like it, others who think it not offensive and some are surprised to find it so harmless.' The text of the address was sent to London for ministerial approval and, though Horace Walpole told Conway that he was 'offended at their [the Patriots] agreeing to an address that avows such deference for prerogative, and is to protest so deeply against having intended to attack it', no one else articulated this view. Thus, the address was returned unchanged, an outcome which was, according to Conway, 'beyond our hopes'. The first hurdle had been easily cleared.[38]

A second obstacle proved more difficult. When the viceroy's address to parliament was debated there were some indications of the source of future dissent. Edmund Pery, Robert French and Mervyn Archdall all attacked Boyle for his deal with Hartington, though the details were not public at this stage.[39] More significant were the rumours that Cox was to allege that the Commons address had been composed in England. This news was followed by the sudden decision by Boyle to amend the address in committee, to express 'our concern at not having an opportunity in the last session of parliament of laying our proceedings before your majesty in their proper light'.[40] Only a few days into the session, Boyle had allowed precisely the censure of the previous administration which the Castle had been seeking to avoid.

Hartington was furious at the way he had been treated, describing the amendment as 'the most unaccountable as well as the most dishonourable action I have ever met with', though he wisely chose to ignore the snub in public. This desire to avoid a quarrel with Boyle was accepted by ministers who faced their own parliamentary difficulties in London. The threat of opposition from Devonshire to subsidy treaties was said to have been avoided by Newcastle 'sacrific[ing] the Stones and Ireland and the Dorsets'.[41] Fox's attitude to Boyle's behaviour can be

ing Kildare's support: PRONI Harrowby papers, T3228/1/70, diary entry of 4 Oct. 1755.
38 PRONI T3019/2670, Conway to Wilmot, 20 Sept. 1755; Conway to Walpole, 16 Sept. 1755 in *Walpole Corr.*, xxxvii, p. 403.   39 Conway to Walpole, 7 Oct. 1755 in *Walpole Corr.*, xxxvii, p. 410; PRONI T3019/2684, Conway to Wilmot, 9 Oct. 1755.   40 Conway to Hertford, 7 Oct. 1755 in *Walpole Corr.*, xxxvii, p. 411; *CJI*, ix, pp. 253 & 261.   41 Memorandum of 7 October 1755 in *Walpole Corr.*, xxxvii, p. 409; J.C.D. Clark, *The Dynamics of Change: The Crisis of the 1750s and English Party Systems* (Cambridge, 1982), pp. 196–230.

explained by his belief that Stone, in collaboration with Newcastle, was directing the Commons opposition of Pery and company in order to undermine the ministry. Fox described one of Stone's letters as far from submissive but 'full of discontent, hurt pride and intention to show his power still'. Fox remained obsessed with this alleged threat during October and November. Reports that Stone had had dinner with 35 MPs, including Pery and Mervyn Archdall, at Leixlip, and rumours that Maxwell was sent back to Dublin by Newcastle, to plot with the primate, made Fox, and then Hartington, wary. After Maxwell's mission, Stone did seem to entertain the idea that Newcastle would force Hartington to retain him in government. By December though, Hartington was scornful of Stone's continuing pretensions to power, which 'shows his ambition to be as great as his folly. I cut it short by treating it as equally absurd and impossible'.[42]

A major success for the Castle was provided by the quiet passage of the money bill. Thereby the government received £300,000 in additional duties, although there was still a surplus of £471,000 in the Treasury. Devonshire observed:

> ... it will be very absurd for any that sincerely wish the good of Ireland not to cooperate in preventing any dispute on account of the great balance in the Treasury; a very unusual thing and which they ought not to discourage.[43]

The administration now considered how to use the surplus to make political management easier. Conway suggested using the surplus to abolish the hearth tax paid by Protestants, saying that this would 'create an interest for conformity among the lower people, which is the only thing that may convert them.' Wilmot disagreed, as he 'doubted whether it was advisable at this time to give the Papists any handle for complaint at this critical time, when invasions from France were daily expected'. He was more keen to extend the appropriations, usually included in the money bill, beyond specific duties paid to the Linen Board, to wider investment in the Irish economy and infrastructure. Once convinced that it would be 'impossible to exclude all schemes of the kind out of our system in the present situation', Conway wanted to act quickly, with his only condition being a refusal to be seen to have made a concession in the direction of 'popularity'.[44]

Avoiding 'popular' schemes was to prove difficult in practice. The use of public money for developing the economy did not start in 1755, but the sums for that session more than doubled previous amounts from nearly £61,000, granted in 1753, to £150,000 in 1755.[45] The viceroy commented:

42 PRONI T3158/945, 955, Fox to Hartington, 21, 28 Oct. 1755; PRONI T3019/2693, 6457/435, Hartington to Wilmot, 21 Oct., 26 Dec. 1755. 43 PRONI T3019/2697, Devonshire to Wilmot, 29 Oct. 1755. 44 PRONI T3158/933, 950, Conway to Wilmot, 16 Oct., Wilmot to Devonshire, 24 Oct. 1755; PRONI T3019/2718, Conway to Wilmot, 30 Nov. 1755. 45 The history of appropriations is found in Kiernan, *Financial Administration*, chapter 6, passim. For the figures for 1753–5: *CJI*, ix, pp. 277–8 & 293–4. For the 1755–6 details: *CJI*, ix, pp. 384–7 & 855–9.

> It might perhaps appear odd to people who did not know the temper and situation of this kingdom, that while the parliament was addressing for money there would be any uneasiness of His Majesty availing himself of any of it and while that was done with moderation nobody would object to it but as great pensions had been given if more were granted now I could not answer for the consequences.[46]

Despite all this rhetoric, a concession to 'popularity' was being made. At the same time the administration were determined not to allow their actions to be construed as *carte blanche* for Patriot schemes. Thus the government forces opposed the introduction of a bounty to aid inland transport of corn, recommended by a committee chaired by Sir Richard Cox. He did not seek to press this recommendation and when Edmund Pery put the resolution to a vote, it was defeated by 128 votes to 53. A bill, drafted by Pery, for the better supplying of Dublin with corn, was actually passed without a division in March, but later dropped in the privy council.[47]

However, contested elections, especially one in County Wexford, threatened this relative parliamentary calm and showed the true balance of political power.[48] These elections had been trials of strength between the Ponsonbys and their enemies in 1754 and now came back to endanger the government's efforts to reconcile the groups. Hartington wanted to help his in-laws, but feared alienating Kildare. The Wexford election was particularly bitter, with the Ponsonbys supporting one candidate and the Gores (with all their allies, including Kildare) backing the petitioner, Abel Ram, who included among his accusations the one that some voters were insincere converts with Catholic wives. The government was forced to publicly proclaim its neutrality, although Wilmot was secretly asked, with Hartington's blessing, to contact all Irish MPs in England who would support the Ponsonbys. Fox, however, insisted on Hartington's neutrality, to keep Kildare loyal to the Castle, and so Ralph Gore was given a leave of absence to travel to Dublin to vote.[49] Conway alternated between boredom and fascination over the election business, which crawled on through November and December. Hartington was more worried that the debates 'created ill blood and keep the spirits of party high.'[50] Matters reached a climax in late November, as the report on the Wexford election came

---

46 PRONI T3158/985, Hartington to Devonshire, 19 Nov. 1755; PRONI T3019/2734, Devonshire to Wilmot, 30 Dec. 1755.   47 *CJI*, ix, pp. 254, 387 & 826. By this time Cox had finally appeared at the Castle which may explain his lack of enthusiasm for Pery's motion: PRONI T3019/2707, Conway to Wilmot, 11 Nov. 1755.   48 NLI O'Hara papers, p. 1576, 'Survey of the Commons' [1755] calculated the figures as 116 MPs for the government and 126 MPs supporting the Patriots; see appendix.   49 PRONI T3019/2692, 2694, Duncannon to Wilmot, 21 Oct., Sackville to Wilmot, 22 Oct. 1755; PRONI T3158/976, Fox to Hartington, 12 Nov. 1755.   50 Conway to Walpole, 27 Nov. 1755 in *Walpole Corr.*, xxxvii, p. 419; PRONI T3019/2717, Hartington to Wilmot, 30 Nov. 1755.

before the Commons and MPs proceeded to debate it for a week. The committee resolution to unseat the Ponsonby candidate, Robert Leigh, in favour of Ram, was finally passed by 115 votes to 112. Another vote on a contested election at Navan quickly followed and the candidate supported by Thomas Carter and Kildare unseated the declared MP, John Preston, by 105 votes to 99.[51] The heat of these contests dissipated very quickly but they show how the legacy of 1753-4 could still recreate a wide gulf between Kildare and the Ponsonbys. This did not endanger government business but it did show that the Castle could not manage parliament with the support of only one of the sides from the money bill crisis years.

Business was then disrupted by the sudden death of the duke of Devonshire, which caused the viceroy to briefly abandon Dublin. Hartington, now the fourth duke of Devonshire, returned to the capital just before the Christmas adjournment to discuss the likely Lords Justices commission.[52] Stone was said to have 'retired' to Leixlip, though he made one last unsuccessful attempt, through Bessborough, to persuade Devonshire to include him in the commission. Despite their election disputes, Kildare and Lord Bessborough were still the two most likely Lords Justices. Fox claimed that Kildare 'hates the Speaker ... [but has the] fear of being thought to have changed sides unworthily'.[53] Boyle's continuing strength in election business and his influence in having the address altered, made it imperative that a deal be finalised if the commission was to be fixed without him. As a Dublin Presbyterian put it:

> They and their friends [the Patriots] are the prevailing party in the House of Commons, which is greatly to the contentment to the people of my country, in general, who have been and still are very zealous on their side.[54]

Thus it was hoped that Boyle would agree to being excluded from the regency and not see this as equating him with Stone. Although there had been no joint undertaking of business by the Kildare/Ponsonby duumvirate, there was still the hope that any remaining management instability would end with Boyle's retirement.

PATRIOTISM UNMASKED?

The signs of a successful settlement were auspicious after parliament returned in early 1756. Boyle seemed to resolve potential problems when he offered to

---

51 D. Goodall, 'All the Cooking that could be Used: A Co. Wexford Election in 1754', *Past*, xii, (1978), pp. 3–22; *CJI*, ix, pp. 401–94 & 573.   52 Conway to Walpole, 11 Dec. 1755 in *Walpole Correspondence*, xxxvii, p. 423.   53 PRONI T3019/2729, Devonshire to Wilmot, 16 Dec. 1755; PRONI T3158/1020, Fox to Devonshire, 8 Dec. 1755.   54 PRONI T3019/ 2729, Devonshire to Wilmot, 16 Dec. 1755; BL Sloane Mss. 4326, f.89, Orr to Birch, [Nov. 1755].

retire as Speaker, signalling his intention not to serve as a lord justice. His price was a settlement for his immediate circle, including the title of earl of Shannon and a £2,000 pension for life for himself, some smaller pensions and places for his relations and the restorations of Malone and Carter as Chancellor of the Exchequer and Secretary of State respectively.[55] These terms were similar to those discussed in May–June 1755, but the delay can be explained by the clear exclusion of Stone from the lords justices by January 1756, which would allow Boyle to claim that his retirement was an honourable one.

Fox and Newcastle quickly agreed to the terms, though George II was slow to give his acquiescence, never mind his approval. Newcastle told the viceroy that the king 'showed the greatest unwillingness to agree to what was proposed, and expressed in the strongest possible terms his dislike towards those who had opposed him.' However, the proposal to replace Boyle with John Ponsonby made the deal slightly more acceptable to the king, especially when Fox promised him that Devonshire hoped to 'lessen the power of the employment as well as change the person'.[56] Devonshire now demanded that Boyle stand down before the end of the session to allow an election of a new Speaker before any opposition to the set-tlement had time to gather strength. At the same time, the viceroy suggested Kildare, Bessborough and Lord Chancellor Newport as his lords justices. George II again proved reluctant to agree to this proposal, especially to the inclusion of Kildare, but Newcastle convinced him that it was the 'preferable measure to that of the Speaker.'[57]

The angry response of Patriot opinion to the deal was probably to be expected. Boyle knew all the dangers from any courtship of popularity, given his long parlia-mentary career and his experience of events since 1750. His sole line of defence was that he had defied Stone and forced his exclusion from government. When one remembers that Boyle was more concerned with convincing his 'country' allies of his integrity, rather than competing for the title of Patriot, this was an under-standable defence. It was not immediately effective, as, in the aftermath of the deal, he was savagely abused. Boyle reacted with great dignity, according to Conway:

> Our late Speaker, dwindled into such an earl as my Lord Bath, still keeps his ground, has taken his seat, and stood all the splattering and clamour with infinite spirit.[58]

In terms of public reputation, the reference made by Conway to Lord Bath's apostasy of patriotism in the wake of Walpole's fall was much more striking than Boyle's calmness.

55 PRONI D619/21/B/149, Rooney to Bayly, 20 Jan. 1756.   56 PRONI T3158/1098–9, Newcastle to Devonshire, 28 Jan., Fox to Devonshire, 28 Jan. 1755.   57 PRONI T3158/1118, Newcastle to Devonshire, 16 Feb. 1756.   58 Conway to Walpole, 29 Apr. 1756 in *Walpole Corr.*, xxxvii, p. 462.

Meanwhile, Kildare escaped criticism, possibly because he had gone into government and replaced Stone, rather than settling for places and pensions. Malone was not so fortunate. His effigy was burnt alongside Boyle's and he was one of the opposition stalwarts who were hustled at their houses and 'cried about the streets three Patriots for three half-pence'. According to Devonshire, 'the settlement has produced far beyond what I had hoped or even wished for; in short it has entirely broke the party and thrown them into confusion.'[59] Malone begged Devonshire to keep quiet about his restoration; Conway reported that Carter was denying all knowledge of the negotiations and Sir Arthur Gore renounced the speaker and told Devonshire he would look to the Castle in future for favours. On this evidence, the viceroy optimistically concluded that 'all the country gentleman declare they have done with parties, and will belong to the government for the future.'[60]

A pamphlet war then began over the rights and wrongs of Boyle's deal with the administration and addressing the wider question of patriotism. One defender described Boyle as 'a steady Patriot before he got into high employment – and I will convince you, that he has never deviated in the smallest instance from the principles upon which he first set out'. The point was once again made that the Speaker had only undertaken to remove Stone, not to negotiate for all those who had voted with him in 1753, though the 'noisiest of them' (Malone) had also been restored. Another apologist pointed out that the 1755-6 session had seen no 'attempt that looked like reasserting the pretensions of prerogative and thus Boyle had served his purpose well'.[61] These sentiments followed the Speaker's own line that the removal of Stone and the avoidance of any mention of previous consent had been his successful aims. Other pamphlets execrated him and his venal followers. One of these authors claimed, in a reference to a potential new Patriot opposition, that a 'remnant is still left to save and defend their country, and point out its enemies to public view'.[62] The apostasy allowed others to pour scorn on opposition in general. In a bitter satire, 'Roger' [Boyle] is tried for the murder of 'Lady Betty Ireland', in other words the betrayal of his Patriot principles. Suddenly the trial is called off, after it is found that 'Lady Betty' is not dead but has suffered a 'Giddiness in her head for a few days', brought on by too much wine and high spirits. Other pamphleteers also addressed the unrest in 1753 and the role of patriotism, including one warning people not to follow false Patriots who were always 'garbling the House of Commons'.[63]

59 PRONI T3019/2770-1, Devonshire to Wilmot, 2 Mar., Conway to Wilmot, 3 Mar. 1756. 60 PRONI T3019/2774-5, Devonshire to Wilmot, 6 Mar., Conway to Wilmot, 6 Mar. 1756; PRONI T3158/1134, Devonshire to Ellis, 2 Mar. 1756. 61 *A Short but Full Defence of a Certain Great Man* (Dublin, 1756), *p. 3–7; Advice to the Patriot Club of Antrim* (Dublin, 1756), p. 6. 62 *Remarks on a late pamphlet entitled 'Advice to the Patriot Club of Antrim'* (Dublin, 1756); *A letter from the side of the Shannon to Roger* (Dublin, 1756), p. 24. 63 *The Tryal of Roger for the Murder of Lady Betty Ireland* (Dublin, 1756), p. 15; *Advice to the Speaker Elect, or a letter to John Ponsonby* (Dublin, 1756), p. 4.

On the surface there seemed to be little basis for opposition to the deal or to the election of John Ponsonby as the next speaker. A County Tyrone MP claimed that, although:

> The Gore family and the country gentlemen are very angry, ... the run of the people is in the general very much against him [Boyle], [and] moderate folks like the present system very well.[64]

This was soon shown to be true, as the anger of the Gores and others did not lay the ground for fresh opposition. At a dinner for forty-six MPs, held in Dublin on 5 April and attended by John Gore and Malone, the discussion turned to what they would do in the latter part of the session. They 'hatched nothing; and on the whole I [Conway] flatter myself will not be able to stir up anything formidable, being broke at present without heads to guide them or strength to support them'. After this there was no obstacle to Ponsonby's election and the Castle were even able to get a supporter of Boyle to second the nomination, albeit at the third attempt.[65]

Across the Channel there were mixed feelings about the deal and the subsequent reactions to it. Newcastle had always been unhappy about Stone's exclusion and was worried about Malone's future intentions, as he believed him to be 'the most material man of them all', but he did concede that Devonshire had won a 'complete victory over patriotism itself.'[66] Fox and Welbore Ellis were again concerned about developments in Irish politics, this time about the surge of anger against Boyle. At first Fox had been optimistic, writing, 'I own I always saw that when the Speaker sold himself publicly, he would be in Lord Bath's situation, not only incapable himself of giving trouble, but a mark to deter others from setting up to give trouble.' However, he later questioned his own opinion, wondering whether the reaction to the deal showed any goodwill for Devonshire's administration or revealed the likelihood of future opposition to this settlement.[67]

Devonshire was not convinced by such arguments and told Ellis that all the politicians were 'out of humour' with one another.[68] The Castle also took heart from the mixed fortunes of the new Patriot opposition, led by Brownlow and Pery. The reaction to Boyle's deal had shown the presence again of a vocal political nation 'out-of-doors', but it was unclear as yet whether this would disappear with the passing of the political crisis. Pery, French and the other Patriot MPs did

64 PRONI Abercorn papers, T2541/IA1/4/9, Pomeroy to Abercorn, 13 Mar. 1756.
65 PRONI T3158/1134, Devonshire to Ellis, 2 Mar. 1756; PRONI T3019/2774–5, Devonshire to Wilmot, 6 Mar., Conway to Wilmot, 6 Mar. 1756.   66 PRONI T3158/1186, Newcastle to Devonshire, 13 Mar. 1756.   67 PRONI T3158/1158, 1153, 1172, Fox to Devonshire, 13 Mar., Ellis to Devonshire, 9 Mar., Ellis to Devonshire, 23 Mar. 1756; Fox to Devonshire, 9 Mar. 1756 in Ilchester, *Henry Fox*, p. 80.   68 PRONI T3158/1220, Devonshire to Ellis, 17 Apr. 1756.

provoke the undertakers into legislative action over the collapse of three Dublin banks in 1754–5, but this did not herald sustained or threatening parliamentary opposition.[69] The legislative limits of this new opposition can be seen with the history of the Place Bill (to make revenue officers stand for re-election), the bill to limit the duration of parliaments and the bill to reform Dublin's corporation, all introduced in the 1755–6 session. The first two were dropped in March 1756, when MPs voted to postpone discussion of them until 1 June, while the City Bill was passed by the Commons in February. Devonshire and Conway were scathing about MPs who were afraid to 'appear the cat's paw in opposing it.' At this point Malone was a central supporter of the bill, sensing its popularity, while the Dublin aldermen timidly dropped a petition to oppose the legislation 'in order to get popularity with them [the Free Citizens] of supporting it and throwing the odium on government of rejecting it'.[70] When the bill returned, after being altered in London, a Commons' motion to defeat it failed by 114 votes to 25, but then MPs voted 55 to 38 to drop the bill, by postponing discussion until 1 June.[71]

There was little affection between these 'new' Patriots, or as they were called, the 'flying squadron', and the former opposition. Indeed, when Pery attacked the privy council over the City Bill, Malone launched into a fearsome defence of prerogative, which embarrassed many MPs who had been called Patriots in previous sessions. The 'new' Patriots were hardly guaranteed the popular support that Boyle and company had enjoyed in 1753–4, since many of these new men, especially Pery, Brownlow and French, had been clearly identified with the government in those years. Pery, in particular, sought to place some distance between his present and former conduct and his recorded speeches from the session accused the former Patriots of being inconsistent. He made the point that he had supported Stone and Dorset until the proroguing of parliament and the sackings, but was consistent in his opposition to faction from wherever that threat came.[72] Several Patriot Clubs accepted these conversions but, because these same societies were savaging Boyle and others for apostasy, they were reluctant to adopt new Patriot icons.

At the end of the session Conway accurately noted that the new opposition, 'which was expected would have increased out of these events is, I think, just where it was ... and not one considerable man among them.'[73] With a money bill and an augmentation of the army by 1,500 men secured, Conway had strong grounds for such confidence. Even those who doubted the wisdom of the settlement, at the time, could find little to criticise in it. Dudley Ryder and Charles Yorke discussed the possibility of an Act of Union but without any

69 *CJI*, ix, pp. 818–9 & 877–8.   **70** PRONI T3019/2766, 2763, Conway to Wilmot, 25 Feb., Devonshire to Wilmot, 23 Feb. 1756.   **71** *CJI*, ix, pp. 907–8.   **72** Pery's various speeches from this session can be found in *HMC Emly Mss.*, pp. 183–9.   **73** *BNL*, 24 Dec. 1755, 12 Mar., 24 Apr. 1756 for the various Patriot Club notices; Conway to Walpole, 29 Apr. 1756 in *Walpole Corr.*, xxxvii, pp. 462–3.

strategy to bring this forward. Fox and Cumberland were less radical, but remained vaguely distracted by rumours that Stone would enter open opposition. Lord Duncannon, the new Speaker's older brother, and Conway doubted whether Stone was capable of mounting an opposition, as 'his passion for power will, I fancy, render him uneasy to himself and others'. Wilmot reported stories, which he did not believe, from an unnamed Irish MP, who had hinted that Ponsonby should be on his guard, as Stone saw him as a traitor, and that Kildare and the Gores were plotting for the next session.[74] The reasons for this confidence were clear in the spring and summer of 1756 as the new, untested regency took power. All that was to change by 1757.

74 PRONI T3228/1/74, entry in Ryder's diary, 28 Mar. 1756; PRONI T3158/1029B, 1236–7, Fox to Devonshire, 23 Apr., Duncannon to Devonshire, 27 Apr., Wilmot to Devonshire, 27 Apr. 1756; Conway to Walpole, 29 Apr. 1756 in *Walpole Corr.*, xxxvii, p. 463.

5

Restoration of the undertakers: the
Bedford viceroyalty, 1757–1760

The duke of Bedford's appointment owed much to the twists and turns in British politics in the autumn and winter of 1756–7. In October 1756 the news began to circulate in Dublin that the Fox/Newcastle ministry had collapsed in a welter of mutual recrimination after the loss of Minorca.[1] Anthony Malone worried about the promise of his office, while Lord Kildare sought confirmation that the lords justices would survive under a new ministry.[2] The eventual consequence of the ministry's collapse was the replacement of Devonshire as viceroy. This was because Fox proved unable to construct an administration and George II turned to Devonshire as an honest broker to talk to Legge and Pitt. The viceroy was then persuaded to head a ministry with Pitt and Legge under him, which led to rumours that Lord Temple, Pitt's brother-in-law, was to be the new lord lieutenant.[3] As Temple proved unwilling, Devonshire made approaches to Bedford, both to curb Pitt's influence and to placate his old ally, Fox. Bedford 'determine[d] to have nothing to do with [the] administration' despite Fox's pleas, though one Irish visitor to London commented that 'it is imagined the Duke will be brought to accept it'. In December 1757, Bedford finally agreed to become the viceroy, after yet another meeting with Fox to discuss political tactics. In all these discussions and offers, Irish affairs had played no part.[4]

No-one expected the new ministry to survive long, given Devonshire's well-known reluctance to become the First Lord, the lack of support at Court and the lack of ministerial supporters in parliament. Within two months of taking over,

---

1 This recrimination reached the Patriot Club of Antrim, who blamed the loss of Minorca on enemies abroad and treachery at home and toasted: 'May no artful pretences prevail on the Patriots of Ireland to suspend that activity which in this critical time of danger must be of the utmost importance and most signal service to their country'; *BNL*, 7 Sept. 1756. 2 PRONI T3087/1/11, Bowes to Pery, 21 Oct. 1756; TCD Clements papers, Ms.1742, Malone to Clements, 28 Oct. 1756; PRONI T3158/1406, Kildare to Devonshire, 26 Oct. 1756. 3 BL Add. Mss. 35416, f.129, Memorandum of Hardwicke on Pitt's plan, 23 Oct. 1756. 4 See Fox's 'Narrative', cited in Ilchester, *Henry Fox*, p. 81; Bedford Mss., xxxii, f.91, Fox to Bedford, 3 Nov. 1756; BL Add. Mss. 51385, f.1184, Bedford to Fox, 22 Nov. 1756; PRONI T3158/1442, Bedford to Devonshire, 19 Nov. 1756; TCD Ms.1742, Blair to Clements, 16 Nov. 1756; Walpole to Mann, 8 Dec. 1756 in *Walpole Correspondence*, xxi, p. 31.

Devonshire told a friend that he was convinced 'more and more in my opinion that the present system cannot last' and Walpole noted that 'the very cement seems disjunctive: If the Duke acts cordially, he disobliges his intimate friend Mr. Fox; if he does not, he offends Pitt.'[5] The expected denouement came in April 1757, with the dismissals of Pitt and Legge after they had opposed the execution of Admiral Byng. Once again Fox entertained high hopes of forming a ministry, yet Conway was surely correct in his assumption that he could not succeed 'when the cry of the people, the general turn of the parliament and the influence of Leicester House are all against him.' By late May 1757 discussions were at a standstill, with George II refusing to have Pitt in his government, despite all the advice from Devonshire and Hardwicke.[6]

It was at this point that the 'arch-schemer', Archbishop Stone, sprang back into the political limelight as the intermediary between Newcastle and Pitt. Lady Kildare informed her husband that 'our Primate has, it seems, done a great deal of mischief; he and Pitt are hand in glove.' Stone's role in the negotiations is borne out by the memorandum he prepared for Newcastle in mid-May, suggesting how he and Pitt could unite in government and his advice was followed in the negotiations of June 1757.[7] Pitt was once again appointed secretary of state with responsibility for Ireland, but this time in a stronger ministry than the previous one. It appeared that Bedford would resign his place in protest, which, according to Walpole, was Stone's wish and Lady Kildare's greatest fear. After a few days reflection, Bedford told Kildare that he feared for their interests under the new ministry, but intended to carry on as viceroy as 'he did not see the necessity of obliging them with government of Ireland too'.[8] The rejuvenation of Stone's fortunes appeared crucial for the future direction of Irish politics. Lady Kildare 'suppose[d] the Primate is in great spirits', despite the primate's gesture of retirement to his country house at Leixlip. Fox was not fooled by this conduct for a moment and instead 'fancie[d] he [Stone] will now throw off all restraint, and declare himself an open enemy, as he is, in connection with all these people [in the ministry] here'. Among observers in Dublin there was a lot of confusion about

5 L. Sutherland, 'The City and the Pitt/Devonshire Ministry of 1757', in A. Newman (ed.), *Politics and Finance in Eighteenth Century England*, (London, 1984), pp. 67–115; PRONI T2812/12/1, Conway to O'Hara, 23 Nov. 1756; PRONI T2541/IA1/4/41, Pomeroy to Abercorn, 20 Nov. 1756; PRONI T3158/1479, Devonshire to Strafford, 23 Dec. 1756; Walpole to Mann, 13 Nov. 1756 in *Walpole Correspondence*, xxi, p. 17.   6 R. Middleton, *The Bells of Victory: The Pitt/Newcastle Ministry and the Conduct of the Seven Years War* (Cambridge, 1985, hereafter Middleton, *Bells of Victory*), p. 15; PRONI T3158/1532, Conway to Devonshire, 8 June 1757; BL Add. Mss. 51375, f.113, Fox to Cumberland, 27 May 1757.   7 BL Add. Mss. 32871, f.15, Stone to Newcastle, 4 May 1757; Kildare to Kildare, 17 May 1757 in *Leinster Correspondence*, p. 33; BL Add. Mss. 32871, f.61, Stone to Newcastle, 12 May 1757.   8 Kildare to Kildare, 14 June 1757 in *Leinster Correspondence*, p. 47; Bedford Mss. xxxiv, f.23, Bedford to Kildare, 16 June 1757; BL Add. Mss. 51385, f.111, Rigby to Fox, 16 June 1757.

the new turn of events, a situation summed up by John Bowes' comment that Dublin was 'perfectly calm at present, I do not say from principle, probably from suspense.'[9]

AN ADMINISTRATION AND STRATEGY FOR IRELAND

Bedford was a proud and impulsive man, not given to political compromise. These characteristics were to prove damaging ones for his viceroyalty, given the delicate political situation he inherited. He was also a political maverick, having been a fixture of the Whig opposition until taking office in the 'Broad Bottom' ministry of 1743 and then being dismissed in 1751.[10] His Irish administration was built around the new chief secretary, Richard Rigby. Walpole's striking portrait is of him is 'a man who was seldom loved or hated with moderation', while Rigby saw himself as a bluff country squire or 'a good four-bottle man.' Because of this it is easy to underestimate Rigby's sharp political intellect, though his indolence did affect, sometimes badly, his time in Ireland.[11] One major change in the Castle was the appointment of John Bowes as lord chancellor after the death of Newport in November 1756. Bowes was 'oddly situated, teased with congratulations on rumours and not believed when I decline them' and was furious that Bedford took so long to make the appointment. This was the beginning of what was to be a rancorous relationship at the heart of the government.[12]

Much more important was the discussion on what strategy would be adopted for political management of the Irish parliament. Bedford has sometimes been associated with an attempt to rule 'above party' and, at the same time (somewhat in contradiction), to lean on a loyal Lord Kildare. This interpretation comes from Horace Walpole and has recently been endorsed by J.C.D. Clark, who argues that Bedford and Hartington had aspirations to break the parties in the Irish parliament, using Kildare as their tool. At one stage Bedford did follow a tactic of dealing impartially with all the undertakers, to prevent fresh parliamentary disputes from breaking out, but this was an approach born out of despair and one designed to placate, not emasculate, factions.[13]

---

9 Kildare to Kildare, 17 June 1757 in *Leinster Correspondence*, p. 48; PRONI T3019/3178, 3184, Clements to Wilmot, 9 June, Bowes to Wilmot, 14 June 1757.   10 Walpole, *George II*, iii, p. 65; A.P.W. Malcomson, 'Introduction to the Bedford Papers', in idem. (ed), *Private Papers of the Eighteenth Century: Volume Two* (Belfast, 1982).   11 Rigby to Bedford, 30 June 1757 in *Bedford Correspondence*, ii, p. 257; F. Hardy (ed), *Memoirs of the Private and Political Life of the Earl of Charlemont* (London, 1812), p. 54. For a perceptive profile see J. Brooke and L. Namier (eds), *House of Commons, 1754–1790* (3 vols, London, 1964), iii, pp. 355–60.   12 PRONI T3019/3013, 3065, 3063, Bowes to Wilmot, 13 Nov., Bowes to Wilmot, 23 Dec., Waite to Wilmot, 23 Dec. 1756.   13 James, *Empire*, pp. 254–5; Clark, 'Whig Tactics', p. 284.

However, the initial strategy was to favour Kildare as the chief undertaker, especially as he was a brother-in-law of Henry Fox and Rigby was complacent about the threat posed by Stone. A letter, written by Lady Kildare in May 1757, claimed that Bedford had been advised by Lord Hillsborough and Dorset to find out which was the strongest party and rule through it, perhaps using another faction for security. Rigby simultaneously advised the viceroy 'not [to] govern by any party', while considering appointing Kildare as a lord deputy during the next interregnum. Bedford seems to have liked the appearance of impartiality, though he wanted also to favour Kildare.[14] The context of these discussions is crucial, as this account dates from May 1757, when Fox was optimistic about heading a new ministry, Stone was apparently despised in London and Lady Kildare had high hopes for the advancement of her family. Within a month all of this had changed. In any case, Bedford's initial strategy, far from breaking party, would have resulted in Kildare enjoying an ascendancy to rival that of Henry Boyle's.

What seems strange is that a management strategy, based on the settlement of 1756 and the cooperation of Kildare and the Ponsonbys, was never attempted. There are a few reasons why. Firstly, the new administration refused to believe that the Speaker of the Commons and potential undertaker, John Ponsonby, was anything other than the dullard described by Lady Kildare. Furthermore, it was expected that the Ponsonby connection would not outlive its creator, Lord Bessborough, who was critically ill throughout 1757. The second reason was that while Kildare 'had no intention of quarrelling with Mr Ponsonby', Lady Kildare 'could not answer by any means for [his] joining particularly, or making any league with him'.[15] A third reason was that Kildare and his allies came to expect unrivalled access and favour from the new viceroy, something they were unwilling to share with the Ponsonbys.[16] However, tensions began opening up among the earl's allies, as Lord Shannon was angry that his requests were ignored by government and the Gore family was also restless, due to the distribution of judicial and ecclesiastical posts.[17] Little of this augured well for any strategy to make Lord Kildare the leading undertaker.

BEDFORD'S INITIAL REPUTATION

Despite such machinations, the popular expectations of Bedford grew throughout 1757. Initially he was lauded by Patriot Clubs and Dublin's Free Citizens as a successor to Lord Russell, a leading Whig hero executed in the wake of the Rye

14 Clark, 'Whig Tactics', p. 292; Kildare to Kildare, 19 May 1757 in *Leinster Correspondence*, pp. 35–6.   15 Kildare to Kildare, 19 May, 5 July 1757 in *Leinster Correspondence*, pp. 35–6, 57; PRONI T3158/1537, O'Hara to Conway, 24 Mar. 1757.   16 PRONI T3158/1532A, Fox to Devonshire, 29 May 1757.   17 PRONI T3158/1515, 1519, 1537, Shannon to Devonshire, 12 Jan., O'Hara to Conway, 24 Mar., Bowes to Devonshire, 28 July 1757.

House plot of 1682.[18] Edmund Pery, in a major pamphlet, pleaded with Bedford to break with past policies and management techniques using the undertakers or parties. He warned that the undertakers would unite 'never to permit a Chief Governor to interfere in the domestic administration of this kingdom'. Bedford should follow the example of Pitt and become a 'Patriot viceroy'.[19] From the opposing perspective of a High Church Whig, Bedford was urged to curb Presbyterians who, since 1753, had been 'carried out of their orbits, raised in their own conceits to the rank of statesmen and philosophers, where you see them aping their betters and setting out the bounds of their authority.'[20]

Bedford spent most of 1757 dealing with two issues, defence and dearth, in a way that enhanced his reputation. As the war delivered fresh blows in America and Germany for Britain, Bedford firmly advised against fresh demands for drafts of troops from the Irish establishment. He also ordered the General Board to come back to full strength, organised an inspection of the coastal defences and went on to address the vital question of Catholic loyalty. With regard to the last, Bedford lent his support to a fresh attempt, by the earl of Clanbrassil, to pass a registration bill in the next parliamentary session. The bill to register Catholic priests was a sensitive one, given the expected opposition from Church of Ireland bishops in the Lords. Clanbrassil's aim was to offer Catholic priests legal recognition, if they registered with the government, took an oath of allegiance and allowed local landowners more of a say in their appointments.[21] Bedford pledged his support for Clanbrassil, though he wondered whether priests would take the oath of allegiance. Catholics were themselves divided over the bill, with the clergy and some laity opposing the 'loyalty clause', while more laity wanted to prove their attachment to the government through loyal addresses. In the event the bill passed the Irish parliament in December 1757, but fell at the privy council stage, a sign that the bishops were still strongly opposed to it.[22] Bedford supported the bill at that stage and gained credit for his loyalty to Clanbrassil, a respected peer.

Bedford's credit rose further after his action to deal with the dearth caused by the failure of the 1756 harvest. Devonshire had already given the lords justices permission to use Treasury funds to support the importation of grain, although Waite argued that 'if we can but keep what we have at home and do not export it we will avoid dearth'. In Dublin and Belfast there were subscription schemes to

18 *BNL*, 20 Dec. 1756; *UA*, 27 July 1757.   19 [Pery], *Letter to Bedford*, pp. 4, 22 & 45–6.   20 *Serious Thoughts concerning the Interests and Exigencies of the State of Ireland in a letter to the Duke of Bedford* (Dublin, 1757), p. 30.   21 M. Wall, 'Government policy towards catholics during the viceroyalty of the Duke of Bedford, 1757–61', in G. O'Brien (ed.), *Catholic Ireland in the Eighteenth Century: The Collected Essays of Maureen Wall* (Dublin, 1989), pp. 103–6; Clanbrassil to Bedford, 17 July 1757 in *Bedford Correspondence*, ii, pp. 263–5; BL Sloane Mss. 4164, f.27, Henry to Secker, 20 Sept. 1755.   22 Bedford to Clanbrassil, 4 Aug. 1757 in *Bedford Correspondence*, pp. 266–7; PRONI T3019/3308, Rigby to Wilmot, 19 Jan. 1758; Barry to Orrery, 24 Jan. 1758 in *Orrery Papers*, ii, p. 131.

support food imports with premiums. Bedford supported this action and asked Wilmot to prepare an estimate of how much it would cost to buy 50,000 barrels of North American wheat. Wilmot calculated that a premium of 3 shillings per barrel and the cost of shipping and storage would amount in total to £20,000, and that each barrel could still be sold at 5 shillings less than the prevailing Dublin price.[23] This sum was agreed though not before food shortages provoked riots and attacks on forestallers and bakers. The Patriots repeated such attacks in parliament, but Bedford gained an enhanced reputation after he spent £5,000 of his own money to import corn for Ulster. Bedford may have been annoyed, when this act was made public by an address from the Armagh grand jury which Stone was rumoured to be behind, though with a stable, well-managed parliament, Bedford could have returned to London in triumph in early 1758.[24]

BEDFORD'S FIRST PARLIAMENTARY SESSION

The signs that trouble could be expected in parliament came when experienced Dublin officials began to worry about attacks on the size of the pensions list. This list showed a substantial increase since May 1755, with some £11,400 in new pensions, making a total of £100,800. Both Clements and Waite, just back from a six week break in England, 'heard on all hands that we are to have a bustle here next winter about the pensions'.[25] The vagueness of these reports may have encouraged Rigby to airily write that:

> [He] had not the least dread at Waite's rumours about the pensions. They will evaporate in fumes, I believe, or if they do not, we must fight with the best force we can muster.[26]

However, a fortnight later, Waite again reported that 'it is talked about town that there will be some stir in parliament concerning the pensions that have been granted since last session, and that Mr Speaker's chair is to be made very uneasy to him'.[27] The threat to Ponsonby from the Patriot opposition, assisted by Stone, and thus the consequent threat to the settlement bequeathed by Devonshire, also seems to have been totally ignored. Bedford was aware of the problems that

---

23 *FDJ*, 2 Nov. 1756; PRONI T3158/1453, Devonshire to the Lords Justices, 25 Nov. 1756; PRONI T3019/3025, 3060, Waite to Wilmot, 27 Nov., Memorandum on corn imports, 26 Dec. 1756; Rigby to Bedford, 23 Jan. 1757 in *Bedford Correspondence*, ii, p. 225.   24 E. Magennis, 'In search of the 'Moral Economy': Food scarcity in 1756–7 and the crowd', in P.J. Jupp & E. Magennis (eds), *The Crowd in Irish History, 1720–1920* (London, forthcoming).   25 *CJI*, ix, pp. 277–8; PRONI T3019/3239, Clements to Wilmot, 3 Sept., Waite to Wilmot, 6 Sept. 1757. 26 PRONI T3019/3249, Rigby to Wilmot, 17 Sept. 1757.   27 PRONI T3019/6457/502, Waite to Wilmot, 18 Sept. 1757.

excessive grants of pensions could cause. When he was told by Newcastle that George II wanted a £6,000 pension for the princess of Hesse, Bedford was clearly reluctant to agree as 'the revenue is at least in an equal degree decreasing, both customs and excise necessarily sinking during a time of war'. However, he told Newcastle that the 'overloaded' Irish list would sustain this request, so long as it was the last one.[28]

When Bedford and Rigby arrived in Dublin there was the usual round of levees and dinners at the Castle, to which all were invited. Rigby wrote of the under-takers that he was 'physiognomist enough to see the heads are not united in their hearts; if they are in their votes, it answers our purpose and they at least promise fair.' His energy went into establishing long-lasting friendships with Pery and Francis Andrews, at the same time as continuing to dismiss reports of problems in parliament:

> Mr Malone, they say, is to be much abused for the one [King's letter] that increases his salary but I believe he is in no dread from that report and I see no reason to be so neither for all the stories of the attack upon the pensions.[29]

Even with the reports of Stone and Ponsonby allying against Kildare and the Cas-tle, Rigby was still confident of a quiet session. One reason for his misreading may have been that the new administration's attention was distracted by the downfall of Bedford's senior ally, the duke of Cumberland, after a military defeat in Hanover and an embarrassing peace with the French, which was rejected in London.[30]

Meanwhile, John Ponsonby and Stone had entered a pact to support one another. Bowes informed Devonshire that Bedford's abandonment of the 1756 settlement left Ponsonby with little option. The rumours that Malone's friend, John Scott, would be made prime serjeant was 'considered [by Ponsonby] as neglect and will be aggravated by some. If these jealousies should be confirmed by future conduct, the consequences will be disagreeable.'[31] Then in a *volte-face* from previous decisions, Bedford suddenly agreed to the commissioning of the adjutant general, Captain Robert Cuninghame, as a lieutenant colonel. This blatant wooing of Stone was seen by Devonshire and Wilmot as a signal of weakness, especially as 'one of the last things Mr Rigby said to me was that the duke of Bedford was determined never to recommend Cuninghame for rank'.[32] As the session approached, Bedford, bereft of allies in London, seemed to be searching for a parliamentary majority in Dublin.

---

28 Newcastle to Bedford, 3 Oct., Bedford to Newcastle, 13 Oct. 1757 in *Bedford Correspondence*, ii, pp. 271, 274–5. 29 PRONI T3019/6457/504–5, 3262, Rigby to Wilmot, 27, 29 Sept., 4 Oct. 1757. 30 Walpole to Conway, 13 Oct. 1757 in *Walpole Correspondence*, xxxvii, p. 518. 31 PRONI T3158/1546, Bowes to Devonshire, 4 Oct. 1757. 32 PRONI T3019/3266. Devonshire to Wilmot, 18 Oct. 1757; PRONI T3158/1548, Wilmot to Devonshire, 20 Oct.

The session itself opened very quietly on 16 October. Addresses were quickly passed, applauding Bedford's 'early and charitable attention to the necessities of the poor of this country in their late distresses' and, in an adjournment vote, the Patriots were only able to muster thirteen votes.[33] When the session resumed a week later, MPs concentrated on gathering the national accounts and different papers on defence and trade issues, while Edmund Pery's populist corn bill was passed without a division. Given the dearth after the harvest of 1756–7, the supply of food was a sensitive issue and therefore the government found it impossible to oppose Pery's bill. Behind the apparent consensus, Rigby was aware that the struggle between the undertakers was 'fairly coming to open war'. As the viceroy 'is here but six months in four and twenty, and they, a majority as they say, will not be rid of Lord Kildare or Malone in His Grace's absence. In short, we are to be bullied or voted to take the primate back into the government.' Despite all of this information, Rigby complacently believed that government business would remain unaffected.[34]

The bubble of complacency burst on 1 November, when the Commons' committee of accounts proposed its eleven resolutions against pensions and not one was challenged. These resolutions included a condemnation of the practice of granting pensions to non-resident persons as a 'prejudice to this kingdom', while the increase in the list was a 'grievance to the nation' which 'demand[ed] redress'. A final resolution attacked the long terms on which the pensions were granted, as 'an alienation for so much of the publick revenue and an injury to the crown and to this kingdom'. John Bowes immediately blamed the affair on Stone's ambition, supported by Ponsonby with his domination of the committee of accounts. At the same time Kildare and Malone were afraid to support government. Bowes pointed out that Rigby had been informed 'that the p[rimate] and the Sp[eaker] have agreed to support each other, that they have the majority and expect to be informed who are to be left in commission'.[35] Despite this development, Bedford refused to alter his approach and so worsened matters. After a Commons adjournment, he called a meeting of the undertakers and government officials and defiantly told the assembled peers and MPs that he would not send the resolutions to George II and demanded that the Commons back down.[36] Few agreed with him; Kildare advised that he send the resolutions, and Malone, Tisdall and Ponsonby all warned him against calling MPs to the Castle to repeat this defiant performance. Bedford ignored the advice and met the entire Commons on 12 November to tell them of his decision not to send the resolutions. It was a stormy meeting, as some MPs

1757. **33** *CJI*, x, pp. 26–9. **34** BL Add. Mss. 51385, f.1393, Rigby to Fox, 31 Oct. 1757. **35** *CJI*, x, pp. 215–6; PRONI T3158/1553, Bowes to Devonshire, 2 Nov. 1757. **36** Bedford may have been prepared to sacrifice the money bill and prorogue or dissolve parliament; PRONI Bedford papers, T2915/3/24, Bedford to Newcastle, 13 Nov. 1757.

attacked the viceroy for ignoring their right to inform the king of their opinions and threats were made to the money bill.

At this point, Bedford demanded that Pitt support his stand and that he be given power to sack disloyal officials. Wilmot was told to check the accuracy of the figures in the resolutions, but when Rigby tried to raise this point in the Commons he was treated dismissively.[37] On the 13th, Bedford met his officials again and was told he no longer had a Commons majority as only Shannon and a few officials supported the government's stance. Ponsonby and Tisdall demanded that the resolutions be sent and Sir Thomas Prendergast, a supporter of Stone, refused to say whether or not he would oppose an adjournment of the money bill. As if to confirm this, Rigby put the issue of adjourning the money bill to the Commons the next day and the Castle lost by 85 votes to 64. With all their options used up, the administration agreed to send the resolutions to London.[38] The threatened money bill was sent to London in December 1757 but was further tarnished in the Castle's eyes by the level of public grants that were agreed by MPs, despite the pressures on expenditure during wartime and the assault on the pensions. Both Bedford and Newcastle were unhappy about the 'clog' or grants of nearly £126,000 but, given the lack of government managers in the Commons, there was little that could be done.[39]

A division list for the adjournment vote, printed in the nineteenth century, shows that the Kildare, Gore and Shannon groups formed the core of the government side, aided by some independent MPs, but they could not command a majority. On the other side were the Patriots and the supporters of Ponsonby and Stone.[40] Knowing the state of the parties, Bowes identified the danger of Kildare's anger at Bedford over the resolutions, which left the government without any effective management in the Commons.[41] Out of doors there was a battle for popularity. Stone's supporters, including Cuninghame and Tisdall, were allegedly trying to get the Patriot Clubs and the Free Citizens to toast the date of the successful resolutions, as they did the rejection of the 1753 money bill. Meanwhile a pamphleteer urged Pery and the Patriots to maintain their good work in parliament, by exposing those MPs who had 'once made a show of sacrificing their all for the publick good [but] have now drank a large portion of the bitter cup [of pensions]'. Rigby noted that 'Malone and his friends did not know whether they can keep their popularity and their places'.[42]

37 PRONI T1060/4, Bedford to Pitt, 12 Nov. 1757; PRONI T3019/3270, Rigby to Wilmot, 18 Nov. 1757. 38 Bedford to Pitt, 17 Nov. 1757 in *Bedford Correspondence*, ii, pp. 289–92. 39 PRONI T3019/3134, Bedford to Pitt, 13 Nov. 1757; Bedford to Newcastle, 18 Nov. 1757 in *Bedford Correspondence*, ii, p. 299; PRONI T2915/3/34, Newcastle to Bedford, 25 Nov. 1757. 40 F. Plowden, *Historical Review of the State of Ireland to 1801* (3 vols, Dublin, 1803), i, appendix lix, pp. 252–60. 41 PRONI T3158/1554–5, Bowes to Devonshire, 15, 16 Nov. 1757. 42 *Ireland Disgraced: or an island of saints become an island of sinners* (Dublin, 1758), pp. 71–2; *A letter to Edmund Sexton Pery and the rest of the Patriot members of the House of Commons, with*

Competition for the mantle of patriotism led to a debate in the *Universal Advertiser*, which had so strongly supported Boyle and Malone in 1753. The newspaper questioned the credentials of the new Patriots like Pery after reports, in November and December, that the Free Citizens and some Patriot Clubs were applauding the resolutions against the pensions. For example, the Newry Patriot Club toasted: 'May our new Patriots demonstrate the sincerity of their conversion by their future steadiness.'[43] Yet the *Universal Advertiser's* correspondents and owner poured scorn on the conversions of Pery and company and questioned their intentions in opposing government just then:

> They were at that time [1753] what they ought not to be; and are at this time what they have no occasion to be: for nothing is asked that an honest man can refuse.[44]

Allegations were also made, as they had been earlier, that these new Patriots were exaggerating problems for factional reasons and that the pensions resolutions were not about Irish freedoms but about the restoration of Stone. Despite such criticism, Pery and company were generally seen as the only Patriot opposition in parliament by late 1757.

As for Bedford, his situation worsened when it became clear that Pitt was critical of his actions over the pensions resolutions. Pitt warned that the crisis 'may be productive of great and serious mischief to his Majesty's service, and materially affect the immediate safety of the kingdom of Ireland'.[45] In his defence, Bedford sent a detailed account of Irish political affairs and pointed out that the two parties of Stone/Ponsonby and Kildare/Shannon were equal in strength and were both willing to go into opposition to intimidate government. His impartiality with all the undertakers, to avoid disappointing any party, had to be accompanied by powers to dismiss any disloyal officials, as 17 of the 85 MPs who had opposed government were placemen. This would 'make the people here look up to their governor, and enable him to set right those defects which faction has brought in too much here, even in the very essence of government'.[46]

In London Pitt was not the only critical voice as the resolutions were printed in the *London Chronicle*. Chesterfield demanded to know whether 'your new Chancellor of the Exchequer [Malone] has lost his tongue, his parts or his credit'. Walpole laid the blame on a combination of Stone's ambition, a lack of diplomacy on the part of Bedford and the fact that government supporters 'dared not say a word against [the resolutions]'.[47] According to Lady Waldegrave, the events in

observations on pensioners (Dublin, 1757), p. 3; PRONI T3158/1557, Rigby to Devonshire, 18 Nov. 1757. **43** *UA*, 12 Nov., 10, 24 Dec. 1757. **44** *UA*, 31 Jan., 4, 11, 14 & 25 Feb. 1758. **45** Pitt to Bedford, 18 Nov. 1757 in *Bedford Correspondence*, ii, p. 301. **46** Bedford to Pitt, 17 Nov. 1757 in ibid., ii, pp. 296–7. **47** Chesterfield to Chevenix, 22 Nov. 1757 in *Chesterfield Correspondence*, v, p. 2265; Walpole to Mann, 20 Nov. 1757 in *Walpole Correspondence*, xxi, p. 154;

Ireland had not hurt Bedford's reputation and ministers 'all talk loudly ... of supporting you and that there is an end of all government if they do not' but she
wondered, 'if they [the ministers] are sincere and in earnest.' Lord Granville's
advice was not to:

> ... withdraw yourself in disgust at the perverseness of such persons, who
> are now thoughtless enough to ruin themselves, which I think it your duty
> to prevent, the reflection on which hereafter will give you honour and
> pleasure.[48]

The influential former viceroy, Devonshire, was furious at the conduct of his
brother-in-law, John Ponsonby, and warned him that he might be abandoned by
the Cavendish family. Yet the duke also wrote to Bowes criticising Bedford for
snubbing Ponsonby and Wilmot was authorised to tell Sir Henry Cavendish that
he should only vote against the administration if he had the approval of the duke.
Henry Fox was largely silent during the crisis though he did ask Kildare to account
for his conduct:

> Is this not as much to say, "In opposition, against the Castle, we are ready to
> assist; but with the Government, when popularity is on the other side, we must
> beg to be excused."[49]

While Bedford's friends and allies were all silent, ambivalent or powerless, his
enemies in the ministry now demanded the restoration of Stone. The primate himself claimed to Newcastle that he 'remained as unengaged and as ignorant of what
was doing as I should have been had I remained in a lodging house in Pall Mall.'[50]
This was totally untrue and, by late November, there were widespread rumours in
Dublin, allegedly originating with Newcastle, that the ministry had no confidence
in Bedford. The undermining of the viceroy continued with Pitt's impatient letter
of 26 November, in which he assured Bedford that the ministry supported his
sending the resolutions, his not endangering the money bill and his clearing up
MPs' misapprehension that the government sought to curb their rights. Pitt went
on to tell Bedford that his analysis 'seems naturally to suggest, and almost necessitate, all softening and healing arts of government, consistent with its dignity, and,
as far as may be practicable, plans of comprehension and harmony'.[51] As Bedford
had done precisely the opposite to Pitt's advice and concluded that compromise
with Stone was impossible, then a clear criticism ran through the minister's letter.

Walpole, George II, iii, p. 68–9.   **48** Waldegrave to Bedford, 26 Nov., Granville to Bedford, 27
Nov. 1757 in *Bedford Correspondence*, ii, pp. 304, 308.   **49** PRONI T3158/1558, Devonshire
to Ponsonby, 19 Nov., Devonshire to Bowes, 19 Nov. 1757; PRONI T3019/3272, Wilmot to
Cavendish, 22 Nov. 1757; Fox to Kildare, 21 Nov. 1757 in Ilchester, *Henry Fox*, p. 83.   **50** BL
Add. Mss. 32876, f.100, Stone to Newcastle, 24 Nov. 1757.   **51** Bedford to Pitt, 5 Dec., Pitt to
Bedford, 26 Nov. 1757 in *Chatham Correspondence*, i, pp. 290, 285–7.

While the money bill was being dealt with, Bedford assessed his options, including Pitt's suggestion to reconcile the 'very disunited parties' in parliament. He again demanded full support from London, including a contradiction of:

> ... reports industriously spread about this town by those of the primate's faction, [saying] that the last despatches I received from you did tie up my hands from taking such measures as I might judge expedient to bring back his Majesty's subjects to a due sense of their duty.

Bedford also complained about the 'rumour [that] the powers of rewards and punishments will be sparingly entrusted to me.'[52] Without these powers and his belief that Ponsonby and Kildare would not work together, Bedford adopted a strategy of appearing to act impartially towards all the undertakers.[53] This impartiality did not placate Ponsonby and Stone, especially when Rigby supported a Commons motion ordering an inquiry into the revenue service. Ponsonby rightly interpreted this as an attack on his family, as the inquiry was proposed by Sir Archibald Acheson, who was both close to Kildare and a brother-in-law of Robert French, a Patriot MP. The fact that Rigby acted as a teller for the majority (98 votes to 50) who supported Acheson's motion was not seen as an act of a neutral.[54] The inquiry was to be carried out by a committee of 31 MPs, chosen by ballot, and Rigby told Wilmot:

> if they can make it appear, as they say they can very fully, that great frauds and mismanagements exist in the collecting of the Revenue, he [Bedford] should be very glad of any means to remedy such an evil.[55]

Walpole's reasoning, that it was 'repelling the war by carrying it into the quarters of the enemy', was closer to the Castle's thinking. Waite confirmed this by asserting that the 'conduct of the members of that Board towards government has been such as by no means to make it necessary for a servant of government to put himself in the gap between them and public justice.' However, the inquiry posed a threat to the government's reputation and, more importantly, countermanded Pitt's wish for a reconciliation between the undertakers.[56] Though the inquiry virtually collapsed, when 28 of the 31 balloted members of the inquiry committee

52 Bedford to Pitt, 5 Dec. 1757 in *Chatham Correspondence*, pp. 289–90; Bedford to Granville, 6 Dec. 1757 in *Bedford Correspondence*, ii, pp. 314–5.   **53** One sign of impartiality was the refusal to intervene in a disputed election between John Hely Hutchinson (supported by Kildare) and Abraham Devonsher (backed by Stone, Ponsonby and Shannon); NLI, Sarsfield papers, Ms.17891; PRONI T3019/3271, Rigby to Wilmot, 2 Nov. 1757; *CJI*, x, pp. 338–44.   **54** *CJI*, x, pp. 371–2.   **55** PRONI T3019/3280, Rigby to Wilmot, 5 Dec. 1757.   **56** Walpole, *George II*, iii, p. 72; PRONI T3019/3281–2, Rigby to Wilmot, 10 Dec., Waite to Wilmot, 10 Dec. 1757.

turned out to be supporters of the Revenue Board, the affair added to the rifts between the different undertakers and between Ponsonby and Bedford.[57]

The uncertainty over parliamentary management allowed the Patriots MPs to make some limited legislative headway. In mid-November, John Bowes warned of an attack on the powers of the Irish privy council and, soon after, Robert French successfully proposed an inquiry into these powers. He demanded that the 'heads of bills' passed by the Commons in the last two sessions be laid before MPs. Subsequently, three bills were found to have been dropped, including two to regulate the coal trade and one to secure a better supply of corn for Dublin.[58] Although this was permitted under Poyning's Law, MPs were sensitive about legislation, particularly these popular bills, whose contents frequently exercised Irish opinion, being lost in this way.[59] When Rigby and Francis Andrews attempted to adjourn this inquiry until 1 June, they were attacked by MPs and the motion was not even put to a division. Rigby pointed out that the privy council itself was divided over the inquiry; Lord Lanesborough and Arthur Hill were said to support a measure of reform to Poynings' Law. In spite of these divisions, the undertakers were not prepared to support French's attempt to introduce a bill, which was defeated by 143 votes to 43.[60] Despite this eventual success for the Castle, Devonshire was shocked that such an inquiry and divisions had taken place at all and at the establishment of a permanent Commons committee to investigate the fate of all bills.[61]

The Patriot agenda was further pursued after this defeat when a bill to limit the duration of parliaments was passed on 23 December without opposition.[62] Rigby's claim, after Christmas, that the parliamentary opposition was melting away was belied by yet more attempted reforms.[63] Foremost among these was Pery's successful proposal to replace military fees paid into the Secretary's office with salaries amounting to £4,000. Waite may have been delighted, given the fact that the fees had declined during wartime, but not Bedford and Rigby.[64] They worried that Rigby would fall a victim to Westminster place legislation and Bedford concluded that the consequence of such a reform would be:

> His Majesty's chief governors here would be deprived of having that choice of proper persons to bring over with them in the capacity of Chief Secretary which they now have.[65]

57 PRONI T3158/1566, Cavendish to Devonshire, 10 Dec. 1757.   58 PRONI T3158/1562, Bowes to Devonshire, 26 Nov. 1757; *CJI*, x, p. 345.   59 *UA*, 1, 29 Jan. 1757; *BNL*, 7 Dec. 1756; PRONI T2812/19, O'Hara's economic survey of Sligo for 1757; PRONI T3087/1/14, Sackville to Pery, 29 Sept. 1757.   60 PRONI T3019/3275, Rigby to Wilmot, 29 Nov. 1757; *CJI*, x, pp. 366–7, 381; [John Monck Mason], *Remarks upon Poynings' Law* (Dublin, 1758).   61 PRONI T3019/3282, 3290, Waite to Wilmot, 10 Dec., Devonshire to Wilmot, 24 Dec. 1757; *CJI*, x, p. 448.   62 The Septennial Bill was later defeated in the privy council; *CJI*, x, p. 469.   63 PRONI T3019/3300, Rigby to Wilmot, 8 Jan. 1758.   64 PRONI T3019/3306–8, Rigby to Wilmot, 15, 19 Jan., Waite to Wilmot, 17 Jan. 1758; *CJI*, x, p. 471.   65 PRONI T2915/4/5,

This Patriot success was accompanied by a fresh bill to reform Dublin's corporation, which eventually passed the Commons in late February, despite a petition from Dublin's mayor and aldermen asking for it to be thrown out.[66] Even embargoes on trade were raised and a resolution attacking them as 'highly prejudicial' was passed on the 16 January.[67] The headway made by the Patriots was limited, but revealed much about the difficulties likely to be encountered by an administration lacking reliable parliamentary management.

THE 1758 SETTLEMENT

By January 1758, the government was still no closer to gaining a dependable majority, with Ponsonby and Stone in open opposition and Kildare sullenly distrustful. Bowes restated his opinion that 'if the Castle can't proceed without the aid of faction, they will want real power.' Fox urged Bedford to name his lords justices as soon as possible, return to London and 'settle with the king and his ministers here, whether, and on what terms, your Grace will remain lord lieutenant.' It was at this stage that Bedford and Rigby suggested the appointment of a lord deputy, rather than lords justices. Bedford had thought of appointing Kildare to this position the previous summer, but now he was convinced that the Castle could not rely on any Irish undertaker and thus a neutral lord deputy must be found. Rigby first lobbied Fox with the idea in late December:

> [N]othing can be done in the present temper of people here, well and effectually to support administration, if he [Bedford] is to remain in the government, or in short, if he is to support any English government whatever, but to appoint an English Deputy in his absence.[69]

Rigby and Bedford considered Lord Bolingbroke for the position, though they knew that no-one, including Kildare, would be happy at the measure. Bedford provided a fuller version of the same thesis in a letter to Pitt in early January. The viceroy divided his analysis into two parts: the longstanding 'poison' of faction that existed in Irish politics and the methods of managing parliament until the next general election. The second was more immediately important as the government had the unquestioning support of only 20 MPs and was faced with two equal parties, each likely to go into opposition, if disappointed. Thus the undertakers could 'distress government in order to force themselves into it'. The Patriots were

14, 18, Bedford to Newcastle, 17 Jan., 14 Feb., Newcastle to Bedford, 11 Feb. 1758. **66** *CJI*, x, pp. 508, 554, 562, 565 & 583. **67** *CJI*, x, pp. 475–6. **68** PRONI T3158/1562, Bowes to Devonshire, 26 Nov. 1757; PRONI T2915/3/55, Fox to Bedford, 21 Dec. 1757. **69** BL Add. Mss. 51835, f.1420, Rigby to Fox, 24 Dec. 1757.

'so infatuated with a vain popularity and so vain a notion of securing their elections in a future parliament, that I cannot depend upon their assistance even in opposition to questions that may be proposed by their most bitter enemies'. This situation left Bedford no alternative but to appoint an English lord deputy. This measure would:

> ... answer the same ends as the continual residence of a Lord Lieutenant here, which must necessarily take off that fear, so continually expressed by those of the different parties, of seeing their antagonists invested with the powers of government.[70]

The ministers finally discussed these suggestions in early February but Pitt stayed silent during the meeting. According to Fox, Lord Mansfield suggested Bowes for the post and the 'others, as usual, talked without even a tendency to come to a decision.' While the Castle awaited Pitt's instructions rumours swept Dublin that Stone had approached Bedford with a deal, which included Rigby's sacking.[71] Pitt finally replied after the ministerial discussions, but did not mention a lord deputy, repeated his earlier wish for conciliation and asked for more information on the state of politics.[72] It was abundantly clear that Pitt favoured a settlement between the Castle and Stone. However, his dismissal of the viceroy's scheme was not unique as Bedford's friends in London told him that he should name three lords justices and then return to England to make the case for a lord deputy. Fox conceded that the latter measure 'may probably be the best way at last', though he preferred a resident viceroy and wisely saw that either would necessitate English control of the Revenue Board for patronage. In any case, Fox made it clear that Bedford's arguments carried little weight in London, when compared to the lobby for Stone's restoration.[73] At the heart of this, Bedford was hardly unaware of the fact that Pitt was in favour of conciliating British subjects in Ireland and North America, as the war with France continued to go badly.[74]

Despite this Bedford made one last attempt to secure the 'appointment of a Lord Deputy, or the continual residence of the Lord Lieutenant [as they] appear to me to be the only possible methods for relieving things from the state of confusion they are now in, and for restoring English authority in Ireland'. He accompanied this request with an offer to resign.[75] While Bedford was considering

70 PRONI T1060/4, Bedford to Pitt, 4 Jan. 1758. 71 BL Add. Mss.51385, f.1427, Fox to Bedford, 3 Feb. 1758; PRONI T3019/3317, Rigby to Wilmot, 6 Feb. 1758. 72 PRONI T1060/4, Pitt to Bedford, 2 Feb. 1758; PRONI T3019/3320, Rigby to Wilmot, 9 Feb. 1758. 73 Fox to Bedford, 7 Jan. 1758 in *Bedford Correspondence*, ii, p. 316–9; Ilchester, *Henry Fox*, ii, p. 84–5. 74 Middleton, *Bells of Victory*, chapter 2, passim; P.J. Marshall, 'A nation defined by Empire, 1755–1776', in A. Grant & K.J. Stringer (eds), *Uniting the Kingdom?: The making of British history* (London, 1995), pp. 208–222. 75 BL Add. Mss. 51385, ff.1425, 1420, Bedford to Fox, 26 Jan., Rigby to Fox, 20 Jan. 1758; Bedford to Granville, 2 Feb. 1758 in *Bedford*

his future, it was clear that Stone was ready to make a settlement with the government and provided a majority for the Castle on the testy issue of embargoes.[76] After this Bowes was clear that settlement with the primate was necessary and inevitable:

> Much indiscretion has been shown by particulars in their unnecessary declarations, which obstruct the only system that can restore peace or preserve government from contempt.[77]

Charles O'Hara's praise for the defiance of Bedford, 'considering how little support he has from the Great Orator [Pitt] and the entanglement of measures here', carried little weight beside Stone's growing momentum.[78] The surrender foreseen by Bowes eventually took place in early February, just after the arrival of Pitt's letter to Bedford. Stone went to the Castle on 10 February and offered Bedford his full support, on condition that he was made one of the lords justices. The viceroy felt he had little option but to accept Stone's offer:

> [to] bring things back to that order and subserviency to British government, which has, since the disputes which arose in the year 1751, been so notoriously incroached upon ... [and granting the] assurance that no proscription will lay upon them for what is passed, and that the favour and countenance of government, shall be dealt out to them on equal terms.

The orchestration of events by London was clear, as Sackville urged Stone to settle with Bedford on 9 February, and Newcastle was able to confirm the primate's offer on the day it was made. In these circumstances the restoration of Stone was assured.[79]

The biggest difficulty with the settlement was to be the reaction of Lord Kildare. The earl refused to serve with Stone, who, he argued, had opposed the government only to force himself into it, something which he believed he had definitely not done in 1753.[80] Bedford hoped that Fox could persuade Kildare to change his mind but the two men had not mentioned Irish politics since a quarrel over the pensions resolutions. Fox did approach the earl with an appeal to public service but no answer is extant.[81] Bedford got Malone and Thomas Pakenham to act as go-betweens, while Rigby hoped that 'the total falling off of all his friends,

Correspondence, ii, pp. 324–5; PRONI, T1060/4, Bedford to Pitt, 9 Feb. 1758.   **76** PRONI T3158/1570, Cavendish to Devonshire, 19 Jan. 1758.   **77** PRONI T3019/3298, Bowes to Wilmot, 5 Jan. 1758.   **78** PRONI T2812/10/9–10, O'Hara to O'Hara, 31 Jan., 6 Feb. 1758. **79** PRONI T1060/4, Bedford to Pitt, 10 Feb. 1758; PRONI T3019/3319, Sackville to Wilmot, 9 Feb. 1758; Newcastle to Bedford, 11 Feb. 1758 in *Bedford Correspondence*, ii, p. 326. **80** PRONI T3019/3322, Rigby to Wilmot, 16 Feb. 1758.   **81** BL Add. Mss.51385, f.1429, Fox to Bedford, 3 Feb. 1758; Fox to Kildare, 25 Feb. 1758 in Ilchester, *Henry Fox*, ii, p. 86.

which may possibly be the case if he resists their united opinion, will at last make him conform'. However, none of this had any effect on Kildare and, in early March, Pakenham told Bedford that Kildare 'could not with truth to the King, consistent with the good of Ireland, nor the restoring government under my [Bedford's] administration to its true rigour, act jointly with the primate's government'. The 'falling off' began and was followed by the successful decision to ask Lord Shannon to be the third lord justice.[82]

After the settlement Rigby was optimistic about the future, arguing that 'peace will be restored to this country and a proper, suffcient and a respectable majority secured in the House of Commons without a single promise of place, pension or peerage.'[83] Waite was less upbeat as he was sorry to lose Kildare and wondered whether the ministers would think it 'necessary to have a new Lord Lieutenant of another disposition of mind and of other connections'.[84] Bowes was also displeased at the outcome since he was excluded from the regency and offered a peerage by way of compensation. He was savagely critical of the viceroy's mismanagement from the start, yet he knew that the chances of continuing with the 1756 settlement had diminished with Pitt and Newcastle, Stone's key supporters, becoming the leading men in London. However, Bowes was correct that Bedford's 'neglect of me will inform others that an invariable attachment to English government in Ireland is not the road for them to travel'.[85] Charles O'Hara agreed with him, and believed that Bedford must have colluded in the deal:

> If the Great Commoner [Pitt] had forced him into this he is a most mighty prince: I mean settling the government in Pluck's [Stone's] favour. If not, his Grace [Bedford] has acted a most wonderful double part.[86]

Pery, though friendly with Rigby, also refused to give his blessing to the settlement, by turning down the offer to serve in an administration 'under the same bottom with the primate'. The Patriots believed that Stone's restoration, like Boyle's in 1756, did little for either the standing of government or the interests of Ireland.[87]

Ministers were less worried by such interpretations. The settlement vindicated those who had championed Stone's restoration from the start. Meanwhile Fox, in a rather stoical letter, told Bedford that the lord deputy scheme would now quietly be forgotten and asked him not be too harsh on Kildare for his refusal to become

---

82 Diary entries of 6–9 Mar. 1758 in *Bedford Correspondence*, ii, pp. 329–31; PRONI T3019/3337, Rigby to Wilmot, 9 Mar. 1758; Fox to Rigby, [early Mar. 1758] in Ilchester, *Henry Fox*, ii, p. 88.   **83** PRONI T3019/3337, Rigby to Wilmot, 9 Mar. 1758.   **84** PRONI T3019/3341, Waite to Wilmot, 14 Mar. 1758.   **85** PRONI T3019/3336, Waite to Wilmot, 5 Mar. 1758; diary entry of 9 Mar. 1758 in *Bedford Correspondence*, ii, p. 332; PRONI T3158/1573–4, 1580, Bowes to Devonshire, 18, 28 Feb., 18 May 1758.   **86** PRONI T2812/10/13, 15, O'Hara to O'Hara, 14, 21 Feb. 1758.   **87** PRONI T3087/1/15, Sackville to Pery, 24 Mar. 1758.

a lord justice.[88] While some ministers may have been uneasy that opposition had again proved the pathway to government, only Chesterfield argued that the settlement reinforced the problems facing any administration in Ireland.[89] Most believed that peace had now been ensured and a rapid dispatch of the remaining parliamentary business seemed to prove that. Three potentially embarrassing committees, looking into the development of the collieries in Tyrone, the state of the barracks and fortifications all came to abrupt and uncontentious ends, while the report into the revenue service passed off without incident.[90] Within a fortnight of the settlement between Stone and the Castle, a working government majority was assured and the Patriots' initiative further curtailed.

Bowes' question of whether 'government here should be deputed to fixed officers or open to contending interests.' was soon answered when Bedford demanded that Sir Richard Cox be made a revenue commissioner.[91] Cox had long been an occasional critic of government and a determined enemy of the Ponsonby ambitions in Cork, but his appointment symbolised the union of the undertakers, bar Kildare, in the settlement of 1758. Newcastle was reluctant, not because of the impression that rewarding such a maverick might create, but because Cox's appointment would reduce the number of Englishmen on the Revenue Board to two. However, Rigby wrote 'we will not suffer that and have insisted upon the thing being done before we quit this country' and Cox was appointed.[92] So another gifted Commons performer was added to the government ranks, with no guarantee of his future good behaviour, confirming Bowes' fears that faction was being rewarded over good service.[93]

Bedford's popularity had rapidly declined from the high point of the summer of 1757. He was defended on the specious grounds of frugality and praised for opposing the city bill, which saved Dublin from the twin evils of the Common Council and the Presbyterians. However, one Patriot pamphlet attacked his 'proud spirit' and his capitulation to Stone, especially as the latter had used tactics in which the 'public good was no way considered in the whole.'[94] Bedford's quiet send-off, when compared to the pomp and ceremony of installing the undertakers as lords justices, seemed to sum up the balance of power in 1758.[95] Walpole caustically commented that Bedford:

> ... like other kings I have known, is grown wonderfully popular there since he was taken prisoner and tied hand and foot. To do faction justice,

88 BL Add. Mss. 51385, f.1431, Fox to Rigby, 25 Feb. 1758.　89 Chesterfield to Chevenix, 14 Apr., 23 May 1758, *Chesterfield Correspondence*, v, pp. 2295 & 2304–5.　90 *CJI*, x, pp. 750–815, 821–848.　91 PRONI T3019/3359, Bowes to Wilmot, 4 Apr. 1758.　92 PRONI T2915/4/34, 40, Newcastle to Bedford, 3, 20 Apr. 1758; PRONI T3019/3367, Rigby to Wilmot, 11 Apr. 1758.　93 PRONI T3019/3359, Bowes to Wilmot, 4 Apr. 1758.　94 *A Farewell to the Duke of Bedford* (Dublin 1758), pp. 6–8 & 15; *Ireland Disgraced*, pp. 59–72. 95 PRONI T3019/3384, 3390, Waite to Wilmot, 7, 10 May 1758.

it is of no cowardly nature: it abuses, while it attacks, and loads with panegyric those it defeats.[96]

No one knew if the settlement of 1758 was the one to finally secure parliamentary management but it had done little to restore the lustre of Dublin Castle.

BEDFORD AND HIS SETTLEMENT

Bedford knew that patronage was the strongest glue to make any political settlement stick. Therefore, on his return to England in May 1758, he met with George II to get royal agreement for his recommendations. The list of demands, for twelve Irish peerages, five new privy councillors and nine pensions to the tune of £2,800, was made more acceptable to the king by the inclusion of a £5,000 pension for the princess of Hesse. Three peerage creations were delayed or refused and, while Bedford was worried at the prospect of £6,500 of the new pensions leaving Ireland, the patronage was regarded as 'the likeliest means to quiet people's minds, who might otherwise be uneasy to see such a great annual sum carried out of their country without having any share of it themselves'.[97] Given Dorset's parsimony in 1754 and Devonshire's tardiness in 1756, the undertakers must have been delighted at this patronage, especially as Shannon's and Kildare's dependants were well represented among the successful claimants.

Indeed Bedford went out of his way to soothe the disappointment of Lord Kildare, once tipped as a lord deputy. This was not an easy task, given the earl's prickliness, which increased sharply in May 1758, when his request for Colonel Henry Sandford to be given the vacant quarter master general's place was refused. As Sandford had recently been appointed to a vacancy on the lucrative Barracks Board, Bedford's refusal seems justified. However, Kildare asked whether he was to be as badly treated in all future requests and was angrily reminded of all the past favours he had received and the continuation of this despite his opposition to the 1758 settlement. Bedford also appealed to Kildare to act with some sense of proportion:

> My refusal to dispose of an employment to a person I may not think so proper as another recommended to me, should [not] be looked upon as renouncing all future intercourse with him.[98]

96 Walpole to Mann, 10 May 1758 in *Walpole Correspondence*, xxi, p. 199. 97 Bedford's diary entry of 24 May 1758 in *Bedford Correspondence*, ii, p. 337. 98 Bedford to Kildare, 24 June 1758 in *Bedford Correspondence*, ii, p. 340.

When tempers had cooled somewhat, Kildare was appointed master of the ordnance in October 1758, with a salary augmentation of £700 a year. Rigby hoped that 'this sugar-plumb will sweeten his lordship to all intents and purposes' and Wilmot told Devonshire, 'it is felt that this must put an end to opposition in Ireland, at least for the next session'.[99]

However, both Rigby and Wilmot were over-confident about the poison having been taken out of the relationship between Kildare and Bedford. Matters worsened once the earl began to take his military duties seriously and clashed with the most senior Irish general, the earl of Rothes, over the disposition of troops and the marching routes of embarking soldiers. When Rothes rightly refused to give way, Kildare once more went to London, with a memorial stating his grievances. Whilst the visit did not prove quite as disastrous as the 1754 one, Kildare told his wife that he was 'worse received by our Lord and Lady Lieutenant than by any in London …There is certainly no such thing as talking of business to either his Grace or his Secretary.' Given this response, the earl had decided to present his memorial directly to the king and then to resign, only six months after being appointed.[100] His friends and family counselled caution, as £1,500 a year was at stake, and Newcastle helped by delaying a royal audience for three weeks, by which time the earl's anger had dissipated.[101] Kildare's wife tactfully told him that it was reported he had won a victory and, in any case, it would be wrong to give up the place, 'because, I hear, all your enemies here triumph so much in it and are delighted at the thought of you giving up so good a thing as this in a huff'.[102] Kildare remained head of the ordnance, but, while his twelve or so Leinster MPs generally supported Bedford's administration, there was little love between the viceroy and Ireland's senior peer. Importantly for the Castle, lack of affection did not translate into open opposition.

With his patronage secure and Lord Kildare a volatile figure within government, Bedford seemed to have secured a stable settlement in 1758. This impression strengthens when one looks at the behaviour of the three lords justices. Shannon was semi-retired, spending all his summers in County Cork.[103] He did not relinquish control of the 'Cork Squadron' just yet, but his days of dominating parliament, as the Speaker and leading undertaker, had ended in 1756. Shannon's desire to provide for his family and closest dependants meant that he did not abdicate his government role completely and, in this way, he kept the 'Squadron' intact for his eldest son, Lord Boyle, to lead in the next decade. With Shannon's semi-retirement, Stone became the major force in the lords justices' commission.

99 PRONI T3158/1605–6, Rigby to Devonshire, 17 Oct., Wilmot to Devonshire, 17 Oct. 1758.
100 Kildare to Kildare, 24 Apr., 3 May 1759 in *Leinster Correspondence*, i, pp. 66, 73–4.
101 Kildare to Kildare, 8 May 1759 in ibid., i, p. 76; PRONI Bedford papers, T2915/7/42, Rigby to Bedford, 22 May 1759.   102 Kildare to Kildare, 22 May 1759 in *Leinster Correspondence*, i, p. 80.   103 PRONI T3019/3405, 3618, Waite to Wilmot, 6 June 1758, 28 Aug. 1759.

The gap in previous experience between himself and Ponsonby was further emphasised by the death of Lord Bessborough in July 1758. The Speaker was devastated by this event and the succeeding dispute over the earl's will, all of which was expected to lead to the decline of the Ponsonby interest.[104]

Though this did not happen, Stone's position was further consolidated by the way in which he courted Bedford after having forced himself on the viceroy only months before. The primate was a changed man since the early 1750s, when his letters had oozed dogmatism in political principles and practice. In his letters to Bedford, Stone showed that he was an assured and politically astute lord justice and stressed his fairness towards each of the contending factions and his role as an arbiter in the government's interest. This meant that ministers believed that the primate was a healing force, especially in January 1759, when he allowed Shannon and Kildare the lion's share of the appointments of sheriffs. Stone was also well aware that, unlike Shannon or Ponsonby, he did not return many MPs. Instead he relied upon the status provided by government office and his disposal of patronage to secure a parliamentary following. Stone never gained much in the way of popularity and some of his original followers, such as Pery and Brownlow, remained in opposition, but he also avoided playing a similar role to that of Archbishop Boulter, as his managers never automatically served the government. These placemen, for example Tisdall and Cuninghame, shared Stone's understanding of the need to avoid unpopularity and to avoid disappointing your friends' expectations, as some felt the primate had done in 1754.[106] Stone stated that, in patronage, it was his 'chief purpose ... that by such a distribution, future combinations might be made less practicable, and to prevent personal disappointments (for such there must ever be) from being resented as a common cause'.[107] Yet his parliamentary following was never a 'Castle party'.

At first glance, John Ponsonby was the natural successor to Henry Boyle, as he was both Speaker of the Commons and first commissioner of the revenue. His failure to do so has often been ascribed to a lack of ability. This can be exaggerated as the expected demise of the Ponsonby connection did not happen. In fact, the position of this connection was consolidated by the Speaker's skilful use of revenue patronage. The patronage at the disposal of the board was huge, with over 1,500 jobs and a salaries and fees bill from 1757–9 of £116,343.[108] Given the fact that, despite the best intentions of the British Treasury, English-born commissioners rarely numbered three and were usually absentee, Ponsonby's control was

104 PRONI T3019/3434, Waite to Wilmot, 20 July 1758; PRONI T3158/1588, Bowes to Devonshire, 21 July 1758. 105 PRONI T2915/7/5, Stone to Bedford, 25 Jan. 1759. 106 [Pery], *Letter to Bedford* , p. 27; Stone to Bedford, 18 Aug., Bedford to Stone, 31 Aug. 1758 in *Bedford Correspondence*, ii, pp. 359, 367–8. 107 Stone to Bedford, 25 July 1758 in ibid., ii, pp. 349–50. 108 *The management of the revenue with queries* (Dublin, 1758), p. 2; *CJI*, xi, pp. 36–9.

largely unchallenged.[109] He continued this reign into the 1760s with safe appointments and cooperation with the likes of Sir Richard Cox.[110] Through this fount of patronage, his use of public money in navigations and turnpike roads and his standing in government, Ponsonby prevented the erosion of his electoral interest, which many had predicted on the death of Lord Bessborough. In fact, he further consolidated his family's grip on county Kilkenny politics. In 1758, when James Agar and Lord Castlecomer, who were allies of Lord Shannon and powerful interests in the county, demanded a say in the nomination of the sheriff, they were refused.[111] Ponsonby used his connections in government to do this and in that way forced Agar and Castlecomer, by the time of the 1761 election, to come to terms with him.[112] He also began to manage the Devonshire electoral interests in counties Cork and Waterford, after the death of Devonshire's wife in September 1758. Ponsonby's initial analysis was that two Waterford boroughs (Lismore and Bandon) were fully in the control of Devonshire and three others (Youghal, Dungarvan and Tallow) could, in time, be recovered from the grip of Lord Shannon. This had not been done by the 1761 general election but, with the continued management of such a huge electoral interest as the Burlington/Devonshire one, the Ponsonbys could expect even brighter times ahead.[113]

In that case why did Ponsonby not succeed William Conolly and Henry Boyle as the unrivalled undertaker for the 1760s and beyond? The answer lies mainly in the changing circumstances and in the fact that each of the undertakers was powerful enough to unsettle government but none of them was able to manage the Commons on his own. Thus any ascendancy had to be based upon cooperation. The upshot of this situation was that the viceroy had to negotiate with all of the undertakers, rather than with one chief, as had been the case before 1753. The appearance of a 'golden age' of undertaking was emphasised by the usual united front of Stone and company. But management was not so easy for the undertakers. They were increasingly constrained by the need to support popular measures, like corn bounties or the attempts to reform Dublin's corporation. Their ability to court popularity was undermined by growing cynicism about the role of undertakers and the fact that the issues pushed by the Patriots were often inimical to the interests of borough patrons.

---

109 *Gentleman and Citizen's Almanac*, (Dublin, 1760), p. 60; PRONI T2915/7/42, 10/41, Rigby to Bedford, 22 May 1759, Newtown to Bedford, 18 Oct. 1760.   110 Stone to Bedford, 25 July 1758 in *Bedford Correspondence*, ii, pp. 348–50; PRONI T3019/3355, Cavendish to Wilmot, 27 Feb. 1759; PRONI T2915/7/21, 27, Rigby to Bedford, 8 Mar., Ponsonby to Bedford, 24 Mar. 1759; PRONI T3019/3567, Ponsonby to Wilmot, 24 Mar. 1759.   111 PRONI T3158/1592, Ellis to Devonshire, 20 Aug. 1758.   112 Bedford to Stone, 31 Aug. 1758 in *Bedford Correspondence*, ii, p. 367; PRONI T2915/5/10, Bedford to Castlecomer, 16 July 1758.   113 PRONI T3158/1601, 'Memorandum on the Burlington boroughs in Counties Cork and Waterford', late Sept. 1758.   114 PRONI T3019/3428, Rigby to Wilmot, 26 July 1758.

The pressure of popularity manifested itself in a number of ways during 1758 and 1759, particularly during trade disputes and when an attempt was made to reform the Barracks Board. In the summer of 1758, the lords justices were consulted by Bedford about a plan, drawn up by Wilmot and Thomas Eyre. The intention was to prevent barracks commissioners and masters from holding the money intended for upkeep and repair, in their own hands. The plan also curbed the discretion of the lords justices to make appointments to the barracks establishment.[114] Stone quickly asked for the reforms to be delayed, on the grounds that more time was needed for the plan to be fully digested and to allow parliamentary input. Simultaneously, he nominated Henry Lyons, an MP of Kildare's, and Robert Cunninghame to the existing board.[115] Despite Bedford's enthusiasm and the need identified by preceding Commons committees, the lords justices were able to prevent change. Waite explained their reason as fear of opinion in parliament, while Wilmot scathingly accused the lords justices of solely protecting a source of patronage.[116] There was probably a mixture of both behind the actions of Stone and his colleagues, as they were anxious to avoid yet another embarrassing and costly (in terms of patronage) inquiry into barracks affairs.

With regard to trade matters, the lords justices avoided unpopularity, even to the extent of allowing the Dublin crowd to riot virtually unhindered. They persuaded ministers to loosen the wartime embargoes, by allowing Irish goods to be traded with neutral countries, using nominated ships. Another potentially explosive issue was the export of live cattle to England, previously banned, now restarted and a threat to the provisions industry in Dublin and Cork. An example of how unpopular such exports were was the May 1759 riot on the Dublin quays, where crowds prevented English merchants from buying Irish cattle. The rigging on two ships was destroyed and, when the city authorities refused to use troops against the crowd, they were weakly defended by Stone. He excused such inaction by referring to fixed dispositions of regiments and other technical matters.[117] Bedford was furious about this response to an overtly anti-English riot, but the lords justices continued a policy of inaction and showed no support for the cattle exporters. Again popularity came first.

Some observers worried what such episodes said about the state of government in Ireland. John Bowes repeatedly made the point that the 1758 settlement marked a continuing decline in the authority of the viceroy. Bowes was undoubtedly disappointed by his removal from the commission and his mood was not improved by Bedford's failure to notice either his life-threatening illness, in the winter of 1758, or his scheme to clarify the legal position of the insane. Yet, he also saw that

115 Stone to Bedford, 25 July 1758 in *Bedford Correspondence*, ii, p. 351.   116 PRONI T3158/1608, Wilmot to Devonshire, 14 Nov. 1758.   117 Bedford to Stone, 22 May, Stone to Bedford, 28 May 1759 in *Bedford Correspondence*, ii, pp. 377, 380; *BNL*, 14 Apr. 1758, 8 May 1759; PRONI T1060/4, Bedford to Pitt, 2 Oct. 1758.

the lords justices were primarily patronage dispensers and that the government and not they, would be blamed for the size of the civil list.[118] Waite and Wilmot were more sympathetic to Bedford and knew how much support he had in London, but they also worried about the weakness of this administration and the part that appeals to popularity played in the behaviour of the undertakers.[119] Beyond the Castle walls, others were concerned about the state of Irish politics. One Anglican champion saw a great threat to tithes, posed by an alliance of Presbyterians and Patriot MPs, which had sprung out of recent political events.[120] Another pamphleteer also connected the self-confidence of 'republican' Presbyterians and the 'mob' to the crisis of 1750–5 and the campaign for reforms of Dublin corporation.[121] These fears increased with the shock victory of the occasional conformist and Free Citizen candidate, James Dunn, over the leading alderman, James Grattan, in a Dublin city by-election in 1758.[122]

A QUIET PARLIAMENTARY SESSION?

Despite concerns about the strength of patriotism in Ireland, a quiet session of parliament was expected in late 1759. Invasion fears meant that wartime demands for money and men were readily accepted by the Dublin politicians. Though 1759 is remembered as Britain's 'year of victories', with victories at Guadeloupe, Minden and Quebec, invasion scares repeatedly worried Irish Protestants. These peaked in the summer of 1759, with the intelligence from Brest, Toulon and Dunkirk of the build-up of French naval forces. News that Irish Jacobite generals were leading these forces increased fears that Ireland was to be the target for invasion. Only 5,000 regular troops were left in Ireland, increasing the rancour between Bedford and Pitt about drafts of troops. Encampments on the Isle of Wight and Admiral Hawke's blockade of Brest were designed to (and did) calm fears in Ireland.[123] Given the concentration on these military worries, historians have either ignored this parliamentary session or treated the riots in Dublin in December 1759 and the landing of Thurot at Carrickfergus in February 1760, as events unconnected with political affairs.[124] The rest of this chapter takes a different approach.

The invasion threat was quickly made a political issue, as Bedford used his information about the French build-up to rally Irish MPs to the government side

118 PRONI T3019/3424, 3448, 3566, Bowes to Wilmot, 1 July, 11 Aug.1758, 24 Mar. 1759. 119 PRONI T3019/3549, Waite to Wilmot, 13 Feb. 1759.   120 *A letter to the people of Ireland on the Subject of Tithes* (Dublin, 1758), p. 16.   121 *Farewell to the Duke of Bedford*, p. 14.   122 *A letter to the Present Electors of the City of Dublin* (Dublin, 1758), p. 7; *BNL*, 12, 16, Feb., 3,14, 17 Mar. 1758.   123 Bedford to Stone, 22 May 1759 in *Bedford Correspondence*, ii, pp. 373–7; BL Add. Mss.32891, f.171, Hardwicke to Newcastle, 18 May 1759.   124 Burns, *Parliamentary Politics*, ii, chapter 7, passim; Dickson, *New Foundations*, p. 94.

and to increase the pace of recruitment to the army. A fortnight after the session began, MPs were told that an invasion attempt, of 13,000 men under the Duc d'Aguillon, was imminent.[125] The news was received grimly and the Commons sent an address to George II, praising the victories at Minden and Quebec and pledging a full contribution to the war effort.[126] The invasion message also provoked offers to 'raise for rank', to reduce recruiting worries, which Pitt quickly agreed to, while also testily reminded Bedford that regular recruiting should not stop.[127] Not all MPs were won over by these schemes and some Patriots accused those involved of wanting rank for status and some martial thrill-seeking. Such talk almost led Pery and Lord Drogheda to blows, but it did not bring a halt to the proposals.[128] Another sign of the willingness of MPs to cooperate with the government was the rapid despatch of the money bill in November 1759, the only delay due to a committee investigating the use of public works money over the previous four years. This committee discovered that on some occasions money that had been granted by parliament was still lying in the hands of trustees, but no attempt was made to amend the practice of appropriating the supplies for public grants.[129]

This muted disposition of parliament had a number of causes. The threat of invasion, although lessened by Hawke's naval victories, did not pass. In October, the French privateer, François Thurot, slipped through Hawke's blockade and headed into the Channel with three frigates. Walpole expected the target to be Ireland, but asked ironically 'Can the lords of America be afraid of half a dozen canoes?'[130] The news had more effect in Dublin where Irish MPs voted a £150,000 loan for the government's use and the newspapers were full of the latest sightings of Thurot.[131] The court-martial of the former chief secretary, Lord George Sackville, for cowardice at the battle of Minden also distracted Irish Protestant opinion.[132] Given the friendship of Stone and Sackville, there were rumours that the primate would be undermined by the trial and he did briefly contemplate retiring to Leixlip in November.[133] Thurot and Sackville seemed more exciting than parliamentary affairs to most Dublin observers in late 1759.

It is thus little wonder that Rigby believed that a quick session was likely, as only about 100 MPs were bothering to attend in mid-October and spent more time socialising than in business.[134] One sign of this mood was that the Patriots failed miserably, defeated by 63 votes to 25, to mobilise MPs on the issue of pensions and the 1757 resolutions.[135] Further Patriot attempts, during debates on the money bill,

---

125 *CJI*, xi, p. 124.   126 *CJI*, xi, p. 127 & 129; *UA*, 3 Nov. 1759.   127 PRONI T1060/5, Pitt to Bedford, 21 Nov. 1759.   128 *A letter from a Commoner in Town to a Noble Lord in the Country* (London, 1760), p. 19.   129 *CJI*, xi, pp. 222–243.   130 Walpole to Mann, 19 Oct. 1759 in *Walpole Correspondence*, xxi, p. 338.   131 *UA*, 6 Nov. 1759.   132 PRONI T3019/3618, Waite to Wilmot, 28 Aug. 1759; Walpole to Conway, 14 Aug. 1759 in *Walpole Correspondence*, xxxviii, p. 20; *UA*, 8, 22 Sept., 6 Oct. 1759.   133 Walpole to Conway, 13 Sept. 1759 in *Walpole Correspondence*, xxxviii, p. 28; PRONI T3019/3647, Waite to Wilmot, 26 Nov. 1759.   134 PRONI T3019/3628, Rigby to Wilmot, 17 Oct. 1759.   135 *CJI*, xi, pp. 182, 218–19.

to have defence estimates laid before the house and to ensure that the loan of £150,000 was only spent on military matters, were both defeated.[136] One potential glimmer of hope for the opposition, when Philip Tisdall opportunistically threatened to leave the government ranks, proved a mirage as he was promised a lucrative office to 'stop his mouth'.[137] The Patriots were cheered by the addition to their ranks of John Hely Hutchinson, a skilful lawyer and talented orator, but they failed to attract more than 25 MPs in any division. According to Rigby, the opposition was 'one man [Hely Hutchinson] who has sense, speech and understanding and about seventeen or eighteen more who have neither'.[138] However, some popular measures were successful, including a militia bill and one to regulate the baking trade. The first was fiercely debated in December and caused a flutter of excitement in the press, where it was 'hoped that the same Patriot zeal to establish such a well-regulated militia, will be amply repaid'.[139] The second was a measure which tapped into anti-catholic feelings in the Dublin bakers' guild and successfully passed, with strong quality controls for wheaten bread.

Despite these limited Patriot gains, the public credit crisis of late 1759 showed the solidity of the 1758 settlement, especially as it involved three government officials in the role of disgraced bankrupts. This sort of crisis was hardly new in the 1750s and reflected both short-term worries about invasion and long-term structural problems in the bias towards dealing in rent remittances and the regular overstretching of credit.[140] One of two Dublin banks which closed was owned by Nathaniel Clements, John Gore and Anthony Malone, all former Patriot stalwarts of the crisis of the early 1750s. Bedford immediately tried to excuse his officials on the grounds that they had stopped payment only because of 'the want of specie to circulate their notes, the substance of the gentlemen concerned in that bank being much more sufficient to discharge all they owe'.[141] Henry Cavendish made the same point for London consumption, even though he and the rest of Dublin's elite knew, from 8 November, that Malone's bank did not have enough specie to cover their circulating banknotes. On that date the bankers had offered notes to their creditors bearing interest rates of 5 per cent. This was a measure approved of by Dublin merchants, but it was not enough to stop closure soon after.[142]

After the closure of Malone's bank, the Castle had to respond quickly to calm fears and stop further runs on the remaining banks. This it did. Once Bedford realised that he could expect little help from the Treasury in England, he drew on

136 *CJI*, xi, pp. 399, 408, 425.   137 PRONI T3019/3636, 3641, Rigby to Wilmot, 9, 12 Nov. 1759; PRONI T2915/9/2, Bedford to Newcastle, 8 Jan. 1760.   138 PRONI T3019/3646, Rigby to Wilmot, 20 Nov. 1759.   139 *FDJ*, 1 Dec. 1759, *UA*, 1 Dec. 1759; Robertson, *Militia Issue*, pp. 106–12, for Scottish attempts at this time.   140 L.M. Cullen, 'Landlords, Merchants and Bankers: Early Irish banking world, 1700–1820', *Hermathena*, cxxxv (1982–3), pp. 25–44.   141 PRONI T2915/8/41, Bedford to Pitt, 6 Nov. 1759.   142 PRONI T3019/3637, 3638, Cavendish to Wilmot, 'Proclamation of the Tholsel meeting', both 8 Nov. 1759

Irish resources.[143] This resulted in a promise to import £45,000 in specie and an association, which was published in the Dublin newspapers, committing merchants and gentry, headed by the viceroy, to accept all bankers' notes.[144] By 15 November, Rigby was confident that the threat to the surviving banks had passed, especially as the Commons quickly legislated to allow the bankrupts to mortgage their estates and schedule repayments to creditors.[145] Although both closures caused administrative difficulties for Bedford, the real political problems seemed likely to come from the outrage in the Commons against Malone and his colleagues.[146] The Patriots had earlier raised the issue of the state of public credit in parliament and Pery and William Harward had argued that the proposed loan of £150,000 was reducing the cash in circulation and causing the crisis.[147] Despite the worries of some MPs and pamphleteers about the problems with a commercialised economy, few had practical suggestions for supporting public credit.[148] In addition, the Commons were more sympathetic than expected to their bankrupt colleagues.[149] Outside parliament, a pamphlet by a 'Free Citizen', written in the style of a dialogue between Malone, Clements and Gore, was as much critical of their 'false Patriotism' as their financial dealings.[150] The government may have been unable to avoid a crisis in public credit or to find a long-term remedy but assured parliamentary management allowed it to avoid any negative political fall-out.

RIOTS AND INVASION

This quietness and political peace in the Commons meant that the anti-union riots in Dublin came as a shock to the Castle. The immediate causes seem to lie in the rumours and pamphlets circulating in Dublin, in late November, about the imminent passing of an Act of Union, perhaps under the guise of a bill to call parliament at fourteen days' notice.[151] Given the invasion fears and potential emergencies, Rigby believed that such a bill was necessary but it was represented as a quick way to call parliament and then dissolve it for good.[152] On 26 November a crowd gathered at College Green; two MPs were struck and others insulted, and

---

143 Newcastle to Bedford, 18 Nov. 1759 in *Bedford Correspondence*, ii, pp. 396–7.   144 Pitt to Bedford, 13 Nov. 1759 in ibid., ii, p. 395; PRONI T3019/3644, Rigby to Wilmot, 15 Nov. 1759. 145 *FDJ*, 10, 13, 17 Nov. 1759.   146 PRONI T3019/3641, Rigby to Wilmot, 12 Nov. 1759. 147 *CJI*, xi, pp. 157–60.   148 *Considerations on the Present Calamities of this kingdom and the Causes of Decay of Public Credit* (Dublin, 1760); *A Proposal for the Restoration of Wealth and Public Credit* (Dublin, 1760); P. Kelly, 'Berkeley, Walpole and the South Sea Bubble Crisis', *ECI*, vii (1992), pp. 54–74. 149 *CJI*, xi, p. 183.   150 [Free Citizen], *The New Bankers Proved Bankrupt* (Dublin, 1760).   151 Walpole, *George II*, iii, p. 239; S. Murphy, 'The Dublin Anti-Union Riot of 3 December 1759', in G. O'Brien (ed.), *Parliament, Politics and People* (Dublin, 1989) pp. 49–68.   152 [Hibernicus], *Advice to the Patriots of the Coombe, the liberties* (Dublin, 1759), pp. 9–10.

John Ponsonby had to come out and promise the crowd that there was no threat of union, upon which they dispersed. This was backed up by statements in *Faulkner's Dublin Journal* that 'the report of a Union between Great Britain and Ireland is without the least foundation' and that Rigby's bill had been withdrawn.[153] Despite these denials, the anti-union cry remained a rallying call on 3 December. The Dublin magistrates seemed paralysed, and a crowd was able to march unhindered from the Liberties, with drummers in front, assemble in College Green and, for a few hours, demand oaths from MPs to oppose an Act of Union. Legal officials, including John Bowes, were targeted, perhaps because it was believed they were to be the architects of the rumoured union, while Rigby, who was absent, had a gallows erected in his honour and received warnings to stay out of the capital.[154] When MPs left the parliament building, it was occupied by the crowd and, only at this stage, were troops called on to disperse the rioters.[155]

One explanation for the riots lies in the volatility of the Dublin crowd in this period. At one level, there existed almost endemic faction fighting between the Protestant Liberty Boys and the Catholic Ormond Boys. This seems to have had more to do with gang warfare than with sectarianism or politics.[156] At another level, Dublin had what could be called a 'moral economy'; this indignation exploded into violent attacks on coal hoarders, live cattle exporters and corn forestallers. There was also a tradition of combining, particularly amongst the Dublin weavers, which had recently led to a notice placed in the Dublin press by the Linen Board, announcing that journeymen weavers in combinations would be severely punished. These kinds of disturbances convinced one pamphleteer, who, in 1760, supported a parliamentary bill to make law and order enforcement in the capital more effective, of the 'licentiousness of the Dublin mob'.[157] The behaviour of the crowd in late 1759, however, suggests that more than economic grievances were at play and that awareness of political issues was crucially important. Perhaps this awareness was a result of the wider audience, which had supported the Patriots in 1753 and, in Dublin, had agitated for the reform of the corporation. The amalgam of politicisation, the usual grievances and a volatile crowd, probably led by Presbyterian radicals rather than French agent provocateurs, was enough to produce an explosive mixture in late 1759.

The anti-union riot is important for the varying responses to it. In Dublin, different groups, including the weavers' guild and the Catholic clergy, attempted

153 PRONI T3019/3649, Rigby to Wilmot, 28 Nov. 1759; *FDJ*, 27 Nov. 1759. 154 James D. La Touche, *A Short but True history of the Rise, Progress and Happy Suppression of several late Insurrections commonly called Rebellions* (Dublin, 1760); Rigby to Pitt, 5 Dec. 1759 in *Chatham Correspondence*, i, pp. 569–70; PRONI T3019/3962, Rigby to Wilmot, 10 Dec. 1759. 155 Walpole,*George II*, iii, pp. 403–4. 156 P. Fagan, 'The Dublin Catholic Mob, 1700–1750', *ECI*, iv, pp. 33–42. 157 *FDJ*, 20 Nov. 1759; *Heads of a Bill, for better regulating the elections of the Lord Mayor, Aldermen, Sheriffs, Commons and other Officers of the city of Dublin, and for preserving the peace, order and good government in the said city* (Dublin, 1760).

to escape blame.[158] Rigby was in no doubt where blame lay as he privately accused Irish MPs of whipping up a torrent of emotion:

> Numbers of men are not to be got in this country for any other species of war, but Civil War. And I do upon my honour, seriously think the seeds of such are deeprooted here.[159]

The Commons was not slow to condemn the actions of the crowd and called the city officials to the bar to explain their behaviour. Nevertheless, Rigby argued that the development of Irish politics in the 1750s had led to the riot and he claimed that 'English government will be kicked out of doors, if such opportunities as these are not laid hold of to act vigorously in support of it'. One of the problems was with civil officials, who were generally reluctant to take action against crowds, and thus Rigby began to think about the utility of a Riot Act.[160] However, it quickly became clear that the only Privy Council supporters of such a bill were the legal officers, while Wilmot was unconvinced, arguing that it would act as a 'check on military execution'. [161]

Government ministers held a special meeting on 19 December, to discuss the events in Dublin and the reports sent by Bedford and Rigby.[162] These reports were intended to counter misinformation in London, but Pitt's letter to Bedford ignored all the available evidence, stressed the threat posed by French agents and dismissed any thesis that rumours of an Act of Union had caused the riot. To rectify the 'loss of energy' in the rule of law, Pitt wanted prosecutions of Dublin's magistrates for failing in their duties, but did not mention a Riot Act.[163] There was talk in London that the Castle had been negligent, ignoring both the first disturbance and a contested election in County Longford where the 'Catholic interest' was allegedly involved and, thus, ministers, once more, failed to vocally approve of Bedford's administration.[164] The viceroy was furious at this misinterpretation of events by Pitt. He, again, demanded support for his administration, dismissed the possibility of trying the city officials and rejected reports of any Catholic initiation of the riot.[165] After this second letter, Wilmot asked Rigby, 'Have you not embarrassed yourselves by representing that Popery had no hand in your disturbances of the 3rd of December?' Perhaps influenced by this advice, the Castle finally

---

158 FDJ, 8 Dec. 1759; M. Wall, 'The Positions of Catholics in mid-18th century Ireland', in G. O'Brien (ed.), *Catholic Ireland in the Eighteenth Century* (Dublin, 1989), pp. 93–101.   **159** PRONI T3019/6458/575, Rigby to Wilmot, 10 Dec. 1759.   **160** PRONI T3019/3660, Rigby to Wilmot, 18 Dec. 1759. For earlier, similar discussions: PRONI T3228/1/65, entry in Dudley Ryder's diary, 27 Feb. 1754.   **161** PRONI T3019/6458/580, 3673, 3662, 3682, Rigby to Wilmot, 26 Dec. 1759, Rigby to Wilmot, 6 Jan. 1760, Rigby to Wood, 23 Dec. 1759, Wilmot to Rigby, 22 Jan. 1760.   **162** PRONI T1060/5, Bedford to Pitt, 5 Dec. 1759.   **163** PRONI T1060/5, Pitt to Bedford, 20 Dec. 1759.   **164** PRONI T3019/3648, Rigby to Wilmot, 26 Nov. 1759.   **165** PRONI T1060/5, Bedford to Pitt, 26 Dec. 1759, Pitt to Bedford, 5 Jan. 1760.

ordered the legal officers to indict the magistrates and concentrate the search for ringleaders on Catholic areas of the city. Rigby was furious at this failure to issue a full-blooded condemnation of the 'spirit of independency' and the decision to initiate hopeless prosecutions and hunt down alleged French spies.[166]

Wilmot's other informants in Dublin agreed with the viceroy's version of events and with his criticism of ministers. Bowes and Waite identified a variety of causes for the riots: erosion of the government's standing, dated by Bowes to 1753, the reports of union and the instability of the Dublin crowd, especially the Presbyterian weavers. Neither believed in the idea of French agents inspiring the riot and it is interesting to note that Bowes fully supported an administration he had little love for and attacked the empty rhetoric coming from London:

> I find they are strongly affected on your side and talk of government, etc., etc.; but when the people have lost all reverence for government or laws, and are prepared to believe the most improbable suggestions to the prejudice of those who rule, what can be done?[167]

The archbishop of Tuam, John Ryder, supported these analyses. According to him, the root of the problem was the attitude of Irishmen, whether Catholic or Protestant, to the relationship with Britain. They were 'unwilling to acknowledge the dependency of this [parliament] on the British legislature; and ... are bred up in a settled antipathy to the latter'.[168] Seen in this light, the anti-union riot was approved of by many Irish MPs and peers and served as a warning shot to ministers who may have been thinking about novel methods of governing Ireland.

In England, Pitt had been able to enforce his views on the Dublin riot because he was at the pinnacle of his power in the winter of 1759–60. Others, including Wilmot, disagreed with his interpretation and hoped that peacetime would provide the opportunity of dealing with deep-seated Irish problems.[169] Devonshire, like Rigby, felt that relying on the civil powers in Ireland was unsatisfactory. He was worried after the first disturbance and described the main riot as 'an expression that in a manner proves they have been too dilatory with their army which I was always apprehensive of'.[170] Chesterfield told George Faulkner that many in London blamed Irish MPs for the trouble in Dublin and asked, 'will the multitude, enraged with whisky, be checked and kept within bounds by their betters, who are full as drunk as they are, only with claret?' Fox's friend, Bubb Dodington, was gloomy at the reports that it had been Protestants who had rioted

---

166 PRONI T3019/3678, 6458/585, Wilmot to Rigby, 14 Jan., Rigby to Wood, 1 Feb. 1760. 167 PRONI T3019/3659, 3664, Waite to Wilmot, 18 Dec. 1759, Bowes to Wilmot, 27 Dec. 1759, Bowes to Dodington, 28 Dec. 1759 in *HMC Various Collections*, vi, p. 70–2.   168 PRONI T3019/3670, Ryder to Wilmot, 1 Jan. 1760.   169 PRONI T3019/3678, Wilmot to Rigby, 14 Jan. 1760.   170 Derbyshire Record Office, Wilmot-Horton Mss., W.H.2945, f.470–1, Devonshire to Wilmot, 2, 26 Dec. 1759.

and worried 'though I am told that all is quiet again, I must be better assured of the foundations of that quiet before I can trust to the surface, calm and serene as it may appear'.[171] However the political reality was that Pitt's views prevailed and the officials in Dublin Castle could only feel further undermined.

To make matters worse, parliament began to grow more restive in the aftermath of the riot. Although MPs had condemned the actions of the Dublin crowd and the inaction of the magistrates, the Patriots successfully raised the issue which had caused earlier crowd unrest in May. Opposition MPs attacked the export of live cattle after a petition from Cork merchants was presented by John Hely Hutchinson. An attempt, by government supporters, to put off further discussion of the issue, was defeated and MPs passed a resolution condemning the exports as prejudicial.[172] A further attempt by the Patriots to address Bedford on this issue was heavily defeated by 104 votes to 7, but their votes did not satisfy Rigby, who pointed out that not one government supporter had actually spoken to oppose Hely Hutchinson. Furthermore, although 104 MPs voted against the motion for an address, they refused to allow their names to be printed. As Rigby put it, 'people in general here are averse to our English Acts, that's the truth of it'.[173]

The period from December 1759 to May 1760 was to reveal the limitations of the 1758 settlement, exposing how timid the undertakers could be in the face of legislation which they should have opposed. Four bills, none of which was sponsored, or supported, by the government, were passed by MPs.[174] The passage of the bills concerning the baking trade and the militia has already been noted. These were soon joined by successful attempts to reform Dublin corporation and to revive the earlier 1756 bill, granting an inland bounty for corn imports to the capital. The corporation, or city, bill was introduced only four days after the riot; despite the long-standing controversy surrounding these reforms. The bill eroded the powers of Dublin's aldermen, reducing their veto over the elected common councillors, while giving the power of electing aldermen to the Common Council. In January, MPs received a petition from the aldermen which accepted the principle of election, but sought to control the candidate selection.[175] Despite the acceptance of this petition and its amendments, the bill was dropped on 12 February by 64 votes to 62. This, however, was not the end of the story and subsequent events showed the timidity of the undertakers. Three days later, another bill, concerning control of the Dublin crowd, was introduced by one of the capital's MPs and friend to the aldermen, Sir Charles Burton. This government-sponsored bill aimed to extend the powers of magistrates in dealing with crowd disturbances and to make building regulations stricter, to stop the ease with which

171 Chesterfield to Faulkner, 7 Feb. 1760 in *Chesterfield Correspondence*, v, p. 2361; Dodington to Bowes, 19 Jan. 1760 in *HMC Various Collections*, vi, pp. 73–4.   172 *CJI*, xi, pp. 439 & 449.   173 PRONI T3019/3655, Rigby to Wilmot, 18 Dec. 1759; *CJI*, xi, pp. 450–1.   174 Ibid., xi, p. 124, 474, 450 & 428.   175 Ibid., xi, p. 506.

houses could be pulled down. A petition from some 'Dublin citizens' then forced the question of the city's government back onto the agenda. The petition argued that:

> the decay of authority in the magistrates of this city and the dissensions ... have arisen from the unequal distribution of power in the constitution of the said city.

This petition should have been ignored but the bill was amended to include far-reaching reforms to open up the corporation.[176] The bill then passed all stages and became an act in May 1760, ending a twenty-year battle for corporation reform in Dublin. The city bill was an example of the undertakers accepting a measure that they had long resisted and, apart from the dropping of the first bill, there is no evidence that they actually intervened to stop its passage.

In stark contrast to the passage of the city bill, the government's legislation to reform the revenue service ran into several difficulties. Rigby angrily attributed all opposition to what he called the 'friends to smuggling', specifically all MPs who sat for boroughs or counties in Connacht and Munster. There was some truth in this, especially as Shannon's 'Cork squadron' was to the fore with amendments, but there was also opposition to allowing revenue officers unlimited search powers. This seems to have come more from 'country' dislike of the potential misuse of a standing army, than from a desire to defend the smuggling trade. The bill did eventually pass, but only after a division in which the government had a majority of eight MPs. Despite all appearances of a trouble-free session, these measures and bills show how the Patriots were consolidating as a small but permanent opposition in two distinct groups: the ten or twelve MPs, like Pery or Brownlow, who were 'independents' or loosely gathered around Lords Belvedere and Tyrone, and the eighteen or so 'eternal opposers', like Hely Hutchinson, who were 'addicted to popularity'.[177]

Parliamentary business was temporarily halted by Thurot's landing at Carrick-fergus in February 1760. In the immediate aftermath, MPs voted for a further £200,000 loan to help with the costs of repelling the attackers and to meet the cost of the earlier-agreed augmentation.[178] Parliament then emptied, as MPs went to join up with their militia corps, while the government concentrated on sending troop reinforcements northwards and getting naval vessels into the Channel. The threat passed as the French commander left Belfast Lough and was killed in a brutal battle off the Isle of Man. However, relief was quickly followed by criticism

176 Ibid., xi, pp. 840–3, 923, 958.   177 PRONI T3019/3695, 3704, Rigby to Wilmot, 9 Feb., Rigby to Wood, 16 Feb. 1760.   178 M. Beresford, 'François Thurot and the French attack at Carrickfergus, 1759–60', *Irish Sword*, x (1971–2), pp. 255–41; PRONI T3019/3712, Rigby to Wilmot, 24 Feb. 1760.

of the Irish administration, particularly in waspish London newspaper coverage. Horace Walpole was typical:

> The negligence of the Duke of Bedford's administration has appeared so gross, that one may believe his entire kingdom would have been lost, if Conflan's [fleet] had not been defeated.[179]

This criticism was very wide of the mark, because Bedford was never as relaxed as Chesterfield had been in 1745 about the threat of invasion and he had issued orders for increased recruitment in Ulster. However, the extent of preparation became a political issue. Once MPs returned to Dublin, the Patriots attempted to attack the government on these grounds, by proposing a motion that, had the militia been well-armed, they could have defeated Thurot on their own. The militia may have been poorly armed when companies arrived in Belfast. This was indeed due to defence priorities and Bedford's jaundiced view of the abilities of the militia, but the motion was defeated by 80 votes to 35.[180]

Having defended itself over the Thurot landing and dealt with the build-up of legislation, there was one final hurdle for the government to cross before the session could be closed. This came in the shape of yet another public credit crisis, as Dawson's bank collapsed in April 1760. Though this was the same old story of bankers with more notes in circulation than specie in support, Thomas Dawson and many Dublin merchants argued that the government should have saved the bank.[181] Furthermore, they attacked the administration for raising a new loan which had allegedly drained all cash out of the capital. Rigby pointed out that the Treasury had only 20,000 guineas in cash and the rest of the loan subscription being in bankers' notes, but this was ignored.[182] A petition about the scarcity of cash gathered thousands of signatures among Dublin's mercantile elite and was presented to the Commons on 14 April by the Dublin MP, James Dunn. The undertakers were only able to secure a postponement of discussion for a week, by a majority of eleven votes, to allow the government to make a deal that £150,000 in Treasury receipts could be used as security for the notes of the remaining three Dublin banks.[183] Rigby was embarrassed by this concession, but excused it on the basis that the security would encourage trade and thus increase the revenue. Bowes agreed, writing that 'whatever [his] personal sentiments may be, affairs on the whole have been sensibly conducted'.[184] MPs were mollified by this appropriation of £150,000 and the session closed soon afterwards.

179 *BNL*, 18 Mar., 1 Apr. 1760; Walpole to Mann, 4 Mar. 1760, in *Walpole Correspondence*, xxi, pp. 376–7.   **180** For similar views, RIA, Ms.12/R/9, f.56, Blacker to Charlemont, 3 Apr. 1756; *CJI*, xi, pp. 907–9.   **181** PRONI T3019/3772, Rigby to Wilmot, 8 Apr. 1760.   **182** PRONI T3019/ 3773–4, Rigby to Newcastle, 10 Apr., Rigby to Wilmot, 10 April 1760.   **183** PRONI T3019/ 3776, Rigby to Wilmot, 15 Apr. 1760, *CJI*, xi, pp. 966–7, 992–4.   **184** PRONI T3019/3785, 3788, 3769, Rigby to Wilmot, 22 Apr., Rigby to Newcastle, 24 April, Bowes to Wilmot, 8 Apr. 1760; *CJI*, xi, pp. 998–9, 1012–13.

CONCLUSION

On balance, the 1758 settlement and the cooperation of the undertakers that followed in its wake did enable Bedford to enjoy a relatively successful parliamentary session. The money bill was not threatened, as it had been in 1757; £350,000 in loans and an augmentation of 4,000 men had been agreed for the war effort. Yet the Patriots had been successful in having secured an inland bounty for corn and reform of Dublin's corporation, and had embarrassed the Castle somewhat over the militia. In addition, Bedford's public reputation remained in the doldrums. When the insane earl of Clanricarde offered to duel Rigby, ostensibly over an Act of Union, the standing of the administration fell further. Even a supporter of the viceroy criticised the chief secretary for his arrogance and excused Bedford his mistakes on the grounds of ignorance.[185] A more jaundiced account justified the anti-union riot by accusing the Castle of:

> An union of the great to oppress the little,...on the fear of adjourning parliament on some pretence, so as to protect persons who have near ruined this country.[186]

In general, the fact that Bedford lacked support from Pitt and the susceptibility of the undertakers to popular pressure meant that the Irish government was, on occasion, weaker than it had been before 1753. Reliable parliamentary management was still outside the grasp of the viceroy and the timidity of the undertakers in the face of public opinion created increasing problems for the Castle. Just how deep these could become was revealed in the 1760–1 interregnum.

185 *Letter from a Commoner in Town to a Noble Lord in the Country* (London, 1760), pp. 3–6.
186 *The Drapier's Ghost's Answer to the Clothier's Letter* (Dublin, 1760) p. 9.

6

A new reign, 1760–1762

On balance, the settlement of 1758 worked well at the start of George III's reign. The patronage demands of the undertakers were largely met and the session of 1761–2 passed more peacefully than many in the past decade, without any threat to the money bills. Opposition was confined to a Patriot minority, while the former enemies (Stone, Shannon and Ponsonby) worked well together, particularly during the 1761 general election. Lord Kildare made a virtue out of his independence, but cooperated with the Castle, while the secondary interests, such as the Gores and Lord Tyrone, saw little advantage in opposition. The distribution of patronage was fair enough to avoid grating discontent and thus, the political initiative lay with the viceroy, Lord Halifax, and the undertakers. Despite this positive outlook for the government, there were still problems with the management system in Ireland. First, constitutional issues (like the money bill used to call a new parliament and a bill to limit the duration of parliaments) acted to encourage popular political forces. Second, the accession of George III, in October 1760, brought new political circumstances that were not altogether helpful to the governing of Ireland. For all the popularity of the new king, the political instability, factionalism and difficulties in political management that came in the wake of his accession, affected Ireland.

THE ACCESSION OF GEORGE III

After the 1759–60 parliamentary session ended, Bedford and Rigby left immediately for Woburn, delighted to escape the 'tedious nonsense' of Irish politics.[1] In England, their attention was soon focused upon developments in the war. In Germany, the French appeared to be gaining an advantage, until an August victory by Frederick II, while there were false rumours that General Murray had lost Quebec.[2] With regard to Ireland, Bedford had to deal with the patronage requests of the undertakers. By mid-July, he had the king's agreement to

---

1 PRONI Wilmot papers, T3019/3797, Rigby to Wilmot, 23 May 1760. 2 PRONI T3019/3811, Wilmot to Waite, 19 June 1760. Wilmot commented on Murray that he 'seems to have acted upon the opinion commonly received, that one Englishman is a match for three Frenchmen and a half'.

four peerage creations and four promotions, plus £5,000 in pensions, £4,000 of this to George II's mistress, the countess of Yarmouth.[3] Of the undertakers, only John Ponsonby was displeased, as his request for a reversion for his eldest son for which he was prepared to offer 4,000 guineas, was refused. Ponsonby was reportedly furious at this turn of events, as were his supporters, one of whom commented:

> It seems somewhat surprising that a favour of this kind that has been granted to many, and lately too...should be refus'd to a person of the Speaker's consequence and figure, especially when there is such a recent memory of his deportment to his Grace last session, how easy his administration was rendered by the Speaker's interposition and how easily he could have made it otherwise.[4]

The death of George II, in late October 1760, soon dominated developments. It quickly became clear that George III and his favourite, Lord Bute, wanted to dispense with the current ministers, but could not do so for the present. This opened a period of great political instability in England. One repercussion of this for Irish politics was that the undertakers, and others, found their English connections of the 1750s rising and falling with dizzying rapidity. There were limits to becoming entangled in British political battles, as few Irish MPs also sat at Westminister. So, when Ponsonby's brother, Lord Bessborough, fell from favour and resigned from the Admiralty in December 1762, the Speaker was told:

> British politics had nothing to do with Irish, and I desire the favour of you upon any account not to think of it [resigning], for in doing it, you will hurt only yourself and do no sort of good to *anyone* but your successor.[5]

Ponsonby took this advice and stayed in office, though he later, in 1763, allowed the Commons to deliver a powerful snub to the authors of the Peace of Paris, which ended the Seven Years War.[6] Stone's connections did better, as his brother, Andrew, continued to serve George III and Bute, after Newcastle resigned in April 1762, while Stone, himself, remained close to the newly resurgent Lord George Sackville. All of these changes, following the collapse of the Pitt-Newcastle ministry in 1761–2, led Irish politicians to expect little direction from London.

Another repercussion, closely connected to the first, was the effect of the rising political temperature in England. First, there was the perception that

3 Bedford to Newcastle, 19 July 1760 in *Bedford Correspondence*, ii, p. 418. 4 PRONI T3019/3867, Caldwell to Wilmot, 9 Sept. 1760. 5 PRONI Grey/Ponsonby papers, T3393/1, Bessborough to Ponsonby, 30 Oct. 1762. 6 PRONI T3019/4700, Bessborough to Wilmot, 29 Aug. 1763.

most 1760s viceroys came from ministries with short lifespans and this led viceroys to be contemptuously regarded. Second, Irish politicians took sides over
affairs across the water. Pitt's acceptance of a pension on his resignation provoked
initial outrage in Ireland, but the savagery of the Court press attacks on him
meant that he remained a hero to Irish Protestants, with merchants in Cork erecting a statue, and Dublin's corporation sending an adulatory address to the 'Patriot
minister'.[7] Irish newspapers continued to acclaim Pitt's behaviour, contrasting his
'lack of invective' with George Grenville's in the parliamentary session of 1761–2,
and savaging Bedford for his venal conduct, in contrast to the virtuous ex-
minister.[8] Pitt's reputation as *the* 'Patriot minister', combining Protestantism,
military success and public virtue appealed to many MPs and out-of-doors voices,
long after his involvement in the war effort ended and is a sign of the development
of an Irish political culture parallel to England's in the early 1760s.[9]

THE MONEY BILL CRISIS OF 1760–1

A political crisis arose almost from nowhere when the Irish privy council refused
to follow past precedents for calling general elections. The 'proper cause' for
issuing election writs was the despatch of a money bill from Dublin. While
Bedford expected the same in 1760, the lords justices, supported by a majority on
the council, sent two bills, one concerning leave to qualify under the penal laws,
and the other to make debt recovery easier.[10] However useful these were, they were
most definitely not money bills and Bowes accused the lords justices of 'ambush-
ing' government supporters on the privy council. When the legal officers, led by
Bowes and William Yorke, argued that only a money bill would do as a 'proper
cause', Anthony Malone led the opposition to them, arguing that the precedents
were unclear and that the current supply would not come to an end until December 1761, leaving parliament time to discuss a supply.[11] The lords justices, and a
majority on the privy council, supported Malone in what Bowes was convinced
was a premeditated action.

    In their letter to the viceroy, the lords justices justified their decision, on
the grounds of necessity and the fact that the role of the privy council, in ini-
tiating legislation, had declined greatly. Although they did not, theoretically, con-

7 PRONI T3019/4201, Waite to Wilmot, 19 Oct. 1761; *FDJ*, 14 Oct. 1761; *BNL*, 13 Oct., 6
Nov. 1761, 5 Jan. 1762. 8 Ibid., 12 Feb. 1762. 9 This combination of Protestant Patriot and
military victor was an effective one; K. Wilson, 'Empire, Trade and Popular Politics in Mid-
Hanoverian England: The case of Admiral Vernon', *Past and Present*, cxxi (1988), pp. 74–109; N.
Rogers, 'Admirals as Heroes: Patriotism and Liberty in Hanoverian England', *Journal of British
Studies*, xxviii (1989), pp. 201–24. 10 Bedford to the Lords Justices, 22 Nov. 1760 in *Bedford
Correspondence*, ii, p. 422; PRONI T1060/6, Lords Justices to Bedford, 26 Nov. 1760. 11
Bowes to Dodington, 30 Nov. 1760, in *HMC Various Collections*, vi, pp. 76–7.

cede the 'sole right' of the Commons to draft money bills, this was a controversial *de facto* recognition of exactly that. The letter finished with a warning that Bedford should accept this reality, in the expectation that ministers would do so.[12] The lords justices were to be sorely disappointed, after Bedford received their letter, as a meeting of ministers was called to discuss precedents that Wilmot prepared a report on.[13] The two-day meeting finished with support for the position of Bedford and Bute that a 'proper cause', in the shape of a money bill, must be sent. Any other path, including a compromise suggestion by Hardwicke, was rejected, as it 'might be interpreted as giving up the point in question'. Behind the scenes, Pitt had been highly critical of the insistence upon a money bill and he absented himself from the signing of the viceroy's strong letter to the lords justices, which told them of the unacceptability of their decision and the need to return to previous practice.[14]

It was now expected that the Irish privy council would capitulate. However, Fox soon wrote, 'what a compliment the Irish Lords make to all the ministers who did sign the letter, by the stress they lay on Pitt's not signing it.' In another letter, he noted:

> Pitt's attitude made a great impression in Dublin, and stiffened the backs of the recalcitrant Lords Justices, who professed to see in it a sign that the English government would not insist upon the terms of their letter.[15]

When the privy council met to discuss Bedford's letter, Malone asked for an adjournment, to allow a wider body of opinion to be consulted. Kildare argued that this made the council more of a weather vane for out-of-doors opinion, than a part of government. At a second meeting, the earl proposed that a money bill be sent, but he was unsuccessful, having only the support of the legal officers. Stone, Ponsonby and Malone managed to avoid any further discussion, by getting a vote to adjourn the meeting until January.[16] After this, the lords justices angrily told Bedford that he was guilty of 'rendering us as contemptible in the eyes of this people as we must appear to have been in your Grace's estimation'. They showed no sign of agreeing to the ministers' instructions, though mention was made of the possibility of sending a short supply bill to extend loan duties to March 1762.[17]

---

12 PRONI Shannon papers, D2707/A1/6/3A, Lords Justices to the Privy Council, 23 Nov. 1760. On an earlier 'sole right' controversy see J. McGuire, 'The Irish Parliament of 1692', in *Penal Age*, pp. 1–31.   13 BL Add. Mss. 32420, f.125, Wilmot to Hardwicke, 2 Dec. 1760.   14 BL Add. Mss. 32420, ff.121–2, Hardwicke to Newcastle, 2 Dec., Newcastle to Hardwicke, 3 Dec. 1760; PRONI D2707/A1/6/5A, Privy Council to the Lords Justices, 3 Dec. 1760.   15 PRONI Bedford papers, T2915/10/66A, Kildare to Fox, 18 Dec. 1760; Fox to Bedford, 30 Dec. 1760 in *Bedford Correspondence*, ii, pp. 428–9; Ilchester, *Henry Fox*, ii, p. 88.   16 PRONI T2915/10/66C, Kildare to Fox, 22 Dec. 1760.   17 PRONI D2707/A1/6/6A, Lords Justices to Bedford, 27 Dec. 1760.

When Newcastle heard that the expected capitulation had not been forth-coming, he described the lords justices' letter as a 'most impudent' one.[18] The ministers met again on 7 January to discuss their response to the suggested compromise of a short money bill and Rigby reported a very heated debate, with Pitt openly critical of Bedford. This time, the other ministers seemed unwilling to confront Pitt and no fresh demand for a money bill was transmitted, though the viceroy was 'directed to write an exhoratory [*sic*] letter to their Excellencies to reconsider – This is for the sake of unanimity.'[19] It was now obvious that the ministers would not force the lords justices and their supporters to give up their point and, at the next Irish privy council meeting, Lord Carrick's proposal of the loan duties compromise was accepted. Kildare's counter-proposal of a full money bill was rejected by 15 votes to 9 and the division list was subsequently released to the public in Dublin's newspapers.[20] This compromise was sent to London, where ministers decided to avoid either a further clash with Pitt or another attempt to dragoon the lords justices. Thus, the short money bill was quietly accepted and the crisis ended as quickly as it had begun.

Bedford's only way of avoiding complete humiliation over this affair was to dismiss someone and the victim was to be Anthony Malone in March 1760. He had been the most vocal opponent of the viceroy in the privy council and was deemed 'not a fit person to be continued in the office of Chancellor of the Exchequer'.[21] That Malone was believed to be 'fit' in the wake of his bank's collapse, is an illustration of the anger at his ingratitude for the administration's assistance at that time. Yet Bedford was not allowed a clear victory, as Pitt told him that, 'had he been consulted on a matter of this consequence, he should have doubted the expediency of such a step, and have thought it required to be more maturely weighed'.[22] For his part, Malone talked of a lucrative return to the bar and a fresh chance to rebuild his political reputation.[23]

The decision, by the ministry, to accept the short money bill was a clear climbdown from their first response in December and both baffled and angered its supporters. Rigby criticised Granville's reading of the dispute that 'the dispute was ... about moonshine, that they have sent you but moonshine, but they have submitted. This is *close reasoning*.'[24] As in December 1759, ministers had been pre-sented with the opportunity to fully support the viceroy and force the undertakers

18 BL Add. Mss. 32420, f.156, Newcastle to Hardwicke, 3 Jan. 1761. 19 PRONI T3019/3963, Rigby to Wilmot, 7 Jan. 1761; PRONI D2707/A1/6/7A, Bedford to the Lords Justices, 17 Jan. 1761. 20 PRONI T2915/11/16, Yorke to Rigby, 24 Jan. 1761; PRONI D2707/A1/6/8, Lords Justices to Bedford, 24 Jan. 1761; *BNL*, 9 Feb. 1761. 21 PRONI D2707/A1/6/11, Bedford to the Lords Justices, 9 Mar. 1761. 22 Pitt to Bedford, 10 Mar. 1761 in *Bedford Correspondence*, iii, p. 6. 23 PRONI D2707/A1/5/41, Shannon to Dennis, 19 Mar. 1761; PRONI T2915/11/48, Rigby to Bedford, 25 Mar. 1761. 24 PRONI T2915/11/17, 20, Bowes to Bedford, 25 Jan., Rigby to Bedford, 1 Feb. 1761.

to behave, but once again they had not taken it. Certainly, Henry Fox had wanted the ministers to use the refusal to send a money bill as an opportunity to remove all three lords justices from the privy council. Newcastle, too, had told Hardwicke that his 'own opinion, *at present*, is that in all events their Excellencies should be removed.' Yet the duke became a crucial element in the capitulation, which suggests that ministers were more concerned with placating Pitt than with tackling Irish political problems. Thus Lord Mansfield and Newcastle vented their real indignation against the privy council, but still supported Pitt against Bedford and Bute.[25]

The decision, therefore, had less to do with Stone's connections and more to do with Newcastle's need for Pitt as a bulwark against Bute's ambitions. At this stage, Bute and George III did not feel strong enough to move against Pitt because of his popularity.[26] For these reasons Pitt's position, that a full money bill was not necessary, either on the grounds of precedent or expediency, became the accepted one in January 1761. Fox blamed the failure to force the lords justices to capitulate on Pitt's vanity and desire for popularity in Ireland. He later accused Pitt of 'being afraid lest his health should not be drunk on Ormond Key and Smock Alley by popish feagues [*sic*] and beggars.'[27] This accusation has some credibility, although Pitt's dislike of Bedford and Bute was undoubtedly also an important factor in his behaviour. Lord Bute argued that he was powerless to refuse the compromise offer of a short money bill, though he agreed with Bubb Dodington that it would be followed by the ridiculing of those on the Irish privy council who had supported past precedent and the orders of the ministers.[28] Fox's gloomy prognosis of the whole affair was that it enouraged those in Ireland, 'who foolishly and seditiously are every day aiming at independency.'[29]

It is not clear whether Fox included the lords justices in his prognosis, but their behaviour raises the question of why the different undertakers acted as they did. On the surface, Kildare's actions certainly seem like a radical change from the Patriot stance he had taken in 1753–4. However, he had always distinguished, in his own mind at least, between factional struggles and threats to the interests of Ireland. He told Fox that the quarrel had been artificially created to court the support of the 'mob' and that, had a money bill been sent initially, 'there would not have been a word said about it till the parliament met'. Therefore he placed this affair in the annals of faction, not patriotism.[30] The other undertakers, Stone, Ponsonby and Shannon, seem to have been driven by their desire to avoid an

25 BL Add. Mss. 51385, ff.1566, 1570, Fox to Bedford, 30 Dec. 1760, Rigby to Fox, 8 Jan. 1761; BL Add. Mss. 32420, f.156, Newcastle to Hardwicke, 3 Jan. 1761. **26** In his memoir of the years 1760–3, Fox emphasised the importance of Stone's connections; Ilchester, *Lady Sarah Lennox*, i, p. 18. **27** Ibid., p. 19. **28** J. Carswell and L.A. Dralle (eds), *The Political Journal of George Bubb Dodington*, (Oxford, 1965), p. 418. **29** Ilchester (ed.), *Lady Sarah Lennox*, p. 19. **30** PRONI T2915/10/66B, Kildare to Fox, 22 Dec. 1760.

unpopular measure, ahead of a general election and a new parliament. According to William Yorke, Stone and the others exaggerated the pressure on them and yet they all offered to resign, rather than send a money bill. Some privy councillors chose to oppose the ministry rather than have to stand in the general election, having voted for the money bill, or having been associated with it, when MPs came to discuss it in the next session. The printing of the privy council division list and the wide circulation of the lords justices' letters, hint at a search for a bigger audience for their defiance.[31]

Others, who had experience of Ireland, saw the affair in the same light as Henry Fox did. Bowes did refer to the forthcoming election, but felt that the behaviour of the privy council had to be seen in the wider context:

> You need not be told by me where power now resides, nor how necessary popularity is to the keeping of it, especially now on the election of a new parliament.[32]

Lord Bessborough was scathing about John Ponsonby's talk of resigning and he also told Devonshire that he was afraid that such opposition would lead to more riots of 'papist mobs' and, ultimately, to the repeal of Poynings' Law.[33] Chesterfield was just as gloomy, because Ireland has 'been lately represented here as being ripe for rebellion ... [which] is believed to be true by too many here.' Devonshire agreed with Bowes and Waite that the search for popularity lay behind the lords justices' manufacturing of the crisis and that this would be encouraged by the outcome of the affair, particularly Pitt's humbling of Bedford. He believed that one symptom of the problem was the transformation of the privy council from an executive check on the Irish parliament, to an extension of the legislature. In support of this, the four MPs appointed in July 1760, Lord Drogheda, Lord Farnham, Benjamin Burton and Sir William Fownes, were all nominated by the lords justices and all in the opposition majority in December 1760.[34]

Despite all this anger, the lords justices were able to escape dismissal, largely because of Bedford's reluctance to return to Ireland. It is just as clear that he would not have been welcome and could have caused more trouble had he returned. Kildare told Fox that 'he thinks the present government not proper to appease the heats of the country, as your Grace [Bedford] is very unpopular, and those about [him] are suspected of evil designs against the country.'[35] Before the

31 PRONI T2915/10/67, Rigby to Bedford, 18 Dec. 1760.   32 Bowes to Dodington, in *HMC Various Collections*, vi, pp. 77–8.   33 PRONI Chatsworth papers, T3158/1630, 1631, Ponsonby to Bessborough, 10 Dec., Bessborough to Devonshire, 18 Dec. 1760; PRONI, T2915/10/66, Rigby to Bedford, 20 Dec. 1760.   34 Chesterfield to Chevenix, 16 Dec. 1760 in *Chesterfield Correspondence*, v, p. 2372; P.D. Brown & K.W. Schweizer (eds.), *The Devonshire Diary, 1759–62* (Camden 4th Series, xxvii, London, 1982), pp. 71–2.   35 BL Add. Mss. 51385, f.1568, Bedford to Fox, 31 Dec. 1760; Rigby to Bedford, 22 Dec. 1760 in *Bedford*

answer to the short money bill became known in Dublin, there were rumours that Bedford was to be replaced, which would have strengthened any resolve to defy him.[36] One also gets the feeling that, despite the consensus of Fox, Devonshire and those ministers who wanted to dismiss the lords justices, there was a lack of any sense of how Irish politics could be altered at this stage. There were concerns that the 1756 and 1758 settlements had solved little and that 'independency' was now at a new high but, as we shall see, there were no serious attempts to alter Irish political management until the end of the 1760s. In early 1761 with a compromise money bill accepted and Bedford looking for a new office, the questions being asked in London centred on his replacement, not on what strategy might be tried to curb the search for popularity by the Irish undertakers.

THE GENERAL ELECTION OF 1761

After the money bill had been eventually agreed, the election writs were issued in March 1761. It immediately became obvious that the borough patrons would, as always, return at least two thirds of the 300 MPs. It is difficult to estimate the numbers returned by the leading undertakers, as some were returned for the undertaker's own boroughs and others for close allies. However, at a rough estimate, Lord Shannon returned 15–20 MPs, John Ponsonby, 14–16, Lord Kildare, 12, and Archbishop Stone, 8. Other important secondary patrons included the Gores, Lord Tyrone, Thomas Connolly, Nathaniel Clements and Lord Abercorn, while many other boroughs were controlled by one patron, or jointly by two. In terms of contests, the 1761 election saw a decline from the 1727 level, when over fifty contests had occurred. This time, there were twenty-six polls in total, nine for counties and seventeen in boroughs.[37] As if to emphasise the smooth running of the general election, there was an electoral pact between the lords justices and Kildare, to avoid expensive or violent contests, as seen in the 1750s. Given the political peace that this engendered, it is not surprising that the extant correspondence of borough patrons show little sign of worry that costly contests would mark the election.[38]

However, the prospect of a general election did not please everyone, even if it was likely to be peaceful. Seat prices rose to £2,000 and some sitting MPs sought to avoid the cost by getting a peerage. One example of this was Charles Gardiner, a recent privy council appointee, who asked Bedford, in November 1760, for a peerage. The viceroy refused, noting that it 'would subject me to so

Correspondence, ii, pp. 427–8.   **36** PRONI T3019/6458/629, Waite to Wilmot, 30 Jan. 1761; PRONI D2707/A1/5/41, Shannon to Dennis, 19 Mar. 1761.   **37** The best guide to the elections in Ireland in this period is J.L. McCracken, 'Irish Parliamentary Elections, 1727–1768', *IHS*, v (1945–6).   **38** PRONI T3019/3920, Waite to Wilmot, 6 Nov. 1760; PRONI Carbery papers, T2966/B/1/128, 2/1, Jackson to Carbery, 8 Dec. 1760, 8 Jan. 1761.

much importunity from others, who might have the like reason of difficulties getting into the House of Commons, that I should not be able to withstand it'.[39] Those historians who have looked at the 1761 election, have not dismissed the importance of this election and have identified Patriot gains, especially among new MPs.[40] Even those undertakers, like Shannon, who had agreed not to oppose each other, were forced to take more than a passing interest in the strength of popular issues. The earl's interest was challenged in the Kinsale and Youghal boroughs, though only in one case did a contest occur. In Kinsale, where Patriot politics had reached a high pitch in corporation battles during 1753–5, Colonel John Folliott emerged as the leading candidate. Shannon chose to support him, although he had reservations over Folliott's promise to support the shortening of the duration of parliaments. In Youghal, the Shannon interest was challenged in a contest, when Edward Hyde stood, having worked assiduously in the previous years to build a popular party among the freemen.[41] Yet Shannon's interest was not overturned anywhere (except, perhaps, in the case of Folliott) because he had long had control of the Burlington electoral interest. Though this had recently passed to the duke of Devonshire and his brother-in-law John Ponsonby, Shannon was still the major patron in the area. Thus Ponsonby came to Shannon to make an agreement, where the earl nominated both MPs for Dungarvan and one for Tallow, while the Speaker had the second Tallow seat and the four seats in Bandon and Lismore. In the case of Bandon, Thomas Adderley was returned against Ponsonby's wishes, but this was something that Shannon was unable to prevent. This was another case where a seat was ceded by the borough patron, rather than pushing matters to a costly contest.[42]

Overall, the undertakers' pact was a moderating influence, though the accommodation did not rule out all conflicts between patrons. In the Ponsonby heartland of County Kilkenny, the 'independent interest', led by Shannon's son-in-law, Lord Carrick, since 1753, was marginalised. The defection of the Agar and Butler interests was crucial, especially when accompanied by the important family of Patrick Wemys.[43] The result was that Wemys was returned for Callan, instead of the county, where John Ponsonby and James Agar gained the seats. All of this sealed the Ponsonby triumph over Carrick, one that Lord Shannon preferred to silently ignore.[44] A different example, where the alteration in relationships isolated

39 PRONI T2915/10/47, Gardiner to Bedford, 4 Nov. 1760; PRONI T3019/3939, Bowes to Wilmot, 18 Nov. 1760. **40** Dickson, *New Foundations*, p. 128; James, *Ireland in the Empire*, p. 263. **41** PRONI D2707/A1/5/31–2, Herrick to Shannon, 2 Dec., Pratt to Shannon, 2 Dec. 1760. **42** Devonshire's agent had told him that Adderley's election, however 'mortifying', was the cost of recovering the borough in the longer term; PRONI D2707/A1/5/33A, Boyle to Shannon, 2 Dec. 1760. **43** PRONI D2707/A1/5/30i-iv, Carrick to Wandesford, 14 Sept., 6 Dec., Wandesford to Carrick, 14 Sept., 1 Dec. 1760. **44** The dispute over Callan borough between Flood and Agar opened up one of the famous electoral contests in eighteenth-century Ireland, which caused a fatal duel in 1768; Kelly, *Henry Flood*, pp. 40–63.

a dissenting voice, came in County Armagh, the scene of a brutal election battle in 1753. This time, Lord Charlemont's candidate was easily defeated by William Brownlow, in alliance with Sir Archibald Acheson, who had been Charlemont's key supporter in former days. Acheson had the backing of both Kildare and Stone, a sign of changed times since 1753.[45]

It would be wrong to paint a picture of absolute control by the patrons. In more open constituencies contests did take place and here, two factors came to the fore: the presence of organised opposition under the guises of Free Citizens or 'independent freeholders', and the mobilising issue of shorter parliaments. One example of this was the election in Cork city, where John Hely Hutchinson, Sir John Freke and Thomas Newenham, a sitting MP and supported by Shannon, contested the two seats. Hutchinson and Freke ran a popular campaign, courting the merchants with ferocious abuse of the revenue service and pledging future support for a septennial bill. In this way they easily defeated Newenham and Hutchinson even had the offer of having his election costs paid.[46] Elsewhere, this mix of local opposition and national politics, through what became known as 'previous promises' of MPs to support a septennial bill, was repeated. In Waterford and Limerick bitter struggles within the corporations were accompanied by appeals for local government reform and more frequent elections.[47] Although the majority of MPs were opposed to a septennial bill, supporters of this measure cited the fact that Britain already had such an act and also that regular elections would make MPs more responsive to the 'sense of the people'.[48] Meetings were held in many counties and towns, asking candidates to give a promise to support a bill in the next session and the newspapers subsequently carried advertisements from fifty-four candidates, pledging their support for any bill shortening parliaments.[49] The sole public response to this was a pamphlet criticism, which centred

45 PRONI Gosford papers, D1606/1/1/30A, Kildare to Acheson, 10 Nov. 1760.   **46** After Newenham's defeat, Shannon bought for him a seat in the borough of Fore at the cost of 1,500 guineas; PRONI D2707/A1/5/40, 42, Shannon to Dennis, 7, 21 Mar. 1761. The offer to Hutchinson was described as 'a noble example for all other places, as the modern expense of elections prevents many gentlemen from offering their services to the public, who would be an honour to their country in parliament'; *BNL*, 15 May 1761.   **47** T.P. Power, 'Electoral Politics in Waterford City, 1692–1832', in W. Nolan & T.P. Power (eds), *Waterford: History and Society* (Dublin, 1992), pp. 236–8; E. O'Flaherty, 'Urban Politics and Municipal Reform in Limerick, 1723–62', *ECI*, vi (1991), pp. 105–20; NLI, Ms.16092–3, List of freeholders voting in the 1761 Limerick city election; *Report of his majesty's attorney and solicitor general upon the bill for better regulating the corporation of Limerick* (Dublin, 1762).   **48** C. Lucas, *Seasonable Advice to the Electors of MPs in the Ensuing General Election* (Dublin, 1760), pp. 22–4. **49** *FDJ*, 17 Feb. 1761; G. O'Brien, 'The Unimportance of Public Opinion in Eighteenth-Century Britain and Ireland', *ECI*, viii (1993), pp. 115–27; P. Kelly, 'Constituents Instructions to Members of Parliament in the Eighteenth Century', in C. Jones (ed.), *Party and Management in Parliament, 1660–1784* (Leicester, 1984), pp. 169–89.

on the question of promises of support being secured from candidates, rather than on the necessity of the bill.[50]

One example of the kind of pressure that could come with more open seats, occurred in the Dublin University election, where the solicitor general, Philip Tisdall, initially refused 'to explain his sentiments in relation to limited parliaments'. After realising that he faced a severe challenge for the seat, he declared that 'he thought limited parliaments were for the good of the kingdom' and was subsequently re-elected.[51] Another case where the issue of shorter parliaments played an important part, involved the former chancellor of the exchequer, Anthony Malone, who was standing for a County Westmeath seat. Although he had led the battle against a money bill in the winter of 1760, Malone struggled to undo the damage done by his banking collapse of November 1759 and his earlier apostasy of patriot ideals.[52] All the other candidates, provoked by George Rochfort's demand that a short money bill be used in the next session, to demand a septennial bill, pledged their support for shorter parliaments, and the Westmeath grand jury did the same. Malone, possibly uncomfortable with this brand of opposition politics, stood down, blaming 'the trouble and fatigue of [polling] which I am not able to undergo' and had to rely upon Shannon's offer of a safe seat in his borough of Castlemartyr.[53] This was a sign of just how much Patriot politics had changed since 1753–4.

The contests in Dublin city, County Tipperary and Ulster revealed the extent of continuity but also Patriot potential. Opposition groups were well-organised, shorter parliaments were raised as an issue and sectarian politics were never far away. The election in Dublin excited most comment, because it marked the return to the city and its politics of Charles Lucas, the radical apothecary.[54] Lucas unsuccessfully petitioned for a pardon for his seditious libel and then returned from England to face legal proceedings, in which he was supported by Pery, Lord Charlemont and Sir Edward King. The lords justices asked that their old enemy be pardoned, following Waite's advice:

> If you should bring him to trial, and he should be acquitted by the jury, which he certainly must be for want of evidence, his acquittal would make as much noise here as the trial of the Seven Bishops.[55]

---

50 *Previous Promises Inconsistent with a Free Parliament and an Ample Vindication of the last Parliament* (Dublin, 1760), p. 8; *Honest Advice to the electors of Ireland on the present most critical time* (Dublin, 1760). **51** *FDJ*, 13 Apr. 1761; *BNL*, 17 Apr. 1761; *Exshaw's Magazine* (1762), p. 182. **52** PRONI D2707/A1/5/33A, Boyle to Shannon, 2 Dec. 1760; TCD Clements papers, Ms.1742, ff. 70, 75, Malone to Clements, 25 July, 12 Oct. 1760. **53** *Pues Occurrences*, 16 Dec. 1760; PRONI T3019/4067, Waite to Wilmot, 28 Apr. 1761; *FDJ*, 23 May 1761. **54** S. Murphy, 'The Lucas Affair: a study of municipal and electoral politics in Dublin, 1742–9' (M.A. thesis, UCD 1981). **55** PRONI T3019/6458/631, 3986, 6458/637, Waite to Wilmot, 5, 12 Feb., 1 Mar. 1761. The reference is to the Anglican

The contest which followed proved a disaster for the sitting MPs, James Dunn and Sir Charles Burton. Dunn had been elected for the city on a radical platform in 1758 and, in 1761, he and Lucas had the support of the Common Council and the Free Citizens. According to observers, Dunn was a credible person to stop Lucas. However, Burton was unpopular with the electorate, not only for opposing Lucas and the Common Council in the 1740s but also for his attempt, in the 1759–60 parliament, to deal with policing in the capital. This unpopularity was compounded by his hypocritical claim to support shorter parliaments.[56] In the event, Lucas gained enough support to be elected alongside the city's Recorder, James Grattan, prompting Bowes to complain that Lucas 'might have been pre-vented had the friends of Sir Charles Burton stopp'd when they saw he could not succeed and cast their votes on Dunn'. This victory worried government, as it gave Lucas a parliamentary platform for his radical brand of politics and boosted the Patriot forces immeasurably.[57]

The Tipperary poll was a very different battle. The contest was the result of a local tradition of convert gentry sitting for seats in the county and in the Fethard borough.[58] One of the converts, Thomas Mathew, stood and raised the issue of shorter parliaments. His large estates in the county and his family's background made him a strong candidate, but also an obvious target for an evangelical Protestant, like his opponent, Sir Thomas Maude.[59] Sectarian bitterness reached a peak when Maude's election agent accused his opposite number of keeping a Catholic wife and a duel ensued, in which Mathew's man was killed. After the poll closed, Maude and Mathew were returned on a double return, to allow parliament to decide and the petitions centred on religious claims and counter-claims.[60] Mathew was forced to withdraw his petition, after MPs voted not to hear it, and Maude was returned. In a sense, the Tipperary election was different, as it marked the rebirth of sectarian hatred in that part of Munster, yet even in such a cockpit, it is interesting to note how 'independent freeholders' raised Patriot demands.[61]

The elections in Ulster also saw religious tensions come to the fore, this time between Presbyterians and established church members. In Antrim town the meeting house was attacked in February 1761, allegedly by an Anglican crowd

bishops tried by James II who were acquitted to poplar acclaim.   **56** A meeting of the Free and Independent Electors of Dublin resolved to support Dunn and Lucas and only those who supported a septennial bill; *FDJ*, 24, Jan., 17 Mar. 1761.   **57** PRONI T3019/6458/642, 646, Bowes to Wilmot, 19 May, Rigby to Wilmot, 11 Apr. 1761.   **58** T.P. Power, *Land, Politics and Society in Eighteenth Century Tipperary* (Oxford, 1993), pp. 222–7.   **59** Mathew was supported by 'independent freeholders' and Patriot clubs in Clonmel and Cashel during the election and was also the grand-master of the freemasons in the county at this time; *FDJ*, 14 Mar. 1761.   **60** J. Kelly, *'That Damned Thing Called Honour': Duelling in Ireland, 1570–1860* (Cork, 1995), p. 98; *BNL*, 22, 29 May 1761.   **61** M. Bric, 'The Whiteboy movement in County Tipperary, 1760–1780', in W. Nolan (ed.), *Tipperary: History and Society* (Dublin, 1985), pp. 148–84.

targetting the Presbyterian minister, William Campbell. The political edge to this was that Campbell supported challenges to established electoral interests in both County Antrim and Newry.[62] In Ulster there was well-organised opposition taking up the issue of shorter parliaments, as the Patriot Clubs shook off their lethargy. In County Armagh, the victorious candidates, William Brownlow and Sir Archibald Acheson, pledged themselves to procure a septennial bill and were recognised independent MPs, despite Charlemont's opposition to them. In other boroughs, such as Newry, Londonderry and Carrickfergus, there were challenges to established interests with complaints of non-resident freemen being allowed to vote in the first two and, in the last, the successful candidates pledging 'zealous endeavours to procure a limitation of parliaments'.[63] County Antrim was to see the most bitter of the Ulster polls with 'independent freeholders', driven by the aim of achieving shorter parliaments, opposing the Massarene and Hertford interests. In December 1760, John O'Neill, son of the Randalstown MP, Charles O'Neill, declared his candidacy and the *News-Letter* editor urged:

> Let your candidates know publickly and boldly but with proper respect, that they alone will be entitled to your approbation, who will in a public manner declare that they will to the best of their abilities promote all proper means for obtaining in Ireland parliaments of shorter duration.[64]

This was followed, in March 1761, by the Antrim grand jury addressing the government in favour of shorter parliaments, and an 'independent electors' meeting in Ballymena, which chose Charles O'Hara as O'Neill's running mate. Despite public support, the Antrim election, when it was held in May, proved a success for the sitting MPs. Once the sheriff had ruled out some of the 'independent' voters, O'Neill believed that hundreds of his voters would be rejected and withdrew, even though he was ahead in the poll. Afterwards, O'Neill was chaired through the streets of Carrickfergus by his supporters and sent a notice to the *Belfast News-Letter* stressing that opposition was necessary for political progress.[65]

The Ulster elections, often ignored by a concentration on the return of Lucas, show a limited emergence of an 'independent interest', predating the radical movement of the 1770s. The result in Dublin was correctly seen by the government as a harbinger of continuing parliamentary opposition, led by the demagogic Lucas, while the Patriots were also boosted by the re-election of Pery and Hely Hutchinson with resounding victories in urban boroughs, and the addition to their ranks of Henry Flood and Lucius O'Brien. Overall, however, the dominant feature of the elections was the lords justices' pact and the success of borough

---

62 *BNL*, 3 & 6 Feb. 1761.   63 Ibid., 5 Jan., 28 Apr., 5 May, 12 May & 12 June 1761. The Newry result was unsuccessfully contested in the following session of parliament: *CJI*, xii, pp. 235, 505, 513 and 521.   64 *BNL*, 12 Dec. 1760.   65 Ibid., 27 Mar, 17 Apr., 12, 15 May 1761.

patrons in continuing to control their interests. Although shorter parliaments had emerged as a significant election issue, there was no doubt that the government could secure a Commons majority by working with the undertakers. The only question was how far the undertakers would bend to the demands of popularity inside and outside the new parliament.

HALIFAX AND IRELAND

The earl of Halifax, the first viceroy after the accession of George III, had much in his favour: a new and still popular king; co-operation among his undertakers; and a successful and ongoing war. Everything looked positive for him to pursue his ambitions with new connections in England and a new start in Ireland.[66] There was one problem in the choice of his chief secretary, William Gerard Hamilton. Though undoubtedly talented, Hamilton's appointment was accompanied by rumours from London, probably originating with Rigby, that John Pownall was to be Halifax's adviser and Hamilton a puppet figure.[67] Waite foolishly decided to behave coolly towards the new Chief Secretary. This led to suspicions that he was 'going native', having already accepted the offer of a Commons seat from John Ponsonby, and, though relationships within the new Castle administration were eventually mended, there remained a legacy of distrust between Hamilton and his office juniors.[68] More importantly, Halifax's appointment sparked rumours that the new reign would produce new beginnings for the government of Ireland. In late March, Henry Cavendish wrote to Wilmot to ask whether Halifax was to be a resident viceroy, commenting 'we shall like his Grace the better upon a long acquaintance with his lordship. Whatever may be thought expedient now, some time or other residence will be found necessary.'[69] Fox recorded in his memoirs that 'Lord Halifax was to go immediately [to Ireland], and remain there till after the second session', though Hamilton's private secretary, Edmund Burke, only mentioned the intention 'not to be absolutely governed ... [and] if possible to do business on an independent footing and at any hazard.'[70] While it is interesting to

66 R. Blackey, 'A Politician in Ireland: Earl of Halifax, 1761–3', *Eire-Ireland*, xiv (1979), pp. 65–82. 67 Waite commented about the rumour that 'an impression may be made to Mr Hamilton's disadvantage, if a report of this kind should be spread about him, which very probably may be the case'; PRONI T3019/4077, Waite to Wilmot, 3 May 1761. 68 Waite had his doubts about accepting this patronage: 'No considerations would have induced me to have gone to the Old Parliament, and perhaps it may be as unpolitick for me to have a seat now'; PRONI T3019/3920, Waite to Wilmot, 6 Nov. 1760. For hostility to Hamilton and its effects: PRONI T3019/4114, 4150, 4188, Waite to Wilmot, pre-12 June, 28 July 1761, Wilmot to Waite, 15 Sept. 1761. 69 PRONI T3019/4033, Cavendish to Wilmot, 31 Mar. 1761. 70 *FDJ*, 4 Apr. 1761; Earl of Ilchester (ed.), *The Life and Letters of Lady Sarah Lennox, 1745–1826* (2 vols, London, 1901), i, p. 35; Burke to O'Hara, 10 July

note that these rumours were widely and enthusiastically disseminated in Dublin, the instructions to the new viceroy were no different from preceding ones, so far as his period of residence was concerned and the lords justices quickly relaxed.[71]

There was nothing innovatory in Halifax's first appointments. When the Common Pleas became vacant normal practice was followed, with an English judge, Richard Aston, being appointed. Though John Bowes was disappointed that his recommendation, the Irishman, William Dawson, was unsuccessful, the Lord Chancellor was soon asked to advise on parliamentary business and told Wilmot that 'I trust my situation here will be more comfortable under the present than the last administration.'[72] Another tried and trusted strategy was used, as the prominent Patriot, John Hely Hutchinson, was brought into 'government hands' as prime serjeant, in October 1761. Rumours followed that he would rival Philip Tisdall as chief Commons manager, while Sir Richard Cox was uneasy, believing that his most prominent opponent was being rewarded to finally make him 'pay costs for Nevill'.[73] Both these fears proved unfounded and a new version of Anthony Malone, a talented if unreliable Patriot, was added to the government ranks.

Halifax arrived in Dublin on 6 October 1761 with two aims: to augment troop numbers, with a war against Spain probable, and to finance this. Despite Horace Walpole's trepidation, Hamilton gained an impression of 'favourable appearances' from the undertakers.[74] This did not, of course, guarantee peace, as the short money bill of the previous winter had to be confronted and rumours soon abounded that the ministry would insist on it being passed.[75] Not knowing that Pitt had resigned, Halifax wrote to remind him of the long-standing opposition in parliament to money bills that did not arise there. While he was not suggesting a concession, he was aware that 'exigencies might exist when it would be more prudent to waive the open and direct assertion of this right.' The previous winter's dispute 'has made the debate of public notoriety and people enter into it with more than the usual warmth' and with a new supply promised, 'many will consider it solely as a superfluous assertion of an invidious claim, without even the usual plea of necessity.'[76] Halifax had quickly realised that the short money bill

1761 in R.J. Hoffmann, *Edmund Burke, New York Agent* (Philadephia, 1956, hereafter Hoffmann, *New York Agent*), pp. 278–9.   71 PRO S.P.63/422, Pitt to Halifax, 1 May 1761; PRONI T3019/4051, 4065, 4068, Waite to Wilmot, 11 Apr. 1761, Wilmot to Waite, 21 Apr. 1761, Lords Justices to Halifax, 28 Apr. 1761.   72 PRONI T3019/4064, 4071, 4087, 4182, Wilmot to Bowes, 21 Apr. 1761, Bowes to Wilmot, 28 Apr., 14 May 1761, Waite to Wilmot, 5 Sept. 1761.   73 PRONI T3019/4198, Waite to Wilmot, 12 Oct. 1761; PRONI Donoughmore papers, T3459/C/2/5, Hely Hutchinson to 'Dear Sir', 29 Nov. 1760; PRONI D2707/ A1/5/44, Cox to Shannon, 1 Aug. 1761.   74 Walpole to Montagu, 16 June 1761 in *Walpole Correspondence*, ix, p. 372; PRONI T/3019/4197, Hamilton to Wilmot, 8 Oct. 1761. 75 PRONI T3019/4182, Waite to Wilmot, 5 Sept. 1761.   76 Halifax to Pitt, 11 Oct. 1761 in *CHOP*, i, pp. 69–70.

would be controversial, especially with stories of unnamed MPs ready to attack those law officers, especially William Yorke and Edward Willes, who had supported Bedford.[77] Anthony Malone promised to have nothing to do with such manouevres, but it was noted by Bowes that, while 'his abilities might be useful, whether his sentiments ever will be, may be questioned'.[78] Halifax certainly did not want to be forced to defend the unpopular Bedford administration.

The reply, which came from Pitt's replacement, Lord Egremont, was an uncompromising one, ordering Halifax to proceed with the short money bill. Egremont pointed out that the Irish privy councillors had been allowed to frame a compromise short bill and, therefore, he was 'surprised that a possibility of resistance should exist' when the undertakers were 'in honour bound to support it'. Given the circumstances, anyone who opposed the bill could only be 'those whose real meaning is to diminish that right in the crown and Privy Council of Great Britain, hitherto allowed to be indubitable, and which His Majesty can never on any consideration relinquish'.[79] Although Stone was reported as saying 'it was impossible that the ministry ... could be absurd and wrong-headed enough to insist on the money bill being pushed in the House of Commons', Halifax was soon able to tell London that the undertakers would support the short bill.[80] Perhaps they recognised that the resignation of Pitt left a ministry in which Bedford was a rising power, thus precluding any support for further Irish resistance.[81]

In the event, the Patriots were not to be curbed by either undertakers or ministers. In early November, Robert French proposed a motion attacking the pension list, because it was £35,129 more than the rest of the civil list put together. The resolution passed, by 82 votes to 80, after what Waite called a 'trifling amendment' moved by Hely Hutchinson. Halifax immediately met the former lords justices, who claimed total surprise at the resolution and, while the viceroy accepted this, he pointed out that such conduct 'could be attended by no other consequence than a confirmation of those unfavourable impressions which had so long and so justly been entertained in England'.[82] Halifax claimed that the undertakers were using the pensions resolution to demand more patronage, or what he called 'low, miserable, narrow reasons of their own.' The earl also privately recorded his dislike of the undertakers: Stone was a 'tedious, starched, unpleasant companion', while Ponsonby was 'never detected of having any thoughts of his own'.[83]

77 Yorke and Willes were also accused of saying that the Irish were 'disaffected towards English government and ... stiffnecked and unruly'; PRONI T3019/4199, Waite to Wilmot, 15 Oct. 1761.   **78** PRONI T3019/4073, Bowes to Wilmot, 30 Apr. 1761.   **79** Egremont to Halifax, 20 Oct. 1761 in *CHOP*, i, p. 71.   **80** The report came through Isaac Barre to Rigby, while Waite also commented 'We are rather angry at your insisting upon it and impute it to the Dukes of Newcastle and Bedford': PRONI, T3019/4206, 4209, Rigby to Wilmot, 27 Oct. 1761; Waite to Wilmot, 31 Oct. 1761.   **81** PRONI T1060/6, Halifax to Egremont, 30 Oct. 1761.   **82** PRONI T3019/4210, Waite to Wilmot, 3 Nov. 1761; Halifax to Egremont, 3 Nov. 1761 in *CHOP*, i, pp. 74–5.   **83** NLI Ms.8064, entries in Halifax's journal of 3, 5 Nov. 1761

More importantly for the government, the undertakers were reluctant to defend pensions and this added strength to the Patriot cause. During a further debate on the money bill, Lucas again attacked the pensions list and accused previous viceroys of 'having conveyed money out of the country.' The Castle defeated further Patriot resolutions against pensions, though with only small majorities.[84] With regard to the debates, only Hamilton and Francis Andrews were vocal supporters of government.[85] The lords justices' refusal to send a full money bill the previous winter was praised by both supporters and opponents of the government, while the Bedford administration was 'publickly called a bad one'. Not a single official rebuked these comments and, when Andrews challenged anyone to debate them with him, he was laughed at. When Lucas spoke, he was consistently applauded from the gallery. This should have been seen as interference by the crowd and should have led to the Commons being cleared, but Waite reported that 'it was not resented as it ought to have been.' This intervention by the crowd was not isolated; there were reports of one government supporter, John St Leger, being threatened outside parliament and of Hamilton being told by the crowd to warn the Speaker against allowing the short money bill to pass.[86] The bill did pass, but the Commons was certainly restless and occasionally defiant, making it difficult to accept Halifax's explanation of the undertaker's actions as being solely due to the 'low reasons' of patronage.

The passing of the short money bill and the main supply bill gave the administration some relief and Waite was confident that the business of the session could be over by February. Behind the scenes, Halifax reported to Egremont that, while he hoped that the undertakers were now firmly behind government, he was 'sorry to say that my expectations do not keep pace with my wishes'. He used a letter from Egremont, recording George III's surprise that the resolution against pensions had been allowed to pass, to try to browbeat the undertakers into supporting the administration.[87] Yet the undertakers still sought concessions to popularity, including a suggestion from Stone and Malone that an absentee tax should be included in the supply bill. Halifax stopped this by rebuking the pair for supporting calls for a sum of near £100,000 to be appropriated for public works, while calling for government frugality over pensions.[88] Halifax did not tell ministers of all these manoeuvres because he hoped to quietly gain the support of the undertakers and thus strengthen his reputation in London. So the viceroy emphasised his firmness with them and told Egremont 'that I would not accept of

84 NLI Ms.8064, entries in Halifax's journal of 13 Nov. 1761; J.A. Eulie, 'Politics and Administration in Ireland, 1760–1766' (PhD thesis, Fordham University, 1965), p. 64.
85 PRONI T3019/4216, Waite to Wilmot, 10 Nov. 1761.   86 PRONI T3019/4222, Waite to Wilmot, 14 Nov. 1761.   87 PRONI T3019/4228, Waite to Wilmot, 26 Nov. 1761; PRONI T1060/6, Halifax to Egremont,16, 20 Nov. 1761; Egremont to Halifax, 12 Nov. 1761 in *CHOP*, i, p. 76.   88 NLI Ms.8064, entries in Halifax's journal of 13, 15 Nov. 1761.

a partial occasional support as a performance of their engagements'. In this way, Halifax was able to convince ministers that the pensions resolutions had been an aberration and in so doing gained Egremont's praise for his conduct so far.[89] The fact that the truth was more complex was not something Halifax wanted to admit.

DEFENCE FEARS AND 'PREVIOUS PROMISES'

The readiness of Ireland to provide more troops for the continuing war effort adds to the picture of a successful administration. In late November, Halifax met with four lieutenant colonels to discuss their plans to 'raise for rank', after which he told the former lords justices that he approved of the scheme and asked them for their recommendations for commissions. His journal entry glows with pleasure as the undertakers 'seemed much pleased with my civility' and eagerly supported the scheme, which was to provide 2,800 men in four new regiments to be completed within four months and to be boosted to 3,500 when a fifth new regiment was added.[90] The only expense to the Castle was to be the cost of arms and accoutrements, as the recruiting levy was provided by each lieutenant colonel selling his current commission with any shortfall being made up by the 'usual advantages on the clothing contracts'.[91]

To sell this proposal to the Commons, Halifax suggested:

> There must be some authorised intelligence, as a ground for my message to the House of Commons, and this they will expect, not only as a regular message in the course of business, but as a proper and precedented compliment to themselves.

Egremont authorised the use of intelligence about the plans of the French Brest squadron, so long as 'needless alarm' was not given by it and the militia in Ulster were provided with some arms.[92] After Christmas, with the undertakers' agreement, Halifax sent this intelligence to the Commons, alongside the British declaration of war with Spain. With new defence assessments, provided by Rothes and Kildare, the Commons unanimously agreed, in February 1762, to vote a new loan of £200,000.[93] The augmentation proved successful, with over 3,600

89 PRONI T1060/6, Halifax to Egremont, 21 Nov. 1761; Egremont to Halifax, 12, 21 Nov. 1761, in *CHOP*, i, pp. 76 & 80.   90 NLI Ms.8064, entry in Halifax's journal of 25 Nov. 1761. By the assessment of Rothes, in December, the effective numbers on the establishment stood at 11,309, requiring nearly 2,500 men to complete the regiments to full strength; PRONI T1060/6, Rothes to Hamilton, 15 Dec. 1761.   91 Halifax to Egremont, 26 Nov. 1761 in *CHOP*, i, p. 81.   92 PRONI T1060/6, Halifax to Egremont, 29 Nov. 1761; Egremont to Halifax, 5, 26 Dec. 1761 in *CHOP*, i, pp. 84, 91–2.   93 *CJI*, xii, p. 729.

men being recruited between January and April 1762, almost half of them to the five new regiments. This allowed Halifax to draft 2,000 men for service in Portugal and to maintain Irish defences, by keeping the establishment at around 12,000 effective men in the country[94]. Halifax's success is confirmed by the address from the Commons, offering to increase his salary by £1,600 per annum. As Archbishop Ryder wrote:

> [I]f it be our way to go into extremities, it is happy for His Majesty, and for both kingdoms, that we are now determined to support government beyond what was ever known or thought of here before.'[95]

Despite his money problems, Halifax declined the offer, on the grounds that it would cause a rush of applications for salary increases. He received further praise from Egremont for this frugality, though the latter also asked that the increase be accepted for the sake of future viceroys. This, perhaps, is another hint that the future residence of viceroys in Ireland might be longer than Halifax's.[96]

Despite the viceroy's popularity, opposition politics did not disappear entirely, while other storms in the Commons arose from older sectarian hatreds. The Patriots took their lead from the general election issues. Thus, on the first day of the session, Lucas got permission to draft a septennial bill, after what was described by Waite as a poor maiden speech. This issue caused Bowes to be more pessimistic about political prospects than Halifax. Though the passage of the money bill 'may convince that we are in a state of repentance' over that matter, Bowes was worried that support for the government might slip away as the septennial bill was 'more explicitly asserted and better supported than I have before known'. As if to add further proof, he noted that the three to one majority among MPs included most of the followers of Stone and Ponsonby.[97] Although the undertakers were expected to oppose a bill that threatened their influence, this issue proved just how far they would now run from unpopularity.

The extent of the undertakers' spinelessness was revealed when the septennial bill received a large majority of ninety votes. A minor amendment, raising property qualifications for MPs, was taken by Halifax, as a way of making the measure unacceptable to borough patrons in the lords or privy council. The viceroy also optimistically interpreted the defeat, by 103 votes to 43, of as a sign that:

94 The recruitment figures are from CJI, xii, pp. 862–6 and for the instructions on drafts see PRONI T1060/8, Egremont to Halifax, 23 Feb. 1762. 95 PRONI T3019/4302, Ryder to Wilmot, 2 Mar. 1762. 96 PRONI T3019/4296, 4300, Waite to Wilmot, 26 Feb. 1762 (with enclosed address); PRONI T1060/8, Halifax to Egremont, 28 Feb., Egremont to Halifax, 20 Mar. 1762. 97 PRONI T3019/4204, 4237, Waite to Wilmot, 22 Oct., Bowes to Wilmot, 3 Dec. 1761.

> the House of Commons have voted the septennial bill to be a proper bill,
> [but] they have in effect voted likewise that it is not a bill which they have
> particularly at heart.[98]

Despite such irritations, the pledges extracted from candidates in the election of
1761 and out-of-doors pressure forced many MPs to vote for a bill that they did not
support in 'a species of parliamentary sanction for these unconstitutional arrange-
ments.' The management malaise had affected government officials and other
friends. Halifax readily admitted that he had 'allowed his new minister [Hely
Hutchinson] and Mr Pery to take the popular side, while Mr Hamilton declared to
everybody his indifference about it'. As the bill moved to the Irish privy council the
viceroy hoped that 'new measures are now to be taken to do with a bad grace what
might have been done at first with dignity and credit'. Yet, even in the privy council
the undertakers hesitated as they and others worried that 'if the bill should pass the
council, it will certainly be returned upon them from England'.[99]

Though Halifax requested assurances that ministers in London would drop
the bill, Egremont refused to say whether they would take the odium of dropping
the measure. The secretary of state argued that Irish politicians should behave as
an arm of government and that 'it might have disagreeable consequences, to signify in Ireland, what the council here would do on a bill to be transmitted from
that kingdom'.[100] The Irish privy council seemed unable to take a decision as the
business of declaring war with Spain and the fresh calls for Pitt's reinstatement
dominated politics.[101] As that body prevaricated, supporters of shorter parliaments lost no time in mobilising out-of-doors opinion. A partisan pamphlet was
published in January 1762, while the press began to carry addresses from various
counties and corporations supporting the septennial bill and urging MPs to continue to do likewise.[102] By late January the lack of any decision by the Irish privy
council provoked one newspaper to ask whether the bill would be dropped and the
'sense of the people' denied. The author finished on the ironic point that 'surely
you cannot think any men would support the bill in public and privately oppose
it'. Given the rumours in Dublin that Stone was going to oppose the bill but then
suddenly 'flew the pit', there were genuine fears of undertakers doing in secret
what they would not do in public.[103]

In the event, the privy council did pass the bill by the narrowest of margins,
seventeen votes to sixteen, on 8 February.[104] John Bowes was praised by the viceroy

---

98 Halifax to Egremont, 8 Dec. 1761 in *CHOP*, i, p. 86; *CJI*, xii, pp. 565–6. 99 PRONI
T1060/6, Halifax to Egremont, 4, 23 Dec. 1761. 100 PRONI T1060/6, Egremont to Halifax,
30 Dec. 1761. 101 PRONI T3019/4248, 4250, Rigby to Wilmot, 31 Dec. 1761, Wilmot to
Halifax, 1 Jan. 1762. 102 *Septennial Parliaments Vindicated* (Dublin, 1762); *FDJ*, 2 Feb. 1762;
BNL, 1, 15 Jan., 16 Feb. 1762. 103 *BNL*, 29 Jan. 1762; PRONI T3019/4275, Waite to
Wilmot, 26 Jan. 1762. 104 PRONI T3019/4277, 4279, Bowes to Wilmot, 28 Jan. 1762, Waite
to Wilmot, 8 Feb. 1762; *BNL*, 26 Mar. 1762.

for his speech against the bill, but other government officials like William Yorke and Edward Willes actually voted in favour of it. This perhaps showed their disinclination to suffer a repeat of the anger directed at them the previous winter, especially when the voting behaviour of privy councillors was reported in the press. Halifax sent the bill to Egremont with the comment that it was growing more unpopular with MPs as the likelihood of its return increased. Opposition to the bill was certainly evident in allegations that it would be a step towards union or that it was a 'dangerous innovation in the constitution'. One author criticised 'those seditious multitudes from whose outrage, and uproar, the sense of a nation is generally collected' and described Lucas as:

> A dry fanatic probationer in the law, who from some foreign republican seminary has brought home just enough learning as will make those stare who have none at all.[105]

At this point Halifax advised that, if the bill was going to be returned from London, it should be amended to fix the length of parliaments at fourteen years. This would provide MPs with a reason to drop the bill on the grounds that it had been amended and their parliament ignored. In such a scenario they could 'suffer the discredit of throwing out this law, even under these circumstances, than have the inconvenience that would arise to themselves from passing it.'[106] Irish MPs were saved from such a dilemma when the bill was dropped in London. This outcome was not unexpected and at a meeting of Dublin merchants on 23 March, speakers blamed the ongoing delay on 'misrepresentations made by some designing men in this kingdom.' Alongside these rumours came later ones arguing that, had the bill been returned, the Commons would have rejected it anyway. To counter such stories, MPs passed a resolution in April stating that these 'suggestions confidently propagated' were 'without foundation'.[107]

The whole affair showed the potential for undertakers, even in their golden age, to abdicate management responsibilities and appeal to London for relief on some issues. Over the septennial bill they seemed powerless to resist Patriot demands. When the 'Catholic question' arose they were caught up in more atavistic currents. The question occurred because Halifax and British ministers began to consider whether or not to accept an offer by a Catholic peer, Lord Trimleston, to raise five Catholic regiments for use in Portugal against the Spanish. However, this search for recruits became derailed by an outbreak of hysteria over 'popish plots' in Munster connected to the Whiteboy agrarian unrest. Trimleston's offer to Halifax fits in the context of the long battle of Irish Catholics under the Hanoverians to fashion a form of loyalty, especially during wartime. Jacobitism

---

105 *The Question about Septennial Parliaments Impartially Examined in two letters to Charles Lucas* (Dublin, 1761), pp. 7, 24–6. 106 PRONI T1060/8, Halifax to Egremont, 19 Feb. 1762. 107 *BNL*, 26 Mar. 1762, *CJI*, xii, p. 913.

may or may not have remained the dominant idiom for Catholic discourse, however this other current became noticed by the Castle.[108] There were loyalty addresses to George III on his accession and in early 1762 messages were read out in many Catholic chapels, which urged loyalty to the Hanoverians and reminded congregations of 'the happy enjoyment of peace and the blessings that attend it'.[109] Further demonstrations of this mood were contained in addresses from Catholics in Dublin, Cork and Waterford.

Though Halifax may have been convinced of the loyalty of the Catholic elite he was cautious enough to ensure that the details of Trimleston's proposals should show an understanding of the ramifications of Catholics being admitted into the British army. All officers were to be Protestant and no arms were to be distributed until the regiments were ready to embark. Oaths of loyalty were to be taken and offers of further service in the Portuguese army were to be given to assuage Protestant fears of Ireland being flooded with Catholic ex-soldiers. When he went to London, Trimleston was to find even more caution, as Egremont refused to discuss the proposals, using the excuse that the Portuguese ambassador was not authorised to deal with such matters. However, what was much more important were the reports in the *London Chronicle* of Jacobite plots and unrest in Munster.[110]

Although the first widespread reports of Whiteboy attacks emerged in the first week of April 1762, the disturbances had begun the previous November in southeast Tipperary and had spread to the borderlands of Cork, Waterford and Tipperary.[111] The reason for the widespread newspaper reports was that, in March 1762, Lismore Castle, property of the Devonshire family, was threatened by hundreds of Whiteboys, while letters had also been sent to Waterford's Protestant gentry demanding their horses and the opening of Tallow gaol. The government responded swiftly, sending regiments of dragoons and light infantry to the area and issuing a proclamation urging magistrates to carry out their duties. However, this did little to calm matters as reports came from Youghal, describing a band of 400 Whiteboys levelling hedges and erecting mock gallows to intimidate informers and recalcitrant gentry.[112] The targets were mainly tithe farmers and landlords who

---

108 For differing interpretations of Catholic Ireland at this time see G.O'Brien (ed.), *Catholic Ireland in the Eighteenth Century* (Dublin, 1989), chapters 5–6; C.D.A. Leighton, *Catholicism in a Protestant Kingdom* (Dublin, 1994), chapter 3; P. Fagan, *Divided Loyalties: The Question of an Oath for Irish Catholics in the Eighteenth Century* (Dublin, 1997), chapter 5; B. O'Buachalla, *Aisling Ghearr* (Dublin, 1997). 109 Trimleston himself had called a meeting of Catholic gentry in counties Westmeath and Kilkenny in January 1761 to discuss a loyalty address to the new king; *FDJ*, 20 Dec. 1760; *BNL*, 29 Jan. 12 Feb. 1762; Halifax to Egremont, [6–12] Feb. 1762 in *CHOP*, i, pp. 154–5. 110 PRONI T1060/8, Egremont to Halifax, 10 Apr. 1762; *London Chronicle*, 8 Apr. 1762. 111 J.S. Donnelly, 'The Whiteboy Movement, 1761–5', *IHS*, xxi (1977–8), pp. 20–59; J. Kelly (ed.), 'The Whiteboys in 1762: A contemporary account', *Journal of the Cork Historical and Archaeological Society*, xciv (1989), pp. 19–26. 112 PRONI T3019/4323, Waite to Wilmot, 10 Apr. 1762, *BNL*, 6 Apr. 1762.

charged conacre rents, or had enclosed common pasture. Thus, whatever the reports of 'disaffected tunes' may have suggested, the grievances were as the Castle believed – economic and belonging to an established tradition of rural unrest.

In all of the contemporary newspaper reports there were recurring claims that the regular clergy and an expectation of French aid were behind the disturbances.[113] However, the Castle refused to believe these stories of Jacobite plots, perhaps partly because the local convert, Edmund Burke, was Hamilton's private secretary.[114] The government's stance seemed to be validated by the acquittals of most of the Whiteboy suspects who had been charged with treason, in counties Limerick and Tipperary. Yet, these decisions by the lord chief justice, Richard Aston, enraged many Munster Protestants and some local army commanders, like Lord Drogheda and General Montague. Certainly in counties Cork and Waterford, outside the ambit of Aston, executions were much more common in 1762.[115] The outbreak of disturbances also spurred on the pamphleteers, who repeated the claims about foreign involvement and clerical leadership, thus laying the ground for the execution of Nicholas Sheehy and the reprinting of Temple's history of 1641.[116]

The Catholic question meant that Halifax now had the difficult task of defending his administration from charges of leniency and complacency. The government was attacked with accusations of courting Catholic support through the favourable treatment of both Trimleston's proposal and the bill which would have allowed Catholics to purchase mortgages in land which they could then transfer. This bill had passed in February 1762, supported in the Commons by government officials like Hutchinson, Hamilton and Nathaniel Clements, and easily went through the privy council, only to be dropped in London.[117] By April, MPs were demanding information on how the militia had been armed to face the Whiteboys and on what was the nature of the 'popish legions'. They also established a committee to 'inquire into the cause and progress of the subsisting Popish insurrection in the province of Munster.' In all three cases the administration

---

113 *The Belfast News-Letter* carried detailed reports of both the government's denial of foreign involvement and all the reports to the contrary: *BNL*, 13 April, 23 April & 21 May 1762.   114 Donnelly, 'The Whiteboy movement, 1761–5', pp. 20–9.   115 Aston sentenced three men to death while in Cork and Waterford 10 were hung. After the assizes in Clonmel Aston was said to have left the town with the roads lined by grateful Catholics, while the Cork judges were lampooned for their leniency by local Protestants; Donnelly, 'Whiteboys', pp. 44–9; PRONI T3019/4346, Waite to Wilmot, 22 June 1762.   116 *An enquiry into the causes of the outrages committed by the Levellers or Whiteboys of Munster* (Dublin, 1762); *An alarm to the unprejudiced and well-minded Protestants of Ireland* (Cork, 1762); T. Bartlett, *The fall and rise of the Irish nation: the Catholic question 1690–1830* (Dublin, 1992), p. 70.   117 For this see *CJI*, xii, pp. 846–7, 855 & 898; James Caldwell, *A Brief Examination of the question whether it is expedient … to pass an act to enable papists to take real securities for money which they may lend* (Dublin, 1764).

struggled to avoid being embarrassed by the 'red hot Protestants' from Munster led by Lord Boyle, who, as Waite put it, 'were much disposed to give his excellency a parting blow.'[118] The militia inquiry was ended before it really began, as government managers allowed information to be given to MPs but prevented any discussion of the damaging papers. Then on 12 April, Lord Carrick (Shannon's son-in-law) proposed an address enquiring whether Halifax had or now intended to raise Catholic recruits, but this was defeated by 113 votes to 63 with Flood and Hutchinson joining forces to tell for the majority. The anger of many MPs was not dissipated as the 'Whiteboy committee' chaired by Lord Boyle was then formed. This did not augur well for its moderation and its report included previous allegations of Jacobitism and attacks on the government's legal officers. The Castle's managers had to respond with a motion to recommit the report which only passed by 58 votes to 44.[119]

Although the administration escaped censure, the flurry of activity shows the mood of anger among some MPs and Halifax's reputation was certainly damaged. It soon became apparent that some in the ministry agreed that the viceroy had not taken the disturbances seriously enough. Before he received any report from the Castle, Egremont told Halifax that he now had information from Cork that Irish-born French officers were in Munster stirring up riots and giving up to 1,500 men military training under Jacobite insignia.[120] Pitt, too, was sent a similar report from County Waterford, perhaps to inspire him to criticise Halifax from a Protestant Patriot position.[121] The secretary of state would hardly have been happy when Halifax reported that he had authorised the use of troops and had dismissed any talk of foreign involvement as 'the suggestion of persons unacquainted with affairs in this kingdom, upon any disorderly motion amongst the people'. Wilmot warned that this letter seemed to 'treat these matters rather too lightly' and advised that the Castle provide proof that the disturbances were economic in origin or else back down.[122] Halifax refused and instead shifted the blame for the Whiteboy disturbances onto 'timid' local magistrates. He also hinted that Egremont's information may have come from those followers of Shannon who were using Whiteboyism to oppose Catholic recruitment which would erode their labour force.[123]

Waite, too, dismissed the reports coming from London, telling Wilmot, 'I never knew anything of their [the Whiteboys] having proclaimed the Pretender until I read it this day in the [London] Chronicle.'[124] He rejected the notion of plots and blamed the disturbances on wider disrespect for the law. Both he and Bowes

---

118 PRONI T3019/4323, Waite to Wilmot, 10 Apr. 1762. 119 *CJI*, xii, pp. 905–6, 861–6, 890. 120 PRONI T1060/8, Egremont to Halifax, 10 Apr. 1762. 121 The contemporary account mentioned in fn.50 above was sent to Pitt in April/May 1762. 122 PRONI T1060/8, Halifax to Egremont, 8 Apr. 1762; PRONI T3019/4324, Wilmot to Waite, 15 Apr. 1762. 123 PRONI T1060/8, Halifax to Egremont, 13 Apr., Halifax to Egremont, 17 Apr. 1762. 124 PRONI T3019/4327, Waite to Wilmot, 17 Apr. 1762.

linked Whiteboyism to the May 1762 Lisburn weavers' riots against a new system of sealing exports of brown linen. Lord Hillsborough had been jostled and forced to take oaths of loyalty to the weavers when he intervened and the army had to be summoned to disperse the rioters. For Bowes, the violence of these weavers' combinations, when taken with the Munster disturbances, pointed to a general 'disregard for all law and decency to government and magistracy'.[125] However, such logic and Halifax's dismissal of Protestant fear as self-interest showed the dangerous gap in perceptions over the 'Catholic question'. In the short term the Whiteboy disturbances had blemished the reputation of a previously popular viceroy. In the longer term it acted as a precedent for ministerial clashes with Irish Protestants over Catholic relief, especially when steps were taken against a background of agrarian unrest.

PEACE AND AUGMENTATION

After his return to London Halifax largely ignored Irish affairs, being thrown fully into the affairs of the new Bute administration.[126] Although the war with Spain continued and led to the capture of Havana in the autumn of 1762, the priority remained that of negotiating a peace settlement. Bedford was sent to France for more negotiations and the peace preliminaries were finally agreed in November 1762. However, these final stages produced more instability in the ministry, as George Grenville was demoted to the admiralty which led to Halifax becoming secretary of state. The negotiations and reshuffles were closely followed in Ireland, the *Belfast News-Letter* commenting that giving up Newfoundland or Guadeloupe:

> might indeed obtain us an insidious truce for a little time, which as it would be of very short duration, could never deserve the name of a Peace.[127]

Others were more pragmatic, so that rumours in August 1762 that a treaty was to be signed imminently, made Waite wonder whether new clothing contracts for the army should be authorised, as peace would mean a reduction in numbers.[128] However, the capture of Havana temporarily hardened attitudes in Ireland towards the negotiations. Bedford was accused in the press of being a friend of France and rumours that Pitt and Newcastle were to rejoin the ministry were reported as

125 PRONI T3019/4338, 4351, Waite to Wilmot, 22 May, Bowes to Wilmot, 27 July 1762; *BNL*, 15 June 1762.   126 The Bute ministry had, at first, the reputation in Ireland of being an unstable one, as Waite told Wilmot, 'most people here think, I had almost say wish, that the present system will not hold till Xmas next'; PRONI T3019/4343, Waite to Wilmot, 9 June 1762.   127 *BNL*, 8 June 1762.   128 PRONI T3019/4358, Waite to Wilmot, 5 Aug. 1762.

being 'heartily wished for by persons of all ranks.'[129] Despite such sentiments, when the news of the preliminaries came to Dublin in early December, Waite told Wilmot that cannons were fired in the Phoenix Park and the lords justices issued a proclamation to announce the end of the war.[130] The fact that the newspapers did not carry coverage of any celebrations outside Dublin just reveals more about the attitude of the editors to the peace.

In any event, peace produced both the end of Halifax's term of office and questions about imperial defence and Ireland's role in that. Even before the peace preliminaries had been signed there were discussions, in October 1762, about the possibility of augmenting the Irish army to 20,000 men.[131] The peace-time 12,000 limit had been broken in 1756 and by the summer of 1762, the establishment was subsisting over 15,000 men. The Irish augmentation was tied to ministerial discussions over the size of a permanent army for the Americas and how to pay for it.[132] In October Stone refused to give more than his personal opinion on the question of an increase to 18 or 20,000 troops. Though he would have been keen not to lose any army patronage by reductions in officer numbers, Stone stressed that the potential problem with an augmentation was not the Limiting Act of William III (which kept the army at 12,000), but how to raise an extra £186,989 each year. With no agreement in sight by December 1762, stories appeared in the press of reductions in every company from 70 men per company to 28. Waite immediately advised that ministers make a decision quickly to avoid the augmentation fiasco of the last peace, when Lord Harrington had tried to get consensus in Dublin and had failed.[133] Waite also hoped that ministers would take into account Ireland's debts and revenue and believed that 18,000 men should be the size of a new, less officer-heavy establishment. Reflecting the ambiguity of Stone and the undertakers on an issue, which mixed patronage and expenditure, he warned that 'we are afraid of ourselves, and of one another'.[134]

Despite this warning, there were no further orders from London for three months, by which time rumours about the names of regiments to be disbanded and, at the same time, how an increase to 20,000 men would be paid for, were rife in Dublin. The discussions in London had become entangled in legal arguments over William III's act and rumours of possible Tory opposition to increases in the standing army.[135] However, Newcastle dismissed any potential Tory threat to a ministerial choice 'to keep up as many men as they please, without being an expense to this country'.[136] This view of likely Tory conduct

129 *BNL*, 24 Sept., 22 Oct. 1762. **130** PRONI T3019/4408, Waite to Wilmot, 2 Dec. 1762. **131** PRONI T3019/4378, Waite to Wilmot, 13 Oct. 1762. **132** J.L. Bullion, *A Great and Necessary Measure: George Grenville and the genesis of the Stamp Act* (London, 1982), pp. 11–15. **133** PRONI T3019/4377, Stone to Halifax, 13 Oct. 1762; *BNL*, 3 Dec. 1762. **134** PRONI T3019/4414, Waite to Wilmot, 5 Dec. 1762. **135** PRONI T3019/4140, Waite to Wilmot, 30 Dec. 1762; BL Add. Mss. 35892, f.31–2, Yorke to [ ], 27 Dec. 1762. **136** BL Add. Mss. 32946, ff.199, 246, Walpole to Newcastle, 24 Jan., Newcastle to Hardwicke, 31 Jan. 1763; P.D.G.

suggests that one should look elsewhere, namely Ireland, for the failure of the augmentation, though one authority claims:

> the weight of precedent and the certain opposition of a subordinate parliament did not deter them [ministers] at all.[137]

It certainly seems that, at least initially, most ministers did not expect resistance from Ireland, despite the example of 1748, which Edward Weston, now an under-secretary to Bute, could have told them about. Because Stone's October response was generally encouraging, Charles Yorke certainly believed that 'no measure [could] be more agreeable to Irish Protestants' than an increase in their army.[138] At this stage only Edmund Burke and perhaps Hamilton wondered if Ireland could afford the revenue increases necessary. In Dublin, Stone continued to balance the patronage needs of the undertakers with the likely unpopularity of an expensive army that might be sent to North America. In December 1762, Colonel Robert Cuninghame was sent to London by the lords justices with a suggested augmentation plan that would increase the numbers of officers and regiments, by making 35 regiments of 300 men instead of 25 of 500. He also carried with him information about likely revenue increases, including a dreaded land tax and cuts in public works grants, and the concession that extra troops should stay in Ireland during peace-time. Hamilton described the scheme thus:

> everything which is frugal is dropped, and everything which is expensive is adopted ... I agree with you in thinking that *an army* is necessary in Ireland for the Protestant interest; but pray is an army of *18,000 men* necessary?[139]

More importantly, ministers did not have any pledge from the undertakers to manage it through parliament. This was 1748 all over again with the possibility of a parliamentary storm and, in January 1763, George III and Bute decided to drop the scheme.[140]

Given this chronology there seems little doubt that ministers were convinced that the time was not right for an Irish augmentation. Hamilton was very quick to claim credit for preventing a massive increase in expenditure, while also blaming Halifax for the negative outcome. According to Hamilton, the viceroy had first suggested 20,000 men and then reduced that to 18,000:

Thomas, 'New Light on the Commons Debate of 1763 on the American Army', *William and Mary Quarterly*, xxxviii (1981), pp. 11–12.   **137** Bullion, *A Great and Necessary Measure*, p. 23.   **138** History of Parliament Trust transcripts, George Grenville papers, Yorke to George III, 17 Dec. 1762.   **139** Hamilton to Hutchinson, 4 Dec. 1762, 5 Jan. 1763 in *HMC Donoughmore Mss.*, 12th report, appendix ix (London, 1891, hereafter *Donoughmore Mss.*), pp. 241–3.   **140** See J. Shy, Towards Lexington, p. 74; J.L. Bullion, 'Security and Economy', pp. 499–507, 503.

> He did the first when he thought of relinquishing Ireland, and the last when he had thought of returning to it.[141]

Although Halifax did plead for the retention of Lord Drogheda's regiment to please Stone, it was clear that during the period of discussion he had never any intention of returning to Ireland. Thus, Hamilton's version of events was driven by an appeal to his friends, Hutchinson and Pery, and a wish to return to Ireland as head of his own 'Castle party' independent of the undertakers.[142] Whether or not Hamilton used his links with Bute to stress the impossible management situation that the augmentation would cause in Ireland, the decision to keep the establishment at 12,000 led Waite to speculate that Hamilton was more popular with Bute than was Halifax.[143] In the longer term the consequences of the failed augmentation scheme were fateful as the ministers announced that a new army was to be based in North America and that the colonists would have to pay for it with taxes. The first part of the imperial crisis jigsaw had been put in place.[144]

141 Hamilton to Hutchinson, 12 Mar. 1763, *Donoughmore Mss.*, p. 245. 142 George III to Lord Bute, 24 Feb. 1763 in R. Sedgewick (ed.), *Letters from George III to Lord Bute, 1756–1766* (London, 1939), p. 191; Hamilton to Hutchinson, 29 Jan. 1763, *Donoughmore Mss.*, p. 244. 143 PRONI T3019/4535, Waite to Wilmot, 18 Mar. 1763. 144 Bullion, 'Security and Economy', pp. 506–7.

7

End of an era, 1763–1766

The failure of the 1756 and 1758 settlements to produce political calm in Ireland certainly produced political frustration in London, but it is questionable whether this led to a reform policy. Indeed, the dominant ministerial thinking in the 1760s was that innovation was to be avoided if the political risks appeared too great. However, several factors made change to the management system inevitable. First, the deaths, in December 1764, of Stone and Shannon, raised great doubts about the undertaker system as it then existed. Second, ministerial demands on the government of Ireland for men and money increased after the Seven Years War, just as the parliamentary undertakers were unwilling or unable to accede to such demands. Third, the popular concessions offered by London in 1765–66 did more to strengthen the Patriots and independent MPs than it did to shore up the reputations of Ponsonby and the second earl of Shannon.

The Seven Years War had created new imperial demands on Britain that had already begun to affect Ireland with the discussion about the use of Catholic recruits in 1762 and this process was to continue. During the augmentation discussions, Wilmot had pointed out that a higher revenue meant that 'a plan for the future government of that kingdom should be well considered and resolved upon.'[1] The concentration by successive ministries on the governance of farther-flung places, especially India and North America, may have influenced thinking about the management of Ireland, but it also prevented any firm decisions being taken until the later 1760s. The government of Ireland continued as before, after the deaths of Stone and Shannon in December 1764, because there seemed no viable alternative to the undertaker system as it then existed.

A SHAMBOLIC VICEROYALTY: NORTHUMBERLAND AND IRELAND

The session of 1763–4 showed how much the undertaker system had changed since 1745 and how it might collapse before ministers decided to abolish it in some imperial overhaul. One of the major influences over the session of 1763–4 was the dreadful relationship between W.G. Hamilton and the earl of Northumberland. The viceroy's appointment had been one of Bute's last before his resignation

---

1 PRONI T3019/4264, Wilmot to Waite, 21 Dec. 1762.

made way for Grenville and Halifax. On top of that, Northumberland had not been Bute and George III's first choice. Lords Waldegrave and Granby refused the viceroyalty, while the duke of Richmond was seen as too close to Kildare, all of which left Northumberland as 'the next best'.[2] Despite all of these manouevres in London, Northumberland and Hamilton shared the same patron, Bute and, yet, they failed to work together.

The main reason for this lies in the schemes Hamilton had been hatching in late 1762 and early 1763 to manage the Irish House of Commons himself or alongside popular MPs like Hely Hutchinson, Marcus Paterson and Pery.[3] This was a dangerous idea, given Hamilton's reliance on his English connections. Thus, his problems began with the resignation of Bute in April 1763 and Halifax's refusal to support his former chief secretary. Given this and the hostility of the Irish undertakers, particularly Stone (who would have known of the chief secretary's schemes), Hamilton changed his tactics. He attempted to reach an accommodation with his Irish rivals, Philip Tisdall and John Gore, but this was rebuffed and Rigby, on a visit to Dublin in June 1763, remarked on the universal dislike of the chief secretary.[4] The appointment of Hamilton as chancellor of the exchequer, when Tisdall and Gore both had brothers for this post, only worsened relations and there were rumours of a possible censure of the chief secretary. His attempt to come to an agreement with Shannon, through a meeting with Bellingham Boyle in London, also ended in disappointment.

Worse was to come for Hamilton and, in consequence, the stability of the Castle administration. In August 1763, Grenville finally forced George III to accept the permanence of Bute's retirement, leaving Hamilton and Northumberland completely isolated.[5] After Northumberland arrived in Dublin, he quickly decided to rely entirely on Stone, and the chief secretary was now utterly marginalised. During the summer there were rumours that Northumberland was 'under the government of his Secretary' and it was this impression that the earl attempted to overturn. This process continued as the viceroy chose to give Philip Tisdall the management of the Commons. By December 1763, Wilmot was writing to Hamilton, sympathising with his predicament, where he was excluded from levees and meetings with the undertakers. After the Christmas recess it became clear that Northumberland would keep Hamilton as his chief secretary, but only until they returned to England and, in the meantime, the viceroy would continue to ignore him.[6]

2 Walpole, *Memoirs of the Reign of George III* (4 vols, London, 1845), i, pp. 169–70; George III to Bute, 7 Apr. 1763 in Sedgewick (ed.), *Letters from George III*, p. 211. 3 Hamilton to Hely Hutchinson, 10–11 Nov. 1762, 20 Jan. 1763 in *Donoughmore Mss*, pp. 239–41, 244–5. 4 Hamilton to Hely Hutchinson, 2 June 1763 in ibid., p. 250; PRONI T3019/4616, Rigby to Wilmot, 18 June 1763. 5 P. Lawson, *George Grenville* (Oxford, 1984), pp. 155–80. 6 PRONI T3019/4750, 4787, Wilmot to Hamilton, 15 Dec. 1763, Waite to Wilmot, 3 Feb. 1764.

With the collapse of Hamilton's schemes to build his own 'Castle following', the management of parliament continued in the hands of the undertakers for another session. The signs of this continuity were apparent from early on as a weakened administration was intimidated by John Ponsonby's refusal to include any reference to the Peace of Paris in the Commons' response to Northumberland's speech. The viceroy cravenly excused the Speaker, who was obviously not going to praise a treaty that his relatives (Bessborough and Devonshire) in England were opposing. In addition, Ponsonby may have been stressing his independence from Stone, as the Speaker had recently married a daughter of Lord Shannon. Instead of condemning Ponsonby's behaviour, the viceroy identified:

> … his good disposition in all other respects towards the King's service, and the ill-humour which the violent pressing of that point might have occasioned … satisfied his Excellency and others acquainted with the state of the country that it would be most imprudent to contend for more than appears in the addresses.[7]

The news that even those favourable to the Peace were loath to discuss it, since the treaty had not been laid before the Irish Commons, angered the ministers. Halifax told the viceroy that George III was surprised at Ponsonby's behaviour and angry that the addresses of both the Lords and Commons omitted any mention of the Peace.[8] The ministry's anger can be attributed to the fact that they had defended the treaty against the savage attacks of the *North Briton* and now had to defend themselves over the use of General Warrants to prosecute Wilkes and his printer. In comparison, Northumberland's problems must have seemed miniscule and his failure to confront the undertakers, infuriating.

Therefore the ministry lost no time in sending the addresses of the Westminster parliament to Northumberland to get him to emulate them. By December, Ponsonby did not oppose references to the Peace, in a Commons address, probably because the Whigs in England had given up that battle. But there was another challenge in the Commons to the address, which condemned the libels of the *North Briton* and thanked the king for the 'honourable and advantageous Peace.' The Patriots, especially Pery, Flood and Brownlow, fiercely attacked this attempt to have them sit in judgement over English quarrels, like 'puppets actuated from without', as William Harward put it. None of the opposition questioned whether libels had occurred, but questions were asked as to why this address had not been presented at the start of the session. Patriot MPs argued that the Peace could not be described as advantageous to Ireland, pointing to falling stock prices in England, which 'rather tended to confirm rather than destroy the [negative] opinion of the Peace.'[9]

7 Northumberland to Halifax, 7 Oct. 1763 in *CHOP*, i, pp. 314–7; PRONI D3312/9/30, Hatch to Waldo, 6 Oct. 1763.   8 PRONI T1060/8, Halifax to Northumberland, 22 Oct. 1763.   9 [Sir James Caldwell], *Debates relative to the affairs of Ireland in the years 1763 and 1764* (2 vols,

Supporters of the government and the treaty, who spoke in favour of the address, talked of a seditious opposition to the Peace and pointed out that Devonshire, Pitt and Legge had not voted against it. Francis Andrews defended Bedford's role in the negotiations, while a dependant of Stone, Sir William Mayne, asked the Patriots to compare the 1763 treaty to that of 1748 and ask which was more advantageous. Hely Hutchinson was more moderate, ambivalent even, about the address, but his attempt to get unanimity failed. Instead, Pery first moved for an adjournment of the discussion until January and then, for an amendment praising Chief Justice Pratt over the General Warrants decision.[10] Both were unsuccessful and the address was finally passed by a large majority, 142 votes to 30.[11] The viceroy insisted that he had always intended to get an this address through parliament, but had been waiting for the right opportunity. The size of the majority confirms that Ponsonby and his followers had supported the address and that only committed Patriots were in opposition.

These battles over the Peace of Paris reflect the longer-term developments in Ireland over the period of the Seven Years War. The growing importance of events in England, the hesitancy of a group of undertakers without a dominant leader and the constancy and widening interests of the Patriot opposition, were all factors in these debates. They should also be seen in their immediate context, where the administration was weakened by the worsening relationship between Northumberland and Hamilton and faced a restless parliament and unrest out-of-doors.[12]

The tentative management of the Commons was shown when MPs, once again, attacked pensions. This happened despite the announcement that George III would no longer grant pensions for life or a fixed term. Northumberland collapsed before this opposition, which the undertakers had refused to curb. Waite believed that the lack of any government leadership in the Commons was the cause of 'such riot, such opposition, such abuse of all pensions and pensioners ... [as would be hard] ... to describe. And Mr H[amilton] openeth not his mouth.'[13] The ministers refused to turn George III's promise on pensions into an address to calm the Commons or, as Grenville put it, give a 'voluntary concession' an 'appearance of force and constraint'. This lack of support from London pushed Northumberland into a closer reliance on Stone and Ponsonby but it did not ensure an easy ride for the Castle. Thus, by the middle of January, Waite was in

London, 1766), i, pp. 608, 618, 636–7, 645. 10 Waite later denied London newspaper reports that a portrait of the Chief Justice was going to be hung in the Guildhall, 'nor have I heard one syllable of any intention in the merchants of Cork to present him with his freedom of that city'; PRONI T3019/4797, Waite to Wilmot, 18 Feb. 1764. 11 PRONI T1060/8, Northumberland to Halifax, 20 Dec. 1763. 12 Hamilton's position was not helped by his very public affair with Lady Newtown, wife of the well-liked revenue commissioner; PRONI T3019/4809, Waite to Wilmot, 4 Mar. 1764. 13 PRONI T1060/8, Northumberland to Halifax, 20 Oct. 1763; PRONI T3019/4729, Waite to Wilmot, 23 Nov. 1763.

despair at the administration's position, telling Wilmot that 'this government never was so cowardly or so low as it is at present.'[14]

The under-secretary's despair was underlined by his concern about continuing and growing unrest, both in Dublin and beyond. In the summer of 1763 the Oakboy disturbances had rocked Ulster; riots in Dublin against silk manufacturers and linen merchants had brought trade to a standstill, while there were still occasional Whiteboy outrages in Munster and south Leinster. The Oakboys had overrun the south Ulster counties and Derry from July until early August, beginning in north Armagh, in protests of up to 10,000 against the county cess.[15] This predominantly Presbyterian unrest and the attacks on tithes and small dues paid to the established church, only increased government worries.[16] The trials afterwards were as much of a disaster for the authorities as the original response of the local magistrates had been. There was only one capital conviction in all the trials, as juries, usually Presbyterian in membership, would not indict on the charge of treason.[17] This did not aid the impression of a clampdown that the government was trying to give. The Oakboy violence was soon followed by economic riots in Dublin, over the employment of women and the prices offered by some linen merchants. Waite was very despondent about all the unrest with the 'spirit of tumult and disorder gone [so] far in this country as is hard to imagine and God knows how it will be quelled.'[18] MPs gloomily accepted John Gore's analysis that 'the treasonable insurrections, which have so frequently, of late, interrupted the public tranquillity in remote parts of the kingdom, have now reached the capital', but they were also at a loss to know what to do.[19]

The unrest in both Ulster and the capital and the continuing restiveness of parliament did nothing to convince Grenville that Northumberland had curbed the 'temper and spirit [of opposition] that has prevailed both in Great Britain and in Ireland.'[20] He was correct that, while the Irish parliament was subordinate, it was hardly compliant. Doubts about the intentions and stability of successive ministries, as well as the actions of viceroys and undertakers, had all undermined the government and encouraged the Patriots. The settlement, made in 1758, had clearly not produced a manageable state of Irish politics by 1764. This raises

---

14 Grenville to Northumberland, 28 Oct. 1763 in *Grenville Papers*, ii, pp. 147–8; PRONI T1060/8, Halifax to Northumberland, 26 Nov. 1763; PRONI T3019/4793, Waite to Wilmot, 10 Jan. 1764.   15 J.S. Donnelly, 'Hearts of Oak, Hearts of Steel', *Studia Hibernica*, xxi (1981), pp. 7–73; E. Magennis, 'A Presbyterian Insurrection?: Reconsidering the Hearts of Oak disturbances of July 1763', *IHS*, xxxi (1999), pp. 31–62.   16 *BNL*, 12 July 1763.   17 *The Respective Charges given to the Armagh Grand Jury at the Assizes of July 1763* (Dublin, 1763). 18 Waite also reported rumours of Oakboy emissaries were in Dublin, where stories abounded that an Act of Union was to be passed; PRONI T3019/4655, 4693, 4702, Waite to Wilmot, 23 July, 18 Aug., 6 Sep. 1763.   19 Caldwell, *Debates*, i, pp. 11–12.   20 Grenville to Northumberland, 28 Oct. 1763 in *Grenville Papers*, ii, p. 148.

questions about what alternatives of governance existed and whether these were seriously intended for use?

THE DEATHS OF STONE AND SHANNON

The viceroyalty of the shambolic, if popular, earl of Northumberland undoubtedly cast fresh doubts about and built upon previous frustration with the management of the Irish parliament. Thus historians see this period as one during which British policy towards Ireland began to change, specifically with the replacement of the undertakers. The historiographical debate about the end of the undertaker system is tied into the larger question of the importance of British ministerial policy for Irish history.[21] As the battle between Anglo-centric and Hiberno-centric histories, between revisionism and post-revisionism, has long been fought in other places, it is not the intention to duplicate those debates here. Suffice to say that the debates have created much more heat than light, in terms of explaining both the modes of governing Ireland and the making of British policy (in particular with regard to the eighteenth century). There is no doubt that British ministers in the mid-eighteenth century had a great influence on Irish politics when they felt the need, not only to draw up policy, but to act upon their musings. The distinction between the two is sometimes missed. Professor Thomas Bartlett made his feelings clear on this very point, most recently in 1992:

> British government itself was ill-equipped to formulate, let alone execute, policy ... None the less, in the mid 1760s the general opinion in British government circles was that a resident Lord Lieutenant should be appointed to Ireland, and indeed in 1766 a modest effort was made to make constant residence a condition of appointment. Nothing came of this; and no such condition was attached to Lord Townshend's appointment to the office in August 1767.[22]

In other words the gap between theory and practice, with regard to Irish policy made in London, could be very large.

But what of the consequences of the deaths of Stone and Shannon in December 1764? At the time, the irony of two longstanding rivals dying within a month of each other provoked most comment. As Pery told Robert Fitzgerald, Shannon

---

21 J.L. McCracken, 'The Irish viceroyalty, 1750–73', in H.A. Cronne, T.W. Moody and D.B. Quinn (eds), *Essays in British and Irish history in honour of James Eadie Todd* (London, 1949), pp. 152–68; T. Bartlett, 'The Townshend Viceroyalty, 1767–72', in Bartlett & Hayton (eds), *Penal Age*, pp. 88–112; M.J. Powell, 'The reform of the undertaker system: Anglo-Irish politics, 1750–67', *IHS*, xxxi (1998), pp. 19–36. 22 T. Bartlett, *The Fall and Rise of the Irish Nation: The Catholic Question, 1690–1830* (Dublin 1992), p. 73.

never 'had the satisfaction to hear of the other's departure, which it is thought both wished.' Pery then went on to speculate on what would happen next. Lord Chancellor Bowes expected to take one of the vacant lord justice places, 'though my private intelligence says it is not determined whether he is to be in government or not.' Lord Kildare was also under consideration for government, but Pery doubted whether 'his high spirit could brook' asking Northumberland and, thus, Lord Arran might be appointed.[23] There was no hint in this letter of any innovation in government policy. Nor was there in Northumberland's letter to John Ponsonby commiserating with him on the death of his fellow lords justices, as the viceroy had hoped to see the Shannon-Ponsonby marriage alliance deliver the political goods.[24]

However, ministers were considering change, as the viceroy's ill-health meant that he was unlikely to return to Ireland.[25] This is confirmed by the famous Grenville ministry cabinet meeting of 1 February 1765, where it was decided that the next viceroy to be appointed would be instructed to reside constantly in Ireland. Should the appointee have to visit England, he would leave a lord deputy, not lords justices behind, while in the meantime, Lord Chancellor Bowes was to join Ponsonby in that commission. There was some comment about the exclusion of Primate Robinson, though Waite caustically commented:

> Whither should the Church go but to the bible. Tho' I suppose at the end of our next session shall return to the old system of Primate, [Lord] Chancellor and Speaker.[26]

However, the long-term import of this decision was clear if it was implemented: the current system of governing Ireland was to be reformed. No decisions were taken about how resident viceroys would manage parliament, if indeed they were to do that differently, but the clock was potentially being turned back to the system of management in the 1690s.

Despite the importance of the decision, none of those present (and they included Bedford, Halifax and Northumberland), mentioned it in correspondence. It was perhaps more important at the time that Northumberland was not to return to Ireland.[27] Having established this, rumours began about who the

---

23 Pery to Fitzgerald, 31 Jan. 1765 in M.A. Hickson, 'Correspondence of the Knight of Kerry', *Old Kerry Records*, 2nd series (1874), p. 279.   24 PRONI Shannon papers, D2707/A2/2/1, Northumberland to Ponsonby, [19] Jan. 1765.   25 Monck Mason to Fitzgerald, 25 Dec. 1764 in Hickson, 'Knight of Kerry', p. 275.   26 Cabinet minutes of 1 Feb. 1765 in J.R.G. Tomlinson (ed.), *Additional Grenville Papers* (Manchester, 1965), p. 335; PRONI T3019/4962, 4966, Waite to Wilmot, 9, 14 Feb. 1765.   27 Only W.G. Hamilton seemed to believe that Grenville would send Northumberland back to Ireland and that, with Stone dead, he could play a management role in the Irish parliament: NLI 15,178, O'Hara papers, Hamilton to [ ], 18 Mar. 1766.

Grenville appointee might be.[28] Lord Weymouth was eventually appointed in May, as a concession to the Bedford faction in the ministry, and, to bestow favour on Lord Holland, his brother-in-law, Sir Charles Bunbury, was made chief secretary. Charles Jenkinson was clear that Grenville was 'evidently ashamed' of appointing Weymouth, but saw it as the price of holding his coalition together.[29] In Dublin, political circles were first surprised and then 'sat in judgement ... and we do not like him [Weymouth] ... We don't believe you can possibly send us such a man.' This reaction is understandable, given the rumours that a Chancery court decision had gone against Weymouth, to the tune of £150,000. The question of residency caused some comment, as a Vatican report noted, 'this arrangement will please the Irish greatly, as they have sought it for a long time.'[30]

Weymouth was never to get the chance to be a resident viceroy, as Grenville's ministry was dismissed not long after this.[31] George III had a strong aversion to his ministers, after a protracted battle over a Regency Bill, but seemed unable to get rid of an administration which had strong Commons backing. In May 1765 he asked Pitt to take office on a number of occasions, but to no avail. Then, later that month, there were rumours in Dublin that 'all those who were turned out for their connections with the Duke of Newcastle and the late Duke of Devonshire would have been turned in last week in the fracas'. Ponsonby was obviously delighted at such stories given his Whig connections.[32] The eventual replacement to the Grenville ministry, in July 1765, was an administration to be led by Cumberland, Newcastle and Rockingham, but not Pitt. Rigby was amazed at this outcome, what he called 'the Duke of Cumberland's political system grafted upon the Earl of Bute's stock', and he did not expect it to survive.[33] However, the ministry did survive and appointed the earl of Hertford, at his fourth time of asking for the position, as viceroy, with no mention of residency or lord deputies.[34]

In Ireland the response to all of these reshuffles, appointments and dismissals is perhaps best summed up by John Ponsonby. He wrote, somewhat wearily, to Anthony Foster in August 1765, lamenting that no viceroy seemed inclined or able to stay more than one session and get to know Ireland better. Given the circumstances:

28 The rivals for the viceroy's place were reported to be Lords Huntingdon, Hertford and Townshend; *FJ*, 16 Feb. 1765.   29 Walpole to Mann, 25 May 1765, in *Walpole Correspondence*, xxii, pp. 302–3; *Jenkinson Papers*, p. 372.   30 PRONI T3019/5013, 5016, Waite to Wilmot, 16, 18 May 1765; 'News from Brussels', 18 June 1765, in 'Nunziatura di Fiandra', *Collectanea Hibernica*, 11 (1968), p. 54.   31 PRONI T3019/5050, 5058, 5064, 5066, Wilmot to Cuninghame, 15 June, Rigby to Wilmot, 25 June, 4 July, Bunbury to Wilmot, 12 July 1765.   32 PRONI T3019/5031, 5052, Waite to Wilmot, 30 May, Rigby to Wilmot, 16 June 1765.   33 PRONI T3019/5065, Rigby to Wilmot, 7 July 1765.   34 Hertford to Walpole, 18 Jan. 1765, in Walpole Correspondence, xxxviii, pp. 491–2; PRONI T3019/5081, Hertford to the Lords Justices, 9 Aug. 1765; PRO S.P.63/424, George III to Hertford, 9 Aug. 1765; Burke to O'Hara, 9 July 1765, in Hoffmann, *New York Agent*, p. 318.

> What matter's it to us who are ministers in England? Let us stick to our
> own circle and manage our own little game as well as we can.[35]

Kildare's attitude was more in keeping with his proud nature. Thwarted once
more of the prize of the lord lieutenancy by Weymouth's appointment, he wrote to
Holland, Grenville and Sandwich in June to tell them of his decision to resign all
his offices. The reason he gave Holland was his anger at the likes of Lord
Drogheda receiving military promotions while he struggled to get any recommendations accepted. Shannon was less concerned with the changes than he was
about their consequences. As the rumours of Kildare's resignation spread he
hoped to replace the earl and wrote 'from the fate of this application I may form
my judgement of what I am to expect and on what terms I am to be with the
Castle.'[36]

There is a danger in recounting these reactions, together with the chaotic
ministerial changes of 1765, that historians miss the importance of the Grenville
cabinet meeting of 1 February. The deaths of Stone and Shannon in December
1764, in retrospect, were a golden opportunity to deal with the recurring problem
of an unreliable system of political management. Looking back, the idea of taking
management into the Castle and ending the use of undertakers, the reform of the
revenue service to centralise control of that, and the appointment of resident viceroys and chief secretaries to accomplish these tasks, seems obvious.[37] And yet,
between 1765 and 1772, these changes were wrought only with much reluctance
in London and after several embarrassing management failures in Dublin. This
prompts the question whether policy created management expedients or *vice
versa*?

Given all of this speculation and supposition about the long-term reform
trends, as against the importance of accident and personality, it is important to
draw out some points. The deaths of the two leading Irish government figures in
December 1764 made a huge difference to Irish politics in the succeeding period.
First, the key undertakers for the previous thirty years had disappeared. Second,
the position was more comparable to 1729 than to 1733. In the former year, there
was no obvious successor to William Conolly as both Speaker of the Commons
and chief government undertaker. Therefore, several Castle officials acted as parliamentary managers in the next two sessions. After 1733, Henry Boyle managed

---

35 PRONI Foster-Masserene papers D562/1757, Ponsonby to Foster, 15 Aug. 1765.
36 Kildare to Grenville, 7 June 1765, in *Grenville Papers*, ii, p. 279; BL Add. Mss. 51386, f.82,
Kildare to Holland, 6 June 1765; PRONI D2707/A2/3/1, Shannon to Dennis, 11 June 1765.
37 In 1778, one traveller commented that had Stone lived, 'of course business would have been
conducted in its usual way ... [so] that the perpetual residence of viceroys would not have been
thought necessary'; T. Campbell, *A Philosophical Survey of the South of Ireland* (Dublin, 1778),
p. 56.

to fill Conolly's shoes. Now, in 1765, the Castle had the prospect of talented managers like Tisdall, Hely Hutchinson and Malone (none with any substantial borough interest) and a Speaker, John Ponsonby, with the numbers to undertake government business, but lacking reliable management ability. Finally, the demands of government increased just at the time when its ability to control the Commons was at a low ebb. All of this became clear during the Hertford vice-royalty and the decisions taken during the Townshend years to dispense with the undertakers became all the easier to make.

HERTFORD AND IRELAND

On the face of it, the earl of Hertford was a perfect choice for viceroy. He owned a huge estate in Antrim, already had an established diplomatic career behind him and, as Charlemont recorded in his memoirs, 'it might well be supposed that even his avarice, the vice most objected to him, would operate in his favour, and that he would be a friend to the soil from which he drew his beloved wealth.'[38] Given his connection with a ministry in which Lord Bessborough also had a post, it was expected that Hertford would work well with Ponsonby and therefore command a large majority in the Commons. As Charles O'Hara told Burke, 'Lord Hertford will find us in good humour with him.'[39]

Hertford had three immediate obstacles to overcome. First, and most transient, was the riot in Dublin by soldiers stationed there, who broke into Newgate and freed some comrades, jailed for earlier disturbances.[40] The lords justices called in another regiment to restore control and bring the ringleaders in Dublin's garrison to justice. Ponsonby was worried that ministers would not approve of their actions and looked to Hertford for backing. This is not altogether surprising, as other voices in the Castle had told of the lords justices being ready to support the demand to remove the existing garrison, as a way of placating the Dublin crowd.[41] The behaviour of the soldiers, though no-one was killed or seriously injured, raised questions of military discipline and expenditure, that the lords justices were keen to keep out of parliament and thus, the court martials were dealt with as quickly as possible.[42]

The second problem was much less amenable to a quick fix. Once more the Irish economy was in recession, through a combination of problems in trade (due to the American non-importation campaign), a general economic downturn and a poor harvest in 1765. These were not things that a new viceroy could solve but the

---

38 *Charlemont Mss*, i, p. 22.   39 O'Hara to Burke, 19 July 1765, in Hoffmann (ed.), *New York Agent*, pp. 321–2.   40 *FJ*, 17, 20 Aug. 1765; *Gentleman's Magazine*, Sept. 1765.   41 PRONI T3019/5085, 5092, 5100, Ponsonby to Wilmot, 14 Aug., Meredyth to Wilmot, 29 Aug., Waite to Wilmot, 7 Sept. 1765.   42 *FJ*, 10, 14, 17, 24 Sept. 1765.

economic problems did raise one political difficulty for Hertford. In Dublin, the rising unemployment among the weavers led to calls for support of native manufactures.[43] Unsurprisingly, warnings were soon coming to the new viceroy, who was a noted Francophile and just coming back from ambassadorial duties in Paris, not to flaunt French goods on his entrance into Dublin. Waite warned that the weavers of the Coombe might riot and that Hertford should leave the yacht 'in an Irish coat, if of rateen so much the better'. Wilmot responded to say that the new viceroy would order liveries for his household in Dublin and that Lady Hertford had expressed 'her resolution to encourage to the utmost of her power, the trade and manufactures of Ireland.' Whatever the countess' intentions may have been, the viceroy was embarrassed at having to woo the Dublin crowd in this way.[44] Economic problems would continue to dog the viceroy during his solitary session and give rise to further attempts to gain the approval of the Irish public.

The third problem was the ever-present one of parliamentary management. Hertford had to balance his wish to reward his own family and followers, with the need to engage support in the Irish Commons. This, as ever, was not easy. The new viceroy made his eldest son, the inexperienced Lord Beauchamp, his chief secretary and followed this by filling the first vacancy on the bishop's bench (in Down and Connor) with his chaplain, James Traill. He noted to Walpole that 'a few such opportunities will satisfy me', though not everyone agreed and there was grumbling about Hertford's distribution of patronage.[45] The viceroy had to be careful, as he still needed managers in the Commons to assist his son. He soon settled on Hely Hutchinson and John Gore, to be appointed lord chief justice of the King's Bench.[46] With these choices, the attorney general, Philip Tisdall, and the Provost, Francis Andrews, appeared to be out of favour, though Hertford did promise Tisdall that he would secure the next Revenue Board place for Bellingham Boyle.[47] On top of this, the favourable opinion of Hertford, expressed by Charlemont, seemed to herald no open warfare from Flood, while Pery was also considering his support for an 'administration on fair principles.'[48]

Despite all the good signs, Waite's analysis of the forthcoming session was thus:

43 PRONI O'Hara papers, T2812/19, 'O'Hara's economic survey of Co. Sligo from 1700'; FJ, 23 Feb. 1765 noted the opening of the Irish Silk Warehouse against the background of trade depression.   44 PRONI T3019/5110, 5126, 5128, Waite to Wilmot [10–16], 24 Sept, Wilmot to Ponsonby, 3 Oct. 1765; Hertford to Walpole, 10 Oct. 1765, in *Walpole Correspondence*, xxxix, pp. 18–21.   45 Hertford to Walpole, 10 Oct. 1765, in *Walpole Correspondence*, xxxix, pp. 18–21; PRONI T3019/5108, Cavendish to Wilmot, 10 Sep. 1765.   46 Hutchinson to Jephson, 17 Sept. 1765, in *Donoughmore Mss.*, p. 257; F. Plowden, *An Historical Review of the State of Ireland* (3 vols, Dublin, 1805), ii, p. 90.   47 PRONI T3019/5178, Waite to Wilmot, 6 Feb. 1766.   48 PRONI Emly papers, T3087/1/35–6, Meredith to Pery, 5 Oct. 1765, Hertford to Andrews, [1765].

The Speaker's members are reported to be very great: But I much doubt whether Lord Shannon will join them unless he succeeds to the Ordnance. People here are vastly affected to my Lord Hertford, but I am afraid we shall have a very troubled winter … Lord Kildare is preparing for hostilities and will be as active as his power will allow in giving us all kinds of disturbances.[49]

Despite the worries about Lord Kildare, the parliamentary session, at first, seemed to justify Hertford's optimism. The public accounts were analysed with the same assiduity as always, but MPs turned to drawing up the money bills with no mention of pension lists. Henry Flood was the sole thorn in the government's side. In November 1765, he began with an attack on the viceroy's address, which had indeed failed to deliver on any of the Patriot expectations.[50] However, with Pery giving Hertford the benefit of the doubt and Kildare's friends supporting government (whatever about the earl's private thoughts), the Patriot forces were reduced to around ten in the first month of the session.[51] Waite's reports comment on 'hostile appearances' in November and early December, but mention that, even when the 'very unpopular question' of pensions was finally raised, the Castle had a majority. His explanation, supported by Archbishop Ryder, was that 'every man and measure bows down to the superior power of the Speaker.'[52] Even the visit of Rigby to Dublin, which was expected to be an occasion of mischief-making, did not ruffle the calm.[53]

However, there were several difficulties which needed more than Ponsonby's support to be overcome. After Flood had uncovered the increasing disposal of secret service monies during peacetime, he pressed the Commons to censure the rise. Though MPs did not support some form of censure, the threat of scrutiny led Hertford to order that several Castle salaries should, in future, be taken from the concordatum fund. This was a more legitimate source of funds, but Waite was worried that the concession would open a 'fresh field for opposition to range in and distress government.'[54] According to O'Hara, the problem for the Castle was that, although Ponsonby had superior numbers, he did not have the ability to manage parliament:

---

49 PRONI T3019/5100, Waite to Wilmot, 7 Sept. 1765; Hertford to Walpole, 10 Oct. 1765, in *Walpole Correspondence*, xxxix, pp. 18–21. 50 Birr Castle, Rosse Papers, F/21, 'Speech on the Address by Henry Flood' [Oct. 1765]. 51 Hertford to Walpole, 1 Nov. 1765, in *Walpole Correspondence*, xxxix, pp. 25–8; Walsh to Townshend, 5 June 1766, in *HMC Townshend Mss.* (London, 1887), p. 402; PRONI T3087/1/37, Hertford to [Pery], 1 Nov. 1765. 52 *CJI*, xiv, pp. 14, 81, 97; PRONI T3019/5130–2, 5140, 5144, Waite to Wilmot, 6, 12, 21 Nov., 7 Dec., Ryder to Wilmot, 17 Dec. 1765. 53 Lady Hertford to Walpole, 16 Dec. 1765, in *Walpole Correspondence*, xxxix, pp. 36–8. 54 PRONI T3019/5135, Waite to Wilmot, 28 Nov. 1765.

[Ponsonby] never governed himself while the Primate governed, [and] must now from political connections have the lead.[55]

The secret service monies were a small problem, however, when compared to the memorial presented to MPs with the aim of assisting Irish sugar merchants. The petition from 103 Dublin merchants asked for aid for their refining industry (which employed 4,000 families). They complained about the extra costs and duties incurred because Irish merchants could not import the raw sugar from the West Indies under the Navigation Acts. There was no demand to change trade regulations, but there was a request for a bounty to assist the merchants. Given the economic problems and also their dislike of the trade restrictions, some MPs suggested an additional duty on English sugars being imported into Ireland. Hertford sought to avoid this kind of protectionism, which he knew would outrage London, but he asked Conway for a 'mark of attention' for the merchants.[56] However, his request was sharply rejected by the Board of Trade and this provoked Pery to report from a Commons committee, with a resolution asking for the direct importation of sugar into Ireland. Ponsonby and government managers were able, at this point, to refer that resolution and report to another committee, from where it never emerged again.[57] Against the background of recession, Hertford was concerned to get some concession for the sugar merchants. Pery and others, like O'Hara and Edmund Burke, concentrated more on creating a fairer system of trade regulations, which would not be as productive of constitutional clashes.[58]

The economic problems and bad harvest produced the threat of food shortages in the winter of 1765. The Commons responded, following the lead of Pery, by passing two bills, one banning the exports of corn and the other prohibiting the use of corn in distilling. These were sent to London in early December, with the urging that they be passed quickly, before merchants sought to beat the export ban and caused dearth that way.[59] What should have been a triumph for the Castle turned into a fiasco, when Flood identified amendments to the corn bill and attacked the privy council for its actions.[60] The Castle was defeated on two motions trying to adjourn scrutiny of the bills, by 60 votes to 17 and 31 votes to 8, though the Corn Bill was passed, on 24 December, by 39 votes to 15. Andrews

---

55 Sheffield City Libraries, Wentworth-Woodhouse Muniments, Burke papers, O'Hara to Burke, 22 Nov. 1765. 56 PRO S.P.63/424, 'The state of the manufacture of refining sugar ... humbly submitted to the Earl of Hertford', Hertford to Conway, 30 Nov. 1765. 57 PRO S.P.63/424, 'Report of the Lord Commissioners of Trade ...' [Dec. 1765]; *CJI*, xiv, pp. 192–5. 58 Burke to O'Hara, 1, 3 Mar., 24 May 1766, O'Hara to Burke, 10 Mar. 1766, in Hoffmann (ed.), *New York Agent*, pp. 331–3, 349–51, 334–8. 59 *CJI*, xiv, p. 114; PRO S.P.63/424, Hertford to Conway, 1, 4 Dec. 1765; PRONI T3019/5137–9, Waite to Wilmot, 1, 3, 5 Dec. 1765. 60 C. Lucas, *A First Address to the Right Honourable Lord Mayor of Dublin* (Dublin, 1766); idem., *A Second Address ...* (Dublin, 1766); idem., *A Third Address ...* (Dublin, 1766).

accused both Beauchamp and Hutchinson of abdicating their management responsibilities. According to Rigby, the Provost was the sole government speaker 'defending the amendment and, in so doing, he thought he was defending both the English and Irish governments.'[61]

Before these defeats for his administration, Hertford had confidently reported that Beauchamp 'is getting praise and reputation very fast'. O'Hara was more circumspect, but reported that, while 'business goes on in a heavy entangled way, our confidence in our Lord Lieutenant keeps us all of one side.'[62] What the corn bill showed was that the government's management of the Commons was by no means unchallangeable, particularly if the right financial or constitutional point arose for the Patriots. Flood, Lucas and Sir William Osborne had very little strength, until a thin Commons attendance and the crucial abdication of Hutchinson had allowed them to land some punches. However, even the Lords was not immune to these feelings, as four peers, led by Charlemont and Tyrone, signed a protest after they were defeated 14 votes to 4 in an attempt to block the corn bill.[63]

Despite this activity, there was talk, by January 1766, that Flood, having dined at the Castle with Hertford, was preparing to accept government office, due to the futility of opposition.[64] One major factor in this feeling of hopelessness, if indeed it existed, was the relatively easy passage of the supplies, by late November. The expenditure was estimated at a lower figure than for 1763–5 and a smaller biennial supply of £1,092,000 was granted. Savings had been made in both the ordnance and the civil list and over £60,000 had been clawed back in military expenditure, while there was also a desire among MPs to curb the grants of money for projects, especially those 'for the encouragement of private undertakings'. With such financial rectitude the Commons was able to grant Ponsonby an increase of £2,000 per session.[65] Given this success, Lord Chancellor Bowes was prepared, in early January, to give Hertford a qualified approval. The reason for the relatively easy passage of government business was quite simple:

> The Speaker's friends are more in number than could be expected, the cement by which they are connected will render them useful to government or the contrary.

Bowes conceded that the accounts of the barracks and ordnance might cause future difficulties, while the 'exhorbitant' public grants still had to be tackled despite the expressions of rectitude. These grants had, in the previous fifteen

61 *CJI*, xiv, pp. 149–50; PRONI T3019/5149, Rigby to Wilmot, 29 Dec. 1765.   62 Hertford to Walpole, 20 Dec. 1765, in *Walpole Correspondence*, xxxix, pp. 39–41; PRONI T2812/15/3, O'Hara to O'Hara, 10 Dec. 1765.   63 *CJI*, xiv, pp. 359–60.   64 NLI, Ms. 1469, Dinner lists for the Earl of Hertford, 1765–6.   65 *CJI*, xiv, pp. 109–13, 126–30, 293–7.

years, eaten up more money (around £100,000 every two years) than the national debt, but Bowes conceded the need for 'an interval to consider what ought or can be done.'[66] The newspapers carried a report on 28 December that a Commons committee, headed by prominent Patriots, would investigate the spending of parliamentary grants. Though the committee did not come to any conclusions, it had the embarrassing potential to either increase the amounts that government spent on the inland navigations, piers and so on, or to identify the worst culprits who had left money lying in the Treasury that should have been spent. One culprit was John Ponsonby, who had left £8,000 in the Treasury, that had been granted to the Dublin committee for widening streets back in 1764, because no decision had been made on competing plans. Little wonder that many were relieved when the Commons did not scrutinise too much.[67]

After the Christmas adjournment the Patriots made few advances, but the government's managers began to look increasingly prone to blundering. Hutchinson and Beauchamp seemed unable to manage the Commons, especially as the more traditional defenders of the Castle, Tisdall and Andrews, took a back seat.[68] This did not mean that government business was threatened, but the Patriot legislative agenda (septennial, militia and habeas corpus bills) got more notice than they should have.[69] The viceroy complained of Lucas and 'ungrateful spirits', but noted his powerful majority and due to this 'I feel less of them [the Patriots] than any of my predecessors.'[70] However, the Hertford administration proved less sound than previous ones, for example, in defending Poynings' Law. In late January 1766, Bowes was worried by the credence allowed to Pery's 'wild scheme' to send a Commons' representative over with bills to London, to explain the 'sense' of these to the privy council there. Bowes had been told by Beauchamp that this idea came from the 'miscarriage of many public bills through lack of such information.' In his eyes, this was an evasive explanation and he had told Hertford that the viceroy and Irish privy council 'were the constitutional informers and to them alone credit could be given.' Because of this intractability, Hertford chose to ignore Bowes' demand, in the Irish privy council, to reject the habeas corpus bill 'on just, rational and legal principles'. According to the Lord Chancellor, to reverse this position would 'reflect on past governments and strengthen the unjustifiable surmises of the evil intentions of English government to this country.'[71]

66 PRONI T3019/5159, Bowes to Wilmot, 2 Jan. 1766. 67 *FJ*, 28 Dec. 1765; PRONI T3019/5089, Ponsonby to Wilmot, 24 Aug. 1765. The figures for 'public monies' are to be found in *CJI*, xiv, pp. 109–13. 68 PRONI T2812/15/7, O'Hara to O'Hara, 11 Feb. [1766]. 69 For the militia bill see Flood to Charlemont, 27 Mar. 1766, *Charlemont Mss.*, i, pp. 279–80; *CJI*, xiv, p. 222. 70 Hertford to Walpole, 13 Jan. 1766, in *Walpole Correspondence*, xxxix, pp. 44–6. 71 PRONI T3019/5170, Bowes to Wilmot, 30 Jan. 1766.

The actions of the Castle and its chief undertaker, Ponsonby, over Poynings' Law and the septennial bill, fully justified Bowes' fears. On the first a Patriot, Lucius O'Brien, attempted, on 24 January, to pass a Commons resolution curbing the powers of the privy council. The management of the resolution was bungled by Ponsonby, until Hutchinson intervened to give the Castle a narrow escape.[72] Then, when the septennial bill was passed from the Commons to the privy council, in late January, Waite described how Archbishop Robinson, Bowes, Gore and Tisdall had spoken against the bill, while Beauchamp and Hutchinson had voted with the majority. Waite said that Ponsonby had spoken so strongly against the bill 'that I wonder it was suffered to pass the House of Commons.'[73] The Irish political elite was still deeply divided over the question of more frequent elections. Some borough patrons and MPs, like Ponsonby and Lord Shannon, were against the measure because of self-interest or for fear of the rising expense of elections and the heightened atmosphere that had been seen in 1761. Others, including Lords Kildare and Tyrone, supported the measure as a boost to the constitution and to public spirit. Because of such divisions in Ireland, the bill's supporters were pessimistic of wrenching the measure from ministerial hands.[74]

Worse was to follow for the standing of the Castle, in April 1766, as MPs grew anxious for the return of the septennial bill. Rumours began to circulate that Ponsonby had used his influence with Lord Bessborough to have the bill dropped in London, while Hertford was seen as being less than active in securing the bill's return.[75] In the Commons, Flood demanded a list of bills sent to London and then moved an address, asking Hertford to seek the return of the septennial bill. Hertford's reply was evasive, saying that he had done his best but that the bill was unlikely to be returned. In despair, the Patriots pressed, on 30 April, for an address to the king, asking for a septennial bill for Ireland, as frequent elections were allowed throughout the British empire.[76] The address was defeated after a division of 117 votes to 29, which revealed the Patriots' true strength at this time. Then, on 5 May, in a twist which amazed several correspondents, Ponsonby backed a motion by Flood to draw up a fresh address to George III. The Castle lost a further three divisions, before the address was drawn up and amended, to make it innocuous, by 80 votes to 62. Some of Hertford's enemies were worried that he 'may communicate part of his terror to his brother [Conway], who is not the most determined minister.'[77] Therefore, once again, the government of Ireland might be discredited.

72 O'Hara to Burke, 25 Jan. 1766, in Hoffmann (ed.), *New York Agent*, pp. 330–1. 73 *CJI*, xiv, p. 180; PRONI T3019/5178, Waite to Wilmot, 6 Feb. 1766. 74 NLI O'Neill papers, Ms. 21293, Maxwell to O'Neill, 21 Apr. 1766. 75 *FJ*, 12, 29 Apr. 1766. 76 *CJI*, xiv, pp. 224, 228–30. 77 Ibid., xiv, pp. 231–3; PRONI Gosford papers, D1606/1/46, Rigby to Acheson, 13 May 1766.

The immediate explanation for the reversal was that Ponsonby had either become confused or 'was frightened or bullied into a support of the opposition.'[78] Soon after this, Hertford told Walpole that Ponsonby had come to the Castle to beg the viceroy's forgiveness. The granting of this was made more easy, as further Patriot attempts to look into the powers of the Irish privy council had been 'beat[en] with disgrace and contempt.' Casting off any 'weak fit', Ponsonby had marshalled his forces behind the Castle and the opposition had lost two divisions by 99 votes to 43 and 106 to 35.[79] The Speaker's reputation, however, had been badly damaged by the management of the septennial bill and the earlier episode, in March, when Pery had been allowed to attack the Irish privy council. After Pery's attack, O'Hara had described the Commons as 'ready for a caning out', while Waite asked 'what is to become of Mr Speaker?'[80] Ponsonby's second desertion of the government side was described as 'unmanly, as well as unpolitic', while he was also bitterly attacked by the Patriots for vacillation.[81]

Such conduct cast question marks over his role as both Speaker and chief undertaker. Charlemont described him as having the 'social qualities for making a party but, from his want of understanding and political courage, ill-qualified to conduct or retain it.' Ponsonby was said to have 'acknowledged his error [more] like a school-boy than in a manner befitting a director of an House of Commons, or to speak more correctly the manager of a party.' This, it was said, could cause his downfall.[82] Hertford concluded, somewhat pompously, that he had 'carried him [Ponsonby] uniformly through the session against his nature' but had been unable to prevent him declaring against the Castle on this popular point.[83] Despite such doubts about the Speaker's abilities, Hertford sailed out of Dublin in June 1766, leaving Ponsonby and Bowes accompanied in the lords justices' commission by his new son-in-law, Lord Drogheda.[84]

HERTFORD'S REPUTATION

Whatever about the Speaker, Hertford's reputation after the 1765–6 session was somewhat tarnished. On the positive side, the supplies had been secured with

78 Sheffield City Library, Rockingham papers, Meredith to [   ], 6 May 1766; PRONI T3019/5229, Waite to Wilmot, 8 May 1766. 79 Hertford to Walpole, 10 May 1766, in *Walpole Correspondence*, xxxix, pp. 67–8. 80 *CJI*, xiv, pp. 195–9; O'Hara to Burke, 10 Mar. 1766, in Hoffman (ed.), New York Agent, pp. 334–8; PRONI T3019/5191, Waite to Wilmot, 5 Mar. 1766; PRONI T2812/15/9, O'Hara to O'Hara, 8 Mar. 1766. 81 For Dublin addresses calling for a short money bill if the septennial bill was not returned for the next session, see *FJ*, 17, 20 May 1766; 'News from Brussels', 10 June 1766, in 'Nunziatura di Fiandra', *Collectanea Hibernica*, 11 (1968), pp. 55–6. 82 *Charlemont Mss.*, i, p. 39; Sheffield City Library, Rockingham papers, Meredith to [   ], 15 May 1766. 83 Hertford to Walpole, 21 May 1766, in *Walpole Correspondence*, xxxix, pp. 70–1. 84 PRO S.P.63/424, Hertford to Richmond, 7, 11 June 1766.

little difficulty and thus the possibility was raised once more of augmenting the army from 12,000 forces to 16,000. Waite remarked in February 1766 that a second vote of £150,000 would be needed for the extra 4,000 men and, after the Commons had already voted £100,000 to the government, 'it will be a very unpopular measure and go down very much against our stomachs.'[85] In the event, the fact that the ministry in London was unable to decide what to do about repealing the limiting act, from William III's time, meant that any augmentation was put off until the next session of 1767–8.[86] Thus, Hertford was able to escape Ireland without having to introduce anything faintly controversial in terms of legislation or additional duties.

The other problem, which might have caused Hertford's reputation great difficulties, was the Whiteboy disturbances. He had referred to the 'insurrections' in Munster, in his opening address to parliament and avoided clashes with the Irish Protestant elite, like Halifax had experienced in 1762. Henry Flood criticised the viceroy for raising this issue in his address, because he argued that repressive government, not those Catholics 'goaded into greater resistance', was a greater danger to the constitution of Ireland.[87] However, Flood was not in tune with the views of most MPs in 1765–66, as addresses from various Dublin guilds and county grand juries thanked Lord Carrick for putting down the disturbances and congratulated those MPs (Flood and other Patriots among them) who had defended the rights of Protestants in the quarterage disputes. In December 1765, MPs passed a bill to charge an entire barony for any disturbances within its boundaries.[88] In reality, Hertford chose to let events take their own course in Munster and Leinster, up to and including the judicial murder of Nicholas Sheehy. Burke's desire for an end to the 'detestable plot mongering' fell on deaf ears during this viceroyalty.[89]

Given this non-intervention on an issue so close to the hearts of many Irish Protestants and his ability to evade onerous tax increases for an augmentation of the army, Hertford must have left Ireland pleased with his experience. Indeed, he had other reasons to feel content, as he had married two of his daughters to rising Irish politicians. His eldest daughter became Lady Drogheda in February 1766, while another married Robert Stewart and became the mother of Lord Castlereagh. Both husbands, especially Lord Drogheda, were suitable and likely to provide strength to the Conway electoral interest in Ulster.[90] The Irish sojourn

85 PRONI T3019/5187, Waite to Wilmot, 22 Feb. 1766. 86 PRONI Grafton papers, T2959/2/2, Conway to Grafton, 7 Apr. 1766. 87 Birr Castle, F/21, 'Speech on the address by Henry Flood', [Oct. 1765]. 88 *FJ*, 28 Dec. 1765; *BNL*, 14 May, 10 June 1766; *CJI*, xiv, pp. 147–8, 185, 229; O'Hara to Burke, 18, 20 Mar. 1766, in Hoffmann (ed.), *New York Agent*, pp. 339–41. 89 This was especially true as London was 'all in a blaze' with Whiteboy stories: Burke to O'Hara, 24 May 1766, in Hoffman (ed.), *New York Agent*, pp. 350–1. 90 Hertford to Walpole, 4 Feb. 1766, in *Walpole Correspondence*, xxxix, pp. 51–2; PRONI T3019/5179, Cavendish to Wilmot, 8 Feb. 1766.

was certainly a profitable one for Hertford and his family, as he had provided for two of his sons, one as Constable of Dublin Castle and another with an exchequer sinecure worth £2,000 per annum. These actions caused some rancour, as Lady Holland contemptuously dismissed the family's avarice and Charles O'Hara asked 'how many sons has he [Hertford], that we may be able to compute when we of this country may hope to get anything.'[91] Rigby's venomous attack on Hertford was hypocritical (given his own place-seeking) but memorable:

> What with sons and daughters and boroughs and employments of all kinds, I never heard of such a trading voyage as his Lordship's has proved.[92]

However, a profitable winter for the lord lieutenant potentially endangered any future management by the same viceroy.[93] There was also some doubt, from January 1766, whether Lady Hertford would have tolerated another Dublin winter season, especially as opposition politics had deprived her of the only company she deemed cultured enough (Lady Kildare and Lord Charlemont).[94] If Hertford was to return, he also needed to mend fences with Tisdall, who was quite marginalised by the end of the session. He had supported Hertford on the promise of the next Revenue Board vacancy for Bellingham Boyle but when, in February 1766, the deceased Sir Richard Cox was replaced by an English appointee of Lord Rockingham's, Tisdall was furious. He fired a warning shot across the Castle's bows by technically supporting Flood's militia bill and thus embarrassing Hutchinson.[95] However, Hertford did not learn from this and managed, by the autumn of 1766, to have utterly alienated Tisdall by granting Hutchinson the reversion to his office of secretary of state and refusing to increase Boyle's pension, as some compensation.[96] This was far from good management for the future.

Public opinion, if taken from the newspapers, was not altogether kind to Hertford either. Much of this has to do with the inflated expectations of a 'Patriot

---

91 Lady Holland to Lady Kildare, 20 Feb. 1766, in *Leinster Correspondence*, i, p. 436; O'Hara to Burke, 14 Aug. 1766, in Hoffman (ed.), *New York Agent*, p. 356.   **92** Rigby to Bedford, 25 Sep. 1766, in *Bedford Correspondence*, iii, pp. 344–6.   **93** For the appointment of new privy councillors (Brinsley Butler, Sir William Mayne and Sir William Brownlow), new peerages and pensions see PRO S.P.63/424, Conway to Hertford, 1, 27 Dec. 1765; *CHOP*, iii, pp. 141–6.   **94** Lady Hertford to Walpole, 20 Jan. 1766, in *Walpole Correspondence*, xxxix, pp. 47–50.   **95** PRONI T3019/5192, 5196, Waite to Wilmot, 8 Mar., La Billiere to Wilmot, 11 Mar. 1766; Flood to Charlemont, 27 Mar. 1766, in *Charlemont Mss.*, i, pp. 279–80.   **96** BL Egerton Ms. 3260, ff.11–22, Tisdall, to Hertford, 28 Aug., 6 Sep., 4 Oct, Hertford to Tisdall, 27 Sep. , [post 4] Oct. 1766. Tisdall was not the only one outraged by Hertford's partiality and also the dominance of Ponsonby at the Revenue Board, all of which promised great discontent: Leland to Charlemont, 11 Mar. 1766, in *Charlemont Mss.*, i, pp. 278–9; PRONI Fitzgerald papers, Mic.639/2/4, Fitzgerald to Day, 3 Apr. 1766.

Chief Governor' that were circulating in the autumn of 1765, something akin to the welcome for Chesterfield in 1745.[97] The *Belfast News-Letter* was less critical, perhaps due to Hertford's local links, his reputed plans to build a house at Lisburn and his assistance in times of dearth. To emphasise this localism, the viceroy visited the north-east in April 1766 and was wined, dined and cheered in Belfast, where he was toasted as a Patriot in expectation of the return of the septennial bill.[98] But it was the failure to secure the latter that damaged Hertford's reputation, at least in the eyes of correspondents in the *Freeman's Journal*. May and June 1766 saw a debate on the viceroyalty, begun by 'Philopolis':

> [Hertford] has promoted, to the utmost of his power, every bill for the encouragement and advantage of this kingdom, and particularly that favourite bill which, for some time past, hath been so much the object of national desire, and the failure of which cannot, without the most extreme ingratitude, as well as injustice, be attributed to him.

The debate continued as others attacked this defence, including 'Paddy Pimlico', who called Hertford's defenders 'Court Querists', and 'Publicola', who launched a defence of Patriot MPs as the real promoters of improvement. Further additions to the debate tried to compare Hertford to the likes of Bedford and Halifax (against whom he measured up well) and Chesterfield and Northumberland (he did not do so well here). On balance, there was an air of disappointment with the present viceroy due, mainly, to the failure of the septennial bill.[99]

The view from veteran administrators was even less flattering to Hertford. His son was dismissed as a shambolic chief secretary who was far too ready to bend to popularity and 'without much knowledge of business or the world'.[100] Waite also gave the impression that Lord Hertford had bought his way out of unpopularity by granting several bounties late in the session, for the export of corn and the encouragement of tillage, which 'set him right again in the opinion and affection of the people.' This sort of conduct, though hardly unique, led Wilmot to bitterly conclude:

> The Spaniards would certainly at the long run find great inconveniences, if they make it a rule to appoint natives of Mexico to be viceroys of that country.[101]

---

97 *FJ*, 5, 19 Aug. 1765; *An Account of Ireland, the Mad Woman* (Dublin, 1745). This last, published by Lucas' printer James Esdall, lamented the death of Swift but praised Chesterfield as a 'hunter of public robbers', (p. 12).   **98** *BNL*, 18 Apr.1766.   **99** *FJ*, 24, 27 May, 3, 7, 10, 14 June 1766.   **100** PRONI T3019/5187, 5189, 5249, Waite to Wilmot, 22 Feb., 1 Mar., 10 June 1766.   **101** *BNL*, 16 May, 10, 17 June 1766; PRONI T3019/5249, 5178, Waite to Wilmot, 10 June, Memorandum of Wilmot, 12 Feb. 1766.

A former chief secretary, Sackville, angrily reported the behaviour of both Hertford and Ponsonby to an army colleague. The Speaker, in particular, deserved censure for his playing 'the old game of dropping in questions where popularity might be lost' and Sackville wondered:

> How surprised such people would be if they were treated with that degree of severity which their conduct naturally calls for, but indeed the lenity of government sets everything afloat in that kingdom.[102]

Given Sackville's experiences in Ireland in the late 1730s and then during the Money Bill crisis his disillusionment was hardly surprising. The unpredictable parliamentary management of the 1750s had settled into a predictable unreliability after the deaths of Stone and Shannon in December 1764. An era had come to an end, but there still seemed little sign of a 'new system of government' for Ireland.[103]

102 Sackville to Irwin, 27 June 1766, in *Stopford-Sackville Mss.*, i, pp. 112–13. 103 PRONI T3019/5249, Memorandum of Wilmot, 12 Feb. 1766.

Conclusion

By the end of the 1760s Ireland was well on its way to acquiring new systems of government and political management. Historians have, as pointed out above, debated the whys, whens and wherefores of this change, but the main consequences were three-fold. First, the viceroy was expected to reside permanently in Ireland. Second, arising from the first point, the input into government of the undertakers, as lords justices, had come to an end. Third, the viceroy, and chief secretary, were expected by ministers to manage the Irish parliament themselves and, thenceforth, disbursed the lion's share of patronage. The combination of these three developments was to ensure that the 'age of the undertakers' had come to an end by 1772.

THE CHATHAM INTERLUDE

Hertford was not long back in England when the inevitable happened and the Rockingham ministry was dismissed by George III, in June 1766. This was not surprising, though the choice of William Pitt to head the succeeding ministry caused consternation:

> What will become of us if Mr Pitt is to return to his old post as guide? I shudder at the consequences.[1]

Some Irish observers, especially those of a Patriot stamp, positively welcomed the change, believing Pitt to be ready to continue his 'Patriot minister' role of the Seven Years War.[2] After a few months of delay, during debate on Pitt's acceptance of a peerage, it became clear that Hertford was to be replaced by Lord Bristol as viceroy.[3] The high expectations for a Pitt-led ministry can be seen through the pages of the newspapers.[4] The disappointment over Pitt's taking a peerage was

---

1 PRONI T3019/5277, Waite to Wilmot, 18 July 1766. 2 PRONI Willes papers, Mic.336, Bowes to Willes, 3 Sept.; Flood to Charlemont, [1766], in R[odd], *Letters to Flood*, pp. 22–9; Bowes to Hely Hutchinson, 17 Sept. 1766, in *HMC Donoughmore Mss.*, p. 182. 3 PRONI T3019/5294, 5301–2, Waite to Wilmot, 21 Aug., 4 Sept., Meredyth to Farnham, 29 Aug. 1766. 4 *FJ*, 14 Jan., 8, 29 July, 2 Aug. 1766, 2 May 1767 (with plans for parliamentary reform).

accompanied by hopes for a dismantling of the undertaker system, a method of management open to savage criticism, by the use of a resident viceroy:

> How such persons [undertakers] could any way be useful for the support of the government, by preserving a fair understanding between the king and his people, but on the contrary, how dangerous to bring in arbitrary power, I leave to every man's judgement. They were so far from being true representatives of the people, that they were a distinct middle interest between the king and the people: and their chief business was to serve some great minister of state, though never so opposite to the true interest of the nation.[5]

The current chief undertaker, John Ponsonby, was advised to retire before the Patriot ministers put him out of business.[6]

The prospect for reform was not only in the minds of journalists and pamphleteers. The residency of Lord Bristol in Ireland was settled on early in the viceroyalty and there were hints that he intended to take a more active role in the dispersal of revenue patronage. Ponsonby, was not slow to respond and, by mid-September, Waite reported:

> Already I am informed that your good friend [Ponsonby] is going about and stopping everyone who sells half a penny of tobacco to tell him of designs that are hatching against Ireland. The gentlemen of the country are all to be removed and set at nought. Not a place to be given away for the future by the Commissioners of the Revenue. A Union. A Land Tax.[7]

Ponsonby had gone to England with Lord and Lady Shannon in the summer of 1766, to see what the future might hold for them.[8] Now that that future seemed likely to include a resident viceroy and political reforms (including a Septennial Act and other Patriot pieces of legislation), others, including Flood and Hutchinson, went to London to see what allies the new ministers were looking for. Given Chatham's Patriot credentials, the new Irish administration might be expected to look beyond the usual parliamentary managers for others to 'take the lead'. Hutchinson was said to be furious at the treatment he received from Bristol, who refused to discuss Irish affairs with this 'person who went over to be announced to king and ministers as the Prime Minister of this kingdom.' Soon after this Hutchinson was reported as being in opposition with Ponsonby.[9] Henry

5 FJ, 16, 20 Sept. 1766, 21 July 1767.   6 *A Letter to the right honourable J[oh]n P[onsonb]y of the H[ous]e of C[ommon]s of I[relan]d* (London, 1767).   7 O'Hara to Burke, 12 Mar. 1767 in Hoffman, *New York Agent*, p. 403; PRONI T3019/5314, 5320B, Waite to Wilmot, 18 Sept., Wilmot to Waite, 18 Sept. 1766.   8 PRONI T3019/5301, Waite to Wilmot, 4 Sept. 1766. 9 PRONI T3019/5350, 5361, 5429, Waite to Wilmot, 25 Oct., 8 Nov. 1766, 12 Feb. 1767.

Flood seemed to fare much better, though his account of his meeting with Chatham at Bath was one of disappointment. It is debatable whether he intended to secure government office, but the example of Pitt surely acted as a prompt towards combining office and Patriotism. In any case, Dublin was full of rumours that Flood would 'take in the lead' in the Commons, that Bristol would work with Lord Tyrone and the duke of Leinster, and that Ponsonby was to suffer the indignity of having Flood forced on him at the Revenue Board. Flood was quick to deny these rumours, once it became clear that his ambition, to purchase a seat in the British parliament, had come to nothing.[10]

All the talk of resident viceroys, removals of Ponsonby and even of Lord Chancellor Bowes, the rise of Flood and the family of Lord Tyrone, and the end of the undertakers, came to nothing for the time being.[11] By August 1767, the internal contradictions of the Chatham ministry meant that Bristol was confessing to Wilmot that his 'dream' of governing Ireland was at an end.[12] The *Freeman's Journal* captured the Dublin mood:

> But, when the people lost the prospect of seeing the promised halcyon days, the tables were once again turned: while these mourned and lamented the kingdom's fate, in the likelihood of its falling again into its too long accustomed thraldom, the ruler and his creatures exulted, strutted, vaunted and domineered.[13]

The Chatham interlude had come to an end and all the hopes for reform seemed to have amounted to nothing.

THE TOWNSHEND VICEROYALTY

It appeared that, with Chatham's retirement, there would be no further threat to the undertakers, especially Speaker Ponsonby. Bristol's chief secretary, Theophilus Jones, did hint that Lord Townshend would pursue reform but, when Robert Cuninghame was sent to London by Ponsonby and Hutchinson, Waite commented:

> We take it for granted that Lord Townshend comes over determined to submit to the great powers here and pay them for doing his business – what else can he do instead?[14]

---

10 For this see Kelly, *Henry Flood*, pp. 109–11; Flood to Charlemont, NLI Headfort papers, Tisdall to Bective, 4 Apr.; PRONI Mic.336, Heany to Willes, 17 Feb.; PRONI T3019/5404, 5465, 5479, Waite to Wilmot, 3 Jan., 4, 16 Apr. 1767. 11 PRONI T3019/5308, 5311, Wilmot to Waite, 11 Sept., Waite to Wilmot, 13 Sept. 1766. 12 PRONI T2959/2/7, Bristol to [Grafton], 26 July; PRONI T3019/5553, Bristol to Wilmot, [1] Aug. 1767. 13 *FJ*, 8 Aug. 1767. 14 PRONI T3019/5580, 5591, Waite to Wilmot, 15, 25 Aug. 1767.

It appeared, in 1767, that the Townshend years would be little more than an adaptation of the management techniques, that is using the undertakers, which had existed for most parliamentary sessions since William III's reign. Indeed, there was little more than hopeful talk that Townshend would be a resident viceroy and the newspapers expected the continuing rule by lords justices.[15]

Despite initial impressions, the Townshend years were to last from 1767 to 1772 and to see the complete overhaul of the Irish political system. The new viceroy, like his brother Charles, was reformist by nature and saw the end of unreliable Irish parliamentary management as a strengthening of British imperial power. In a period when the American colonists were attempting to redefine their relationship with the metropolitan power and, when Wilkes and his supporters were upsetting political complacency in Britain itself, Lord Townshend was keen to ensure that Irish politics were tightly managed. After initial disasters, as he failed to get an augmentation of the Irish army undertaken by his managers in 1767–8 and then saw these very managers lead the opposition to a supply bill in 1769, the viceroy demanded, and finally got from ministers, the powers that a resident viceroy would need to control the Irish parliament. The fact that ministers proved unwilling to grant Townshend the power to disburse revenue patronage may have had something to do with his difficult reputation, but there was also reluctance to dispense with the undertaker system, until it proved clearly useless for British needs. Townshend's failures as a manager, in refusing to trust successive chief secretaries and his occasional reliance on the notoriously unreliable country gentlemen MPs, especially in the 1771–2 parliamentary session, meant that a 'Castle party' was built during later viceroyalties, but the foundations of the 'new system of government' were laid between 1767 and 1772.

Townshend, himself, went through a short period of experimentation with the existing undertaker system in the 1767–8 session. This was because of the necessity for getting the measure of army augmentation through the Irish Commons, without much ministerial support from London.[16] Townshend negotiated with the undertakers (including Ponsonby, Leinster and Lord Tyrone), sought to meet their patronage demands, got ministerial approval to shorten the duration of Irish parliaments, and make judges answerable for their conduct to that parliament. Thus, by October 1767, he hoped for a quiet session, especially if concessions on a security clause were made to the augmentation scheme.[17] However, the failure to

---

15 O'Hara to Burke, 16 Aug. 1767, in Hoffman, *New York Agent*, p. 407; *FJ*, 8 Sept. 1767. The question whether Townshend was to be a resident viceroy or not is well treated in Bartlett, 'Townshend viceroyalty', pp. 49–50. 16 Grenville to Whateley, 20 Oct. in Smith, *Grenville Papers*, iv, p. 176; Burke to O'Hara, 27 Oct. 1767 in Copeland, *Correspondence of Burke*, i, p. 330. 17 PRO SP63/425, Townshend to Shannon, 6 Sept., Townshend to Leinster, 9 Sept., Townshend to Grafton, 27 Oct.; *FJ*, 15 Sept.; PRONI T3019/5634, Waite to Wilmot, 24 Oct. 1767.

make either Tisdall or Hely Hutchinson lord chancellor, followed by the collapse of the judges' bill, seriously undermined Townshend's standing with both the undertakers and a wider audience. These issues paled into insignificance once it became clear that ministers were not prepared to grant a security clause that guaranteed 12,000 troops would remain in Ireland.[18] The fact that an Octennial Act passed the Irish parliament in 1768, may have given Townshend some popularity, but his relationship with the undertakers had completely broken down. The Castle was left with a restive parliament, non-existent managers and with unlikely materials from which to rebuild a parliamentary majority. The wheel seemed to have turned full circle to the position in which Dorset and Sackville had found themselves in 1754.

CONCLUSION

It is sometimes believed that it was at this point, with the augmentation scheme defeated and Townshend lacking a parliamentary majority that British ministers decided to abolish the undertaker system. However, given the twists and turns since 1750, one would be foolish to believe that Townshend's instruction to stay in Ireland in March 1768 meant the end of the undertakers. Indeed his failure to rebuild a majority, ahead of the 1769 session, resulted in the defeat of a supply bill and prorogation of parliament and could have cost him his office, as it had done to Dorset in 1755. The main reason that it did not was, perhaps, the experience that the Castle had gained since the end of that earlier Money Bill crisis. The frustration at repeated failures of the undertakers (in 1757–8, 1760, 1763–4 and 1765–6) to deliver reliable political management led finally to the conclusion that Townshend needed real power to sack officials, reward loyal supporters, and, ultimately, to reshape the revenue system to pass control of its patronage to the Castle. Ministerial reform finally passed from words to actions.

    The end of the undertakers was also, arguably, a self-inflicted demise as the question arises as to whether Henry Boyle would ever have opposed Townshend in the same way that John Ponsonby and his allies did. This is in the realm of speculation, given the Irish developments since the early 1750s and the changed political realities in Britain under George III. Professor Bartlett is surely correct in saying that an opposition, dominated by the agenda of undertakers, had passed its sell-by date by 1772.[19] Indeed, the end of the undertakers led to a new dynamic in

18 Hely Hutchinson to Hamilton, 9 Oct. in *HMC Donoughmore Mss.*; PRO SP63/425, Townshend to Grafton, 27 Oct., 4 Nov., Townshend to Shelburne, 27 Oct., 5 Nov., 12 Dec., Shelburne to Townshend, 28 Oct., 18 Nov., 28 Dec.; PRONI T3019/5679, 5691, Waite to Wilmot, 26 Nov., Campbell to Wilmot, 31 Dec. 1767. Also the Baratariana series of satires attacking both Townshend and the undertakers, especially Hely Hutchinson, were published in January 1768 in the *Freeman's Journal.*   19 T. Bartlett, 'Opposition in late eighteenth-century

the relationship between Castle and Commons after the Townshend years. The forces of the secondary political interests and the Patriots, that had been flexing their muscles since 1750, now came into the open making the management of parliament a much more fluid affair. This development was given extra impetus by more frequent elections after 1768. The government also lost its middlemen and, between 1770 and 1800, had to curb both patriotism and the ferocious defence of Protestant political privilege, by drawing on its own resources.[20] The demise of the undertakers did lead to a new political system in Ireland. It was not, however, one that guaranteed any more political calm than had existed before 1750.

Ireland: the case of the Townshend viceroyalty', *IHS*, 22 (1981), pp. 66–87.   **20** The work of James Kelly best captures these developments: J. Kelly, *Prelude to Union: Anglo-Irish politics in the 1780s* (Cork, 1992); idem, *Henry Flood*; idem, 'The genesis of Protestant Ascendancy', in G. O'Brien (ed.), *Politics, Parliament and People* (Dublin, 1989), pp. 93–129.

Appendix

'OBSERVATIONS ON THE DIFFERENT INTERESTS IN THE IRISH
HOUSE OF COMMONS' BY CHARLES O'HARA, [1755]

Observations on the Country Side

1. Henry Boyle (Co. Cork)
2. Richard Boyle (Dungarvan)
3. Henry Walsingham (Tallagh)
4. Bellingham Boyle (Bandon)
5. Michael O'Brien Dilkes (Castlemartyr)
6. John Lysaght Snr. (Charleville)
7. John Lysaght Jnr. (Castlemartyr)
8. John Magill (Rathcormack)
9. Sir John Colthurst (Doneraile)
10. Sir Richard Cox (Clonakilty)

'These are immediately under the direction of the Speaker, so connected by blood, dependencies or positive engagements that nothing can move from him.'

11. Kingsmill Pennefeather (Cashel)
12. Richard Pennefeather (Cashel)

'These two have discovered so close an attachment to the Speaker that they may be counted entirely his.'

13. John Eyre (Galway)

'A nephew of Sir Richard Cox and entirely under his direction. Also attached to the Speaker as the only chance to retrieve his interest in the County of Galway. To help him government would have to sacrifice French, Staunton and the Dalys.'

14. Dr Edward Barry (Charleville)

'His attachment to the Speaker is great but can be forced to serve government and has done before.'

15. William Cooper (Hillsborough)

'Attached to the Speaker but his nephew and heir has a patent employment, the Chancellor [Newport], must have influence there.'

16. John Colthurst (Tallagh)

'Dependent on the Speaker for his seat.'

17. Caesar Colclough (County Wexford)

'Must go with the Speaker in opposition to Lord Loftus, who is Lord Bessborough's brother-in-law.'

'These people [Nos. 1–17] must be considered as the Speaker's detached party, exclusive of any connection he may have with other people.'

18. Thomas Carter (Hillsborough)
19. Thomas Carter Jnr. (Old Leighlin)
20. Stephen Trotter (Carysfort)

'The late Master of the Rolls [Carter] formed the opposition out of aversion to the Primate and is intimately connected with the Speaker as head of the opposition; farther his attachment does not go.'

21. Anthony Malone (County Westmeath)
22. Edmund Malone (Askeatown)
23. Richard Malone (Fore)
24. Sir Ralph Gore (County Donegal)
25. Henry Gore (Killybegs)
26. Frederick Gore (Tulsk)
27. Edmund Malone K.C. (Ardfert)

'These seven, from a marriage with a Gore and personal obligations in money matters to the late Prime Serjeant [Anthony Malone], may be reckoned entirely at his disposal, but however closely he may be with the Speaker in opposition, his attachment to him is not personal; his views are much more extensive. He wants to raise a Gore to the Chair, Sir Ralph if he will apply himself to business, if not, Sir Arthur, but this he would not do by subserviency to government; he thinks the constitution of Ireland needs alteration and principally from this opinion it was that he laboured the expulsion of Nevill and headed the opposition to the preamble of the [Money] Bill last session. Suspicion arose that the money he lent to Sir Ralph, Henry and Frederick Gore was underhand had of Mr Clements, but in a late transaction this has appeared not to be the case. Suspicions however still remain as the matter was not pushed to eternity.'

28. Arthur Gore (County Longford)
29. John Gore (Jamestown)
30. Ralph Gore (Kilkenny)
31. William Gore (County Leitrim)

'None of these are personally attached to the Speaker. They joined in the opposition upon a promise that a Gore was to succeed Mr Boyle in the Chair and the honour of the name will ever be their ruling motive.'

32. Sir Arthur Gore (Donegal)
33. Annesley Gore (County Mayo)

'Neither have any personal attachment to the Speaker. Sir Arthur was promised to succeed to the Chair; if this hope has removed from him he would probably look for honour.'

34. Sir Arthur Newcomen (County Longford)
35. Thomas Newcomen (St Johnstown)
36. Hugh Crofton (County Leitrim)
37. Gilbert King (Jamestown)
38. John French (County Roscommon)
39. James Cuffe (County Mayo)
40. Sir Edward King (Boyle)

'They are all allied to the Gores and would support them and they have been of late connected with the Speaker in opposition but upon the Gore plan.'

41. Nathaniel Clements (Duleek)
42. Henry Mitchell (Castlebar)

'There has been for many [years] a secret connection between the Speaker and the Treasury arising from mutual support and of all arts of office the best understood is that of extending influence without securing to have any particular interest.'

43. Nehemiah Donnellan (County Tipperary)

'Has hitherto been with the Speaker, not out of personal attachment, but out of a deluded Patriotism.'

44. Robert Sandford Snr. (Newcastle)
45. Robert Sandford Jnr. (Athy)
46. Henry Sandford (County Roscommon)
47. Kildare Burrowes (County Kildare)
48. John Digby (Kildare)
49. Thomas Burgh (Naas)
50. William Sandford (Roscommon)
51. Borough of Kildare

'These seven belong absolutely to Lord Kildare; and he will return an eight [h] for Kildare.'

52. Thomas Pakenham (Longford)

'Will always go with Lord Kildare unless he should imagine the interest of his country attacked and in that case he'll separate.'

53. Sir Edward O'Brien (County Clare)

'Would willingly have Lord Kildare and the Speaker remain united, that the O'Brien might be entire when they separate he would probably stick to him who should be most against government.'

54. Sir Samuel Cooke (Dublin city)

'Would be entirely directed by the City of Dublin.'

55. Sir Maurice Crosbie (County Kerry)
56. William Crosbie (Ardfert)
57. John Blennerhasset (County Kerry)
58. John Blennerhasset Jnr. (Tralee)
59. Thomas Mahon (Roscommon)

'These five commonly called the Kerry members, tho' Mahon be of Connacht and only connected with the rest by marriage; they have always gone with the Speaker but 'twas from thinking him right, not that they are under his influence, even so much as to prevent their having been suspected of a design to go over to the other side.'

60. John Caulfield (Charlemont)

    'Went over last time to serve his nephew [Lord Charlemont], and I believe dislikes the Primate; but has an employment, and certainly would vote for government, or stay away.'

61. Edward Herbert (Ennisteogue)

    'Most certainly in the same circumstances [as Caulfield], his natural direction is with the Kerry squadron.'

62. Cosby Nesbit (Cavan)

    'In the same circumstances.'

63. Gustavus Lambert (Kilbeggan)

    Is in employment and naturally would go with Lord Belfield but from his aversion to the Primate on account of Dr Andrews.'

64. Sir Compton Domville (County Dublin)

    'Will go with government in all government questions. In private affairs divided between the Speaker and Mr Clements.'

65. Patrick Wemys (County Kilkenny)
66. James Wemys (Callan)

    'These two will go against Lord Bessborough and merely for that reason.'

67. Henry Southwell (County Limerick)

    'Related to the Speaker but has got a pension and will hardly live to attend.'

68. Robert Hickman (County Clare)

    'Thought himself a Patriot but was lately taken off.'

69. Robert Roberts (Dungarvan)

    'Was for and against last session but may be easily secured.'

70. Thomas Loftus (Bannow)

    'Was also for and against, upon principle, but is inclined to the government side.'

71. Thomas Southwell (Enniscorthy)
72. Charles Gardiner (Taghmon)
73. Francis Macartney (Blessington)
74. Edward Smyth (Lisburn)
75. Abraham Creichton (Lifford)
76. Arthur Hyde (County Cork)
77. Emmanuel Pigott (Cork)
78. James Tynte (Youghal)
79. Sir John Freke (Baltimore)
80. William Harward (Doneraile)
81. John Bingham (Tuam)
82. Richard Dawson (Irishtown)
83. Joseph Deane (Ennisteogue)
84. Henry Lestrange (Banagher)
85. Edward Taylor (Askeaton)
86. Edward Cary (County Londonderry)
87. Arthur Francis Meredyth (County Meath)
88. Joseph Ashe (Trim)
89. Chichester Fortescue (Trim)
90. Thomas Cooley (Duleek)
91. Gorges Lowther (Ratoath)
92. Marcus Crofton (Ratoath)
93. Thomas Dawson (County Monaghan)
94. Warren Westenra (Maryborough)
95. William Henry Dawson (Portarlington)
96. Joshua Cooper (County Sligo)
97. Richard Vincent (Clogher)
98. Beverley Usher (County Waterford)
99. Aland Mason (County Waterford)
100. Shapland Carew (Waterford)
101. Richard Aldworth (Lismore)
102. John Rochfort (Mullingar)
103. Robert Doyne (Wexford)
104. Abel Ram (Gorey)
105. Daniel Faulkiner (Baltinglass)

'These 24 members are quite detached from all party, and had not among them any connection than what arose by their uniting in opposition. Some of them as were thrown into it by disappointment might easily be regained.'

106. Thomas Adderley (Charlemont)
107. Arthur Upton (Carrickfergus)

108. James Hamilton (Carlow)
109. Thomas Montgomery (Lifford)
110. Bernard Ward (County Down)
111. James Stevenson (Killyleagh)
112. Alexander Hamilton (Killyleagh)
113. Sir Archibald Acheson (Dublin University)
114. John Cole (Enniskillen)
115. [Robert] Scott (Newry)
116. Henry Hamilton (Londonderry)
117. Henry Cary (Coleraine)
118. Robert Parkinson (Ardee)
119. John Ruxton (Ardee)
120. Alexander Montgomery (County Monaghan)
121. William Hamilton (Strabane)
122. Andrew Ram (County Wexford)

'These seventeen members are in the Dissenting interest, and have no other connection with the Speaker, than what arose from the late opposition. Their motive to oppose is distinct from the rest.'

123. George St. George (Athlone)
124. Charles Echlin (Dungannon)

'Both dead. 'Tis doubtful how St George's place will be filled up. Thomas Knox will return a friend to the Primate in Echlin's place.'

125. [Edward] Southwell (Downpatrick)

'Lately got a pension.'

'OBSERVATIONS ON THE COURT PARTY'

1. Lord George Sackville (Portarlington)

'To be replaced by Colonel Conway.'

2. John Ponsonby (Newtown)
3. William Bristow (Lismore)
4. Richard Ponsonby (Knocktopher)
5. Robert Burton (County Carlow)
6. Samuel Bindon (Ennis)
7. Sir Charles Burton (Dublin City)

   8. Sir William Fownes (Dingle)
   9. Thomas Tenison (Dunleer)
  10. Henry Loftus (Bannow)
  11. Joseph Leeson (Thomastown)
  12. Brabazon Ponsonby (Newtown)
  13. Francis Leigh (Drogheda)
  14. Maurice Keating (County Kildare)
  15. William Evan Morres (Kilkenny)
  16. Harvey Morres (Irishtown)
  17. Benjamin Burton (Knocktopher)
  18. Eyre Evans (County Limerick)
  19. George Evans (Queen's County)
  20. Stephen Moore (County Tipperary)
  21. John Leigh (New Ross)
  22. Nicholas Loftus Hume (Bannow)
  23. Anthony Brabazon (County Wicklow)
  24. Robert Perceval (Fore)

   'All 23 under the influence of Lord Bessborough, most of them of his family, the rest bound to him by obligations so fast that they have always gone with him. Keating may not live 'til next session, in which case [Lord] Kildare would probably put a friend in for the county, though Lords Moore, Grandison and Bessborough would run him very hard. If George Evans should die, Mr Pole who is married to Lord Moore's sister would succeed.'

  25. John Maxwell (County Cavan)
  26. Robert Maxwell (Lisburn)
  27. Thomas Fortescue (Dundalk)
  28. William Henry Fortescue (County Louth)
  29. Edmund Sexten Pery (Wicklow)
  30. William Brownlow (County Armagh)
  31. William Richardson (Augher)
  32. William Richardson of Richhill (County Armagh)
  33. Robert Cuninghame (Tulsk)
  34. Owen Wynne Jnr. (County Sligo)

   'These ten are personally attached to the Primate [Stone] and will, I believe, be entirely directed by him.'

  35. Robert Handcock (Athlone)
  36. Henry Lyons (King's County)

'These two are under the influence of Lord Belfield, who I think cannot be detached from the Primate.'

37. Owen Wynne Snr. (County Sligo)
38. John Browne (Castlebar)
39. James Daly (Athenry)
40. [Charles] Daly (County Galway)
41. Robert French (County Galway)
42. Thomas Knox (Dungannon)
43. Matthew Forde (Downpatrick)
44. Richard Whaley (County Wicklow)
45. Richard Jackson (Coleraine)
46. Jonah Barrington (Ballinakill)
47. William Stewart (County Tyrone)

'These eleven have been particularly obliged to the Primate and would unwillingly be detached from him, but I think they would adhere to government for private reasons; Stewart I should have added to the Primate's list for he is attached to him by interest as well as by inclination.'

48. Brinsley Butler (County Cavan)
49. Thomas Butler (Belturbet)
50. John Butler (Newcastle)
51. Robert Butler (Belturbet)

'Lord Lanesborough's family would go with government but have hitherto gone hand in hand with the Primate. Tom Butler is dead but will certainly be replaced by one of the family.'

52. Attorney General [Warden Flood] (Callan)
53. Solicitor General [Philip Tisdall] (Dublin University)
54. William Bristow (Lismore)
55. John Bourke (Naas)
56. [General] Philip Bragg (Armagh)
57. Robert Jocelyn (Old Leighlin)
58. David Bindon (Ennis)
59. James O'Brien (Youghal)
60. Anthony Jephson (Mallow)
61. Richard Tonson (Baltimore)
62. John Folliott (Donegal)
63. Arthur Hill (County Down)
64. Bysse Molesworth (Swords)

65. Robert Fitzgerald (Dingle)
66. John Graydon (Harristown)
67. Luke Gardiner (Thomastown)
68. Boleyn Whitney (Philipstown)
69. Alexander Nesbit (Limavady)
70. Anthony Marlay (Lanesborough)
71. Thomas Bligh (Athboy)
72. Sir Thomas Prendergast (Clonmel)
73. Walter Hore (Taghmon)
74. Lord Forbes (Mullingar)
75. Hugh Skeffington (County Antrim)
76. James Smyth (Antrim)
77. Hungerford Skeffington (Antrim)
78. John Graham (Drogheda)
79. Edward Bolton (Swords)
80. James Saunderson (Enniskillen)
81. Robert Blakeney (Athenry)
82. Henry Bingham (Tuam)
83. Thomas Burgh (Lanesborough)
84. James Agar (Gowran)
85. Richard Aldworth (Lismore)
86. Sir Lawrence Parsons (King's County)
87. William Molesworth (Philipstown)
88. Charles Smyth (Limerick)
89. Richard Maunsel (Limerick)
90. Robert Ross (Carlingford)
91. [Nathaniel] Preston (Navan)
92. Sir Thomas Taylor (Kells)
93. Thomas Taylor (Kells)
94. William Wall (Maryborough)
95. James Stopford (Fethard)
96. William Tighe (Clonmines)
97. [John] Stratford (Baltinglass)
98. Charles Usher (Blessington))

'These 47 will vote with government. They are pretty much divided in affection between the Primate and Lord Bessborough's family but may be detached from either for the service of government.'

99. William Sharman (Randalstown)

100. Sir Richard Butler (County Carlow)
101. Sir Richard Wolseley (Carlow)
102. William Annesley (Midleton)
103. Philip Oliver (Kilmallock)
104. Hercules Langford Rowley (County Londonderry)
105. Henry Bingham (Tuam)
106. Anthony Foster (Dunleer)
107. Samuel Barker (Waterford)
108. Charles Tottenham (Fethard)
109. Thomas Loftus (Clonmines)

'These 12 have hitherto gone against the Speaker, and consequently of late with the government, the first however was in great measure the cause of the latter.'

110. Arthur Dobbs (Carrickfergus)
111. Thomas Staunton (Galway)
112. George Hamilton (St Johnstown)
113. John Folliott Jnr. (Granard)

'The first is gone is search of the North West Passage. Staunton and Hamilton may attend. Folliott has lately pacified but must be again applied to.'

114. John Preston (Navan)
115. Eaton Stannard (Midleton)
116. Robert Marshall (Clonmel)

'The two first dead, the latter a Judge. The two first will be succeeded by friends to government. I doubt as to the last.'

'NB: [William] Napper (Athboy) is left out on the Country Side because he won't attend next session.

'Of the new elections, four will go for the Court, two doubtful: two of the four taken for the opposition reduce their [majority] to six. Nicholas Archdall (County Fermanagh), Robert Hickman and Southwell since come over and make the numbers equal but the Speaker being one leaves the casting vote to the Court. Of such as did not attend last session the majority would be for the Court.'

Bibliography

MANUSCRIPT SOURCES

Armagh Public Library
   Physico-Historical Society papers (Ms.G.1.14)
Boston Public Library
   Townshend papers (Ms.Eng.180)
British Library
   Berkeley papers (Add. Mss.39315)
   Egerton Ms 3435
   Hardwicke papers (Add. Mss. 35585–6, 35919, 35892, 35591–6)
   Holland House papers (Add. Mss. 51385, 51388–9)
   Lansdowne papers (Add. Mss.24137, 1235)
   Liverpool papers (Add. Mss. 38204–5)
   Mitchell papers (Add. Mss. 6818–39)
   Newcastle papers (Add. Mss.32420, 32690–2, 32705, 32725–7, 32732–7,
      32852–76, 32920, 32939–41)
   Rothes' defence survey (Add Mss. 30196)
   Sloane Ms 4164, 4326
   Southwell papers (Add. Mss. 21121–3)
   Townshend papers (Add. Mss. 38497)
Derbyshire Record Office
   Wilmot-Horton papers (WH 1772, 2945)
Dublin Public Library
   Harcourt papers (Gilbert Ms.94)
   Accounts of Dorset and Devonshire, 1730–1741 (M.199)
House of Lords Record Office
   Tickell papers
National Archives, Dublin
   Adjutant-General's entry-book (M.2554)
   Calendars of miscellaneous official papers (M.1A/52/63,
      M.1A/52/166–7, M.2446)
   Townshend papers (M.724–35)

National Library, Dublin
   Account books of Sir Henry Cavendish (Ms.9835)
   Adjutant General's entry book, 1757–1763 (Ms.681)
   Fitzgerald papers (Ms.624–31)
   French papers (Ms.2745, 7375, 19821)
   Holloden papers (Special list 416)
   Inchiquin papers (Ms.1986, 2789, 2835)
   Lane papers (Ms.8645)
   Lord Halifax's journal, 1761 (Ms.8064)
   Lord Lieutenants' dinner lists, 1755–1772 (Ms.1466–71)
   O'Hara papers (Ms.20393–5, microfilm p. 1576)
   O'Neill papers (Ms.21293)
   Poll book for Limerick city, 1761 (Ms.16092–3)
   Sarsfield papers (Ms.17891)
   Talbot-Crosbie papers (Ms.2054)
   Tighe papers (Ms.8470)
   Townshend papers (Ms.14299)
   Treatise on taxes paid by Ireland, 1691–c.1730 (Ms.694)
   Wynne papers (Ms.22252)
Northumberland Record Office
   Potter papers (Ms.650/19–22)
Nottingham University Library
   Newcastle (Clumber) papers (some in PRONI T2863)
Public Record Office, London
   Chatham papers (PRONI Mic.207)
   State Papers, Ireland
   War Office papers, 1750–1763 (WO 1/609, 8/4–5, 30/54)
Public Record Office of Northern Ireland
   Abercorn papers (T2541)
   Alnwick papers (T2872)
   Anglesey papers (D619)
   Armagh diocesan papers (DIO4)
   Arran papers (T3200)
   Bedford papers (T2915)
   Bristol papers (T2960)
   Brownlow papers (T2718)
   Carbery papers (T2966)
   Castleward papers (D2092)
   Chatsworth papers (T3158)
   Dobbs papers (Mic.533)
   Donoughmore papers (T3459)

Emly (Pery) papers (T3052, 3087)
Foster-Massarene papers (D562)
Gosford papers (D1606)
Harrowby papers (T3228)
'History of the Irish parliament' papers (ENV5)
Lenox-Conyngham papers (D1449)
Letters on Thurot's landing, 1760 (T1180)
Macartney papers (D572, Mic.227)
Malcomson 'working papers' (D3312/9)
Midleton papers (Mic.207)
Mussenden papers (D354)
O'Hara papers (T2812)
Pelham papers (T2863)
Roden papers (Mic.149/9)
Shannon papers (D2707)
Stopford-Sackville letter (T2789)
Tenison Groves papers (T808)
Transcipts of State Papers (T1060)
Villiers-Stuart papers (T3131)
Wicklow papers (Mic.246)
Willes papers (Mic.336)
Wilmot papers (T3019)
Royal Irish Academy, Dublin
Charlemont papers (Ms.12/R/9)
Colonel Roy's tour in Ireland, 1766 (Stowe Ms.G/I/2)
List of gentry in Counties Antrim and Down worth more than £100, 1710
(Ms.24/K/19)
Military establishment of Ireland, March 1755 (Ms.12/B1/8)
Southwell papers (Ms.12/W/35)
Trinity College, Dublin
Arran papers (Ms.7576)
Barker-Ponsonby papers
Clements papers (Ms.1741–3)
West Sussex Record Office
Bunbury papers (PRONI Mic.238)
Yale University, Beinecke Library
Smith-Townshend papers
Townshend papers
Waite-Macartney papers
Private Collections
Rosse papers, Birr Castle, County Offaly (printed in a calendar by Registry
of Irish Archives)

PRINTED PRIMARY MATERIAL

Bedford: Lord John Russell (ed.), *The Correspondence of John, fourth Duke of Bedford* (3 vols, London, 1842–6).

Boulter: *Letters written by His Excellency Hugh Boulter, Lord Primate of all Ireland* (2 vols, Dublin, 1770).

Bowen: E.A. MacLysaght (ed.), 'Bowen Papers: Reports on private collections', *Analecta Hibernica* xv (1944).

Burke: T.W. Copeland (ed.), *The Correspondence of Edmund Burke* (10 vols, Cambridge, 1958–70).

Burke: Fitzwilliam and Bourke (eds), *Correspondence of Edmund Burke* (4 vols, London, 1814).

Burke: R.J. Hoffmann (ed.), *Edmund Burke, New York Agent...* (Philadelphia, 1956).

Chatham: W.J. Taylor and J.H. Pringle (eds), *Correspondence of William Pitt, Earl of Chatham* (4 vols, London, 1838–40).

Chesterfield: B. Dobree (ed.), *The Letters of Philip Dormer Stanhope, fourth Earl of Chesterfield* (5 vols, London, 1932).

Delany: Lady Llanover (ed.), *Autobiography and Correspondence of Mary Granville, Mrs Delany* (6 vols, London, 1861–2).

Devonshire: P.D. Brown and K.W. Schweizer (eds), *The Devonshire Diary, 1759–1762*, Camden 4th series, xxvii (London, 1982).

Dodington: J. Carswell and L.A. Dralle (eds), *The Journal of Bubb Dodington* (Oxford, 1965).

Fitzgerald: M.A. Hickson, 'Correspondence of the Knight of Kerry', *Old Kerry Records*, 2nd series (1874), pp. 261–95.

Flood: Warden Flood, *Memoirs and Correspondence of the Right Hon. Henry Flood, MP* (Dublin, 1838).

Flood: [T. Rodd], *Original Letters ... to the Right Hon. Henry Flood* (London, 1820).

Fox: Earl of Ilchester (ed.), *Henry Fox, first Lord Holland, his family and relations* (2 vols, London, 1920).

George III: Sir John Fortescue (ed.), *The Correspondence of George III* (6 vols, London, 1927–8).

Grafton: Lord Anson (ed.), *Autobiography and Political Correspondence of Augustus Henry, third Duke of Grafton* (London, 1898).

Grenville: W.J. Smith (ed.), *The Grenville Papers* (4 vols, London, 1852–3).

Grenville: J.R.G. Tomlinson (ed.), *Additional Grenville Papers, 1763–1765* (Manchester, 1962).

HMC: *Charlemont Mss*, 12th Report, appendix x (2 vols, London, 1891).

HMC: *Donoughmore Mss*, 12th Report, appendix ix (London, 1891).

HMC: *Egmont Diary* (3 vols, London 1902), vol. iii.

HMC: *Emly Mss*, 8th Report, appendix i (London, 1881).

HMC: *Eyre-Matcham Mss*, Reports on various collection, volume vi (London, 1905).

HMC: *Hastings Mss* (3 vols, London, 1934), vol iii.

HMC: *Knox Mss*, Reports on various collections, vi (London, 1909).

HMC: *Stopford-Sackville Mss* (2 vols, London, 1904), vol i.

HMC: *Townshend Mss*, 11th Report, appendix iv (London, 1888).

HMC: *Weston Mss*, 10th Report, appendix i (London, 1885).

Hardwicke: P.C. Yorke (ed.), *Life and Correspondence of Philip Yorke, first Earl of Hardwicke* (3 vols, London, 1915).

Home Office: *Calendar of the Home Office Papers, 1760–1775* (4 vols, London, 1878–90).

Inchiquin: John Ainsworth (ed.), *Inchiquin Manuscripts* (Dublin, 1943).

Irish papers: A.P.W. Malcomson (ed.), *Eighteenth-century Irish Official Papers in Great Britain* (2 vols, Belfast, 1973–90).

Irish parliament: *Journals of the Irish House of Commons, 1613–1800* (20 vols, Dublin, 1796–1800).

Irish parliament: [Sir James Caldwell], *Debates relative to the affairs of Ireland in the years 1763 and 1764* (2 vols, London, 1766).

Irish parliament: D. Large, 'The Irish House of Commons in 1769', *IHS*, xi (1958), pp. 18–45.

Irish parliament: M. Bodkin, 'The Irish parliament in 1773', *Proceedings of the RIA*, 48C (1942), pp. 145–232.

Irish parliament: W. Hunt (ed.), *The Irish Parliament in 1775* (Dublin, 1907).

Leinster: B. Fitzgerald (ed.), *Correspondence of Emily, Duchess of Leinster* (3 vols, Dublin, 1949).

Lennox: Countess of Ilchester and Lord Stavordale (eds), *The Life and Letters of Lady Sarah Lennox, 1745–1826* (2 vols, London, 1901).

Liber Munorum Publicorum Hiberniae (2 vols, London, 1852).

Macartney: T. Bartlett (ed.), *Macartney in Ireland, 1769–1772* (Belfast, 1978).

Oakboys: E. Magennis, 'The Hearts of Oak in County Armagh', *Seanchas Ard Mhaca*, 17 (1998), pp. 19–31.

O'Conor: C.C. Ward and R.E. Ward (eds), *The Letters of Charles O'Conor of Belangare, 1731–90* (2 vols, Ann Arbor, 1980).

Orrery: Countess of Cork and Orrery (ed.), *The Orrery Papers* (2 vols, London, 1903).

Pococke: J. McVeagh (ed.), *Richard Pococke's Irish Tours* (Dublin, 1995).

Shelburne: Lord Fitzmaurice (ed.), *Life of William, Earl of Shelburne* (3 vols, London, 1875–6).

Stone: C. Litton Falkiner (ed.), 'The Correspondence of Archbishop Stone and the Duke of Newcastle', *English Historical Review*, xx (1905), pp. 509–42, 735–63.

Vatican Archives: Cathaldus Giblin, 'Catalogue of material of Irish interest in the collection Nunziatura di Fiandra', parts 6–7, *Collectanea Hibernica*, x-xi (1967–8), pp. 72–138, 53–90.

Walpole: William Coxe, *Memoirs of the life and administration of Sir Robert Walpole, Earl of Orford* (3 vols, London, 1798).

Walpole: W.S. Lewis (ed.), *The correspondence of Horace Walpole* (48 vols, New Haven, 1937–83).

Walpole: Lord Holland (ed.), *Horace Walpole's Memoirs of the reign of George II* (3 vols, London, 1846).

Walpole: G.F. Russell-Barker (ed.), *Memoirs of the reign of George III* (4 vols, London, 1894).

Whiteboys: J. Kelly (ed.), 'The Whiteboys in 1762: a contemporary account', *Journal of the Cork Historical and Archaeological Society*, 94 (1989), pp. 19–26.

Willes: J. Kelly (ed.), *The Letters of Lord Chief Baron Edward Willes to the Earl of Warwick, 1757–62* (Aberyswyth, 1990).

Wilmot: J. Walton (ed.), *The King's Business* (New York, 1997).

NEWSPAPERS

Belfast News-Letter, 1737–1772
The Censor, 1748–1749
Corke Journal, 1757–1762
Dublin Courant, 1733–1747
Dublin Evening Post, 1733
Dublin Gazette, 1759–1765
Exshaw's Magazine, 1760–1763
Universal Advertiser, 1753–1761

Faulkner's Dublin Journal, 1741–1763
Freeman's Journal, 1763–1772
Gentleman's Magazine, 1740–1770
London Magazine, 1754
The Patriot, 1753
Pue's Occurrences, 1745–1754
The Tickler, 1749

PAMPHLETS (IN CHRONOLOGICAL ORDER)

[Henry Brooke], *The Farmer's Letters to the Protestants of Ireland, I–VI* (Dublin, 1745).

An Account of Mrs Ireland, the Mad-Woman (Dublin, 1745).

[James Moody], *A Sermon occasioned by the present Rebellion in Scotland, Preached at Newry ...* (Belfast, 1745).

[Rev. William Henry], *The Beauty, Deliverances and Security of the British Constitution* (Dublin, 1746).

The Necessity of a well-disciplined Militia in Ireland (Dublin, 1746).

The History of the Rise, Progress and Tendencies of Patriotism (Dublin, 1747).

The Secret History of the Barracks of Ireland (Dublin, 1747).

[Sir Richard Cox], *The Cork Surgeon's Antidote, I-VII* (Dublin, 1749).

[William Henry], *An Appeal to the People of Ireland* (Dublin, 1749).

[Bishop George Berkeley], *Maxims concerning Patriotism* (Dublin, 1750).

A humble address to the Nobility, Gentry and Freeholders of the Kingdom of Ireland (Dublin, 1751).

[Nicholas Archdall], *An alarm to the people of Ireland* (Dublin, 1751).

[Lord Hillsborough], *A proposal for uniting the Kingdoms of Ireland and Great Britain* (London, 1751).

[Rev. Peter Bristow], *Honesty the Best Policy or the History of Roger* (Dublin, 1752).

Philo-Militum, *The Case of the Infantry in Ireland* (Dublin, 1753).

Seasonable Advice to the Freeholders of the County of Armagh (Dublin, 1753).

Letter from a Free Citizen of Dublin to a Freeholder in the County of Armagh, I-II (Dublin, 1753).

[Thomas Tell-Truth], *A Letter from a Gentleman in the County of Armagh to his friend in Dublin occasioned by the late robbery of the Northern Mail* (Dublin, 1753).

The Parson's Letter to Sir R[ichar]d C[o]x, Bart. (Dublin, 1753).

[William Bruce], *Some Facts and Observations relative to the Fate of the Late Linen Bill* (Dublin, 1753).

A Letter of Advice to the I[ris]h members (Dublin, 1753).

A Letter of advice from an Old Party-Writer to a Novice in the Trade (n.p. , 1753).

The Spirit of Party (n.p. , 1753).

Letter from a Kilkenny Clergyman [Bishop Michael Cox] to Sir Richard Cox (Dublin, 1753).

A Letter of Sir R[ichar]d C[o]x to a certain great man and his son on the present state of affairs in Ireland (Dublin, 1753).

[Hibernicus], *Dedication on a Dedication...* (London, 1753).

Political Pastime of Faction Displayed.. (Dublin, 1753).

[Christopher Robinson], *Considerations on the late bill for payment of the remainder of the national debt* (Dublin, 1754).

[William Bruce], *Remarks on a late pamphlet entitled Considerations on the late bill for paying the National Debt, etc.* (Dublin, 1754).

[Sir Richard Cox], *The proceedings of the honourable House of Commons of Ireland in rejecting the altered Money Bill on December 17th 1753 Vindicated, etc.* (Dublin, 1754).

The Universal Advertiser or a collection of essays, moral political and entertaining (Dublin, 1754).

Joshua Pym to Dionysius [Cox] the Aeropagite (Dublin, 1754).

[Rev. John Brett], *A friendly call to the People of the Roman Catholic Religion in Ireland* (Dublin, 1755).

Policy and Justice: An Essay being a proposal for augmenting the power and wealth of Great Britain by uniting with Ireland (Dublin, 1755).

The State of Ireland laid open to the view of His Majesty's Subjects (Dublin, 1755).

A Short but Full Defence of a Certain Great Man (Dublin, 1756).

Advice to the Patriot Club of Antrim (Dublin, 1756).

A letter from the side of the Shannon to Roger (Dublin, 1756).

The Tryal of Roger for the Murder of Lady Betty Ireland (Dublin, 1756).

Advice to the Speaker Elect, or a letter to John Ponsonby (Dublin, 1756).

Remarks on a late pamphlet entitled 'Advice to the Patriot Club of Antrim' (Dublin, 1756).

A Few Thoughts on the Times from a Free Citizen in Dublin to his Friend in the North (Dublin, 1756).

[Charles O'Conor], *The Principles of the Roman Catholics of Ireland* (Dublin, 1756).

[E.S. Pery], *A Letter to the Duke of Bedford* (Dublin, 1757).

Serious Thoughts concerning the Interests and Exigencies of the State of Ireland in a letter to the Duke of Bedford (Dublin, 1757).

Northern Revolutions or the principle causes of the declensions and dissolution of once flourishing Gothic Constitutions in Europe (Dublin, 1757).

A letter to Edmund Sexton Pery and the rest of the Patriot members of the House of Commons, with observations on pensioners (Dublin, 1757).

Some Proceedings of the Freeholders' Society (Dublin, 1757).

Ireland Disgraced: or an island of saints become an island of sinners (Dublin, 1758).

[John Monck Mason], *Remarks upon Poynings' Law* (Dublin, 1758).

The Management of the Revenue with Queries (2nd edition, Dublin, 1758).

John Brown, *Estimate of the Manners and Principles of the Times* (Dublin, 1758).

A Farewell to the Duke of Bedford (Dublin 1758).

[John Curry], *Historical Memoirs of the Irish Rebellion of the year 1641* (London, 1758).

A letter to the people of Ireland on the Subject of Tithes (Dublin, 1758).

A letter to the Present Electors of the City of Dublin (Dublin, 1758).

[Hibernicus], *Advice to the Patriots of the Coombe, the liberties* (Dublin, 1759).

A letter from a Commoner in Town to a Noble Lord in the Country (London, 1760).

Considerations on the Present Calamities of this kingdom and the Causes of Decay of Public Credit (Dublin, 1760).

A Proposal for the Restoration of Wealth and Public Credit (Dublin, 1760).

[Free Citizen], *The New Bankers Proved Bankrupt* (Dublin, 1760).

James D. La Touche, *A Short but True history of the Rise, Progress and Happy Suppression of several late Insurrections commonly called Rebellions* (Dublin, 1760).

Heads of a Bill, for better regulating the elections of the Lord Mayor, Aldermen, Sheriffs, Commons and other Officers of the city of Dublin, and for preserving the peace, order and good government in the said city (Dublin, 1760).

The Drapier's Ghost's Answer to the Clothier's Letter (Dublin, 1760).

C. Lucas, *Seasonable Advice to the Electors of MPs in the Ensuing General Election* (Dublin, 1760).

Previous Promises Inconsistent with a Free Parliament and an Ample Vindication of the last Parliament (Dublin, 1760).

Honest Advice to the electors of Ireland on the present most critical time (Dublin, 1760).

A Comment on a letter from the Earl of Clanrickarde to the Duke of Bedford (Dublin, 1760).

An answer to a comment on a letter from the Earl of Clanrickarde to the Duke of Bedford (Dublin, 1761).

The Question about Septennial Parliaments Impartially Examined in two letters to Charles Lucas (Dublin, 1761).

Liberty or Bondage for the Citizens of Dublin or queries humbly offered to those Citizens who have Votes (Dublin, 1761).

Septennial Parliaments Vindicated (Dublin, 1762).

A slight review of the transactions of the late long Parliament with some observations on the rise and progress of the Septennial Bill (Dublin, 1762).

Report of his majesty's attorney and solicitor general upon the bill for better regulating the corporation of Limerick (Dublin, 1762).

An enquiry into the causes of the outrages committed by the Levellers or Whiteboys of Munster (Dublin, 1762).

An alarm to the unprejudiced and well-minded Protestants of Ireland (Cork, 1762).

The Respective Charges given to the Armagh Grand Jury at the Assizes of July 1763 (Dublin, 1763).

James Caldwell, *A Brief Examination of the question whether it is expedient ... to pass an act to enable papists to take real securities for money which they may lend* (Dublin, 1764).

C. Lucas, *A First, Second and Third Address to the Right Honourable Lord Mayor of Dublin* (Dublin, 1766).

A Letter to the right honourable J[oh]n P[onsonb]y of the H[ous]e of C[ommon]s of I[relan]d (London, 1767).

T. Campbell, *A Philosophical Survey of the South of Ireland* (Dublin, 1778).

SECONDARY WORKS

T.C. Barnard, 'The political, mental and material culture of the Cork settlers, c.1650–1750', in P. O'Flanagan (ed.), *Cork: History and Society* (Dublin, 1993), pp. 309–67.

——, 'The government and Irish Dissent, 1704–1780', in K. Herlihy (ed.), *The Politics of Irish Dissent* (Dublin, 1997), pp. 9–27.

T. Bartlett, 'The Townshend Viceroyalty, 1767–1772' (PhD. thesis, Queen's University Belfast, 1976).

——, 'Townshend and the Irish Revenue board, 1769–1772', *Proceedings of the Royal Irish Academy*, lxxix (1979), pp. 153–76.

——, 'The Townshend Viceroyalty, 1767–72', in T. Bartlett & D.W. Hayton (eds), *Penal Age and Golden Era* (Belfast, 1979), pp. 88–112

——, 'The augmentation of the army in Ireland, 1767–69', *English Historical Review*, 96 (1981), pp. 540–73.

——, 'Opposition in late eighteenth-century Ireland: the case of the Townshend viceroyalty', *IHS*, 22 (1981), pp. 66–87.

——, 'Army and Society in eighteenth-century Ireland', in W.A. Maguire (ed.), *Kings in Conflict* (Belfast, 1990), pp. 173–82.

——, *The fall and rise of the Irish nation: the Catholic question 1690–1830* (Dublin, 1992).

M. Beresford, 'Francois Thurot and the French attack at Carrickfergus, 1759–60', *Irish Sword*, x (1971–2), pp. 255–41.

R. Blackey, 'A Politician in Ireland: Earl of Halifax, 1761–3', *Eire-Ireland*, xiv (1979), pp. 65–82.

J. Brady, 'The proposal to register Irish priests, 1756–7', *Irish Ecclesiastical Record*, xcvii (1961), pp. 209–22.

John Brewer, *Party Ideology and Popular Politics at the Accession of George III* (Cambridge, 1976).

——, *The Sinews of Power: War, Money and the English State, 1688–1783* (London, 1989).

M. Bric, 'The Whiteboy movement in County Tipperary, 1760–1780', in W. Nolan (ed.), *Tipperary: History and Society* (Dublin, 1985), pp. 148–84.

J. Brooke and L. Namier (eds), *The House of Commons, 1754–1790* (3 vols, London, 1964).

J.L. Bullion, *A Great and Necessary Measure: George Grenville and the genesis of the Stamp Act, 1763–5* (Missouri, 1982).

——, 'The Ten Thousand in America: More Light on the Decision on the American Army, 1762–3', *William and Mary Quarterly*, xliii (1986), pp. 646–57.

——, 'Security and Economy: The Bute Administration's Plans for the American Army and Revenue, 1762–3', *William and Mary Quarterly*, xlv (1988), pp. 499–507.

R.E. Burns, *Irish Parliamentary Politics in the Eighteenth Century* (2 vols, Washington, 1989–1990).

J.C.D. Clark, 'Whig Tactics and Parliamentary Precedents: The English management of Irish politics, 1754–6', *Historical Journal*, xxi (1978), pp. 275–301.

——, *The Dynamics of Change: The Crisis of the 1750s and English Party Systems* (Cambridge, 1982).

L. Clarkson & E.M. Crawford, *Ways to Wealth* (Belfast, 1985).

S.J. Connolly, *Religion, Law and Power: The Making of Protestant Ireland, 1660–1760* (Oxford, 1992).

——, 'The defence of Protestant Ireland, 1660–1760', in T. Bartlett & K. Jeffery (eds), *The Military History of Ireland* (Cambridge, 1995), pp. 231–246.

D.A. Cronin, *A Galway Gentleman in the Age of Improvement: Robert French of Monivea, 1716–1779* (Dublin, 1995).

L.M. Cullen, 'Landlords, Merchants and Bankers: Early Irish banking world, 1700–1820', *Hermathena*, cxxxv (1982–3), pp. 25–44.

——, *An Economic History of Ireland since 1660* (2nd edn., London, 1986).

D. Dickson, *New Foundations: Ireland, 1690–1800* (Dublin, 1987).

J.S. Donnelly, 'The Whiteboy Movement, 1761–5', *IHS*, xxi (1977–8), pp. 20–59.

——, 'Hearts of Oak, Hearts of Steel', *Studia Hibernica*, xxi (1981), pp. 7–73.

J.A. Eulie, 'Politics and Administration in Ireland, 1760–1766' (PhD thesis, Fordham University, 1965).

P. Fagan, 'The Dublin Catholic Mob, 1700–1750', *ECI*, iv, pp. 33–42.

——, *Divided Loyalties: The Question of an Oath for Irish Catholics in the Eighteenth Century* (Dublin, 1997).

C. Litton Falkiner, 'Archbishop Stone', in idem., *Essays Relating to Ireland* (London, 1909).

K.P. Ferguson, 'The Army in Eighteenth Century Ireland' (PhD thesis, TCD, 1980).

F. Forde, 'The Royal Irish Artillery, 1755–1801', *Irish Sword*, xi (1973), pp. 1–15.

R.F. Foster, *Modern Ireland, 1600–1972* (London, 1988).

N. Garnham, *The Courts, Crime and the Criminal Law in Ireland, 1692–1760* (Dublin, 1996).

D. Goodall, 'All the Cooking that could be Used: A Co. Wexford Election in 1754', *Past*, xii, (1978), pp. 3–22.

E.H. Gould, 'To Strengthen the King's Hands: Dynastic Legitimacy, Militia Reform and Ideas of National Unity in England, 1745–60', *Historical Journal*, xxxiv (1991), pp. 329–48.

A. Guy, *Economy and Discipline: Training of the British Army, 1715–95* (Manchester, 1985).

——, ' "A whole army ruined in Ireland": Aspects of the Irish Establishment, 1715–1773', *Annual Report of the National Army Museum* (1978–9), pp. 33–49.

——, 'The Irish military establishment, 1660–1776', in Bartlett and Jeffery (eds), *Military History of Ireland*, pp. 211–230.

R. Harris, *A Patriot Press: London Newspapers and National Politics in the 1740s* (Oxford, 1993).

C. Haydon, *Anti-Catholicism in eighteenth century England* (Manchester, 1993).

D. Hayton, 'The Beginnings of the "Undertaker System"', in Bartlett and Hayton (eds), *Penal Age*, pp. 32–54.

——, 'Walpole and Ireland', in J. Black (ed.), *Britain in the Age of Walpole* (London, 1984), pp. 95–119

—— and D. Szechi, 'John Bull's other kingdoms: the English government of Scotland and Ireland', in C. Jones (ed.), *Britain in the first age of party, 1680–1750* (London 1987), pp. 241–80.

——, 'Anglo-Irish attitudes: Changing perception of national identity among the Protestant Ascendancy', *Studies in Eighteenth-Century Culture*, xvii (1987), pp. 145–57.

——, 'Exclusion, conformity and representation: The impact of the sacramental test on Irish dissenting politics', in Herlihy (ed.), *The Politics of Irish Dissent*, pp. 52–73.

——, 'British Whig Ministers and the Irish Question 1714–1725', in S. Taylor, J. Connors & C. Jones (eds), *Hanoverian Britain and Empire: Essays in Memory of Philip Lawson* (Woodbridge, 1998), pp. 37–64.

J.R. Hill, *From Patriots to Unionists: Dublin Civic Politics and Irish Protestant Patriotism, 1660–1840* (Oxford, 1997).

J.H. Houlding, *Fit for Service: The Training of the British Army, 1715–1790* (Oxford, 1981).

J.L.T. Hughes, 'The Chief Secretaries, 1561–1921', *IHS*, viii (1952–3).

F.G. James, 'Irish Smuggling in the eighteenth century', *IHS*, xii (1960–1).

——, 'The Irish lobby in the early eighteenth century', *EHR*, lxxxi (1966), pp. 543–77.

——, *Ireland in the Empire, 1688–1770* (Cambridge, Mass., 1973).

E.M. Johnston, *Great Britain and Ireland, 1760–1800* (Edinburgh, 1963).

——, *Ireland in the Eighteenth Century* (Dublin, 1974).

P.J. Jupp, 'The landed elite and political authority in Britain, c.1760–1850', *Journal of British Studies*, 29 (1990), pp. 53–79.

M.G. Kammen, *A Rope of Sand: Colonial Agents, British Politics and the American Revolution* (New York, 1968).

J. Kelly, 'The origins of the Act of Union: an examination of unionist opinion, 1660–1800', *IHS*, xxxv (1987), pp. 236–63.

——(ed.), 'The Whiteboys in 1762: A contemporary account', *Journal of the Cork Historical and Archaeological Society*, xciv (1989), pp. 19–26.

——, 'The genesis of Protestant Ascendancy', in G. O'Brien (ed.), *Politics, Parliament and People* (Dublin, 1989), pp. 93–129.

——, *Prelude to Union: Anglo-Irish Politics in the 1780s* (Cork, 1992).

——, *'That Damned Thing Called Honour': Duelling in Ireland, 1570–1860* (Cork, 1995).

——, *Henry Flood: Patriots and Politics in Eighteenth Century Ireland* (Dublin, 1998).

Paul Kelly, 'Constituents Instructions to Members of Parliament in the Eighteenth Century', in C. Jones (ed.), *Party and Management in Parliament, 1660–1784* (Leicester, 1984), pp. 169–89.

Patrick Kelly, 'Berkeley, Walpole and the South Sea Bubble Crisis', *ECI*, vii (1992), pp. 54–74.

T.J. Kiernan, *History of the Financial Administration of Ireland to 1817* (London, 1930).

P. Langford, *A Polite and Commercial People: England 1727–83* (Oxford, 1992).

P. Lawson, *George Grenville* (Oxford, 1984).

W.E.H. Lecky, *A History of Ireland in the Eighteenth Century* (5 vols, London, 1892).

C.D.A. Leighton, *Catholicism in a Protestant Kingdom* (Dublin, 1994).

H. McAnally, 'The Militia Array of 1756', *Irish Sword*, i (1950), pp. 94–104.

D. McCartney, *W.E.H. Lecky: Historian and Politician, 1838–1903* (Dublin, 1994).

J.L. McCracken, 'The Undertakers in Ireland and their Relations with the lord lieutenants, 1727–1771' (MA thesis, Queen's University Belfast, 1941).

——, 'The Central and Local Administration under George II, 1727–60', (PhD thesis, Queen's University Belfast, 1948).

——, 'The conflict between the Irish administration and parliament, 1753–1756', *IHS*, iii (1942–3), pp. 159–79.

——, 'Irish Parliamentary Elections, 1727–1768', *IHS*, v (1945–6), pp. 209–30.

——, 'The Irish Viceroyalty, 1760–1773', in H.A. Cronne, T.W. Moody and D.B. Quinn (eds), *Essays in British and Irish History in honour of J.E. Todd* (Dublin, 1949).

R.B. McDowell, *Ireland in the Age of Imperialism and Revolution, 1760–1800* (Oxford, 1992).

J. McGuire, 'The Irish parliament of 1692', in Bartlett and Hayton (eds), *Penal Age*, pp. 1–31.

P. McNally, 'Patronage and politics in Ireland, 1714–1727' (PhD thesis, Queen's University, Belfast, 1993).

——, *Parties, Patriots and Undertakers: Parliamentary Politics in early Hanoverian Ireland* (Dublin, 1997).

——, '"Irish and English Interests": National conflict within the Church of Ireland episcopate in the reign of George I', *IHS*, 115 (1995), pp. 295–314.

——, 'Wood's Halfpence, Carteret, and the government of Ireland, 1723–6', *IHS*, xxx (1997), pp. 354–76.

E. Magennis, 'A 'Beleaguered Protestant'?: Walter Harris and the writing of Fiction Unmasked', *ECI*, 13 (1998), pp. 86–111.

——, 'A Presbyterian Insurrection?: Reconsidering the Hearts of Oak disturbances of July 1763', *IHS*, xxxi (1999), pp. 31–62.

——, 'Popery, Patriotism and Politics: The Armagh election of 1753', in A. Hughes & R. Weatherup (eds), *Armagh: History and Politics* (Dublin, forthcoming).

——, 'In search of the "Moral Economy": Food scarcity in 1756–7 and the crowd', in P.J. Jupp & E. Magennis (eds), *The Crowd in Irish History, 1720–1920* (London, forthcoming).

A.P.W. Malcomson, 'The Newtown Act: Revision and Reconstruction', *IHS*, xviii (1973), pp. 313–44.

——, 'Speaker Pery and the Pery papers', *North Munster Antiquarian Journal*, xvi (1973), pp. 33–60.

——, *John Foster: The politics of the Anglo-Irish Ascendancy* (Oxford, 1978).

[——], 'Introduction: Part Three', in E. Hewitt (ed.), *Lord Shannon's Letters to his son* (Belfast, 1982), pp. xxiii–lxxix.

P.J. Marshall, 'A nation defined by Empire, 1755–1776', in A. Grant & K.J. Stringer (eds), *Uniting the Kingdom?: The making of British history* (London, 1995), pp. 208–22.

R. Middleton, *The Bells of Victory: The Pitt/Newcastle Ministry and the Conduct of the Seven Years War* (Cambridge, 1985).

R. Munter, *The History of the Irish Newspaper to 1750* (Cambridge, 1967).

S. Murphy, 'The Lucas Affair: a study of municipal and electoral politics in Dublin, 1742–9' (M.A. thesis, UCD 1981).

——, 'The Dublin Anti-Union Riot of 3 December 1759', in G. O'Brien (ed.), *Parliament, Politics and People* (Dublin, 1989) pp. 49–68.

——, 'Charles Lucas: A forgotten Patriot?', *History Ireland*, ii, (1994), pp. 26–9.

G. O'Brien, 'The Unimportance of Public Opinion in Eighteenth-Century Britain and Ireland', *ECI*, viii (1993), pp. 115–27.

B. O'Buachalla, *Aisling Ghearr* (Dublin, 1997).

D. O'Donovan, 'The Money Bill Dispute of 1753', in Bartlett & Hayton (eds), *Penal Age*, pp. 55–87.

J. O'Donovan, 'The Militia in Munster, 1715–78' in O'Brien (ed.), *Parliament, Politics and People*, pp. 31–48.

E. O'Flaherty, 'Urban Politics and Municipal Reform in Limerick, 1723–62', *ECI*, vi (1991), pp. 105–20.

M. Peters, *Pitt and Popularity: The Patriot Minister and London Opinion during the Seven Years War* (Oxford, 1980).

F. Plowden, *Historical Review of the State of Ireland to 1801* (3 vols, Dublin, 1803).

Martyn J. Powell, 'The reform of the undertaker system: Anglo-Irish politics, 1750–1767', *IHS*, xxxi (1998), pp. 19–36.

T.P. Power, 'Electoral Politics in Waterford City, 1692–1832', in W. Nolan and T.P. Power (eds), *Waterford: History and Society* (Dublin, 1992), pp. 236–8.

——, Land, Politics and Society in Eighteenth Century Tipperary, (Oxford, 1993).

J. Robertson, *The Scottish Enlightenment and the Militia Issue* (Edinburgh, 1985).

N. Rogers, *Whigs and Cities: Popular Politics in the Age of Walpole and Pitt* (Oxford, 1980).

N. Rogers, 'Admirals as Heroes: Patriotism and Liberty in Hanoverian England', *Journal of British Studies*, xxviii (1989), pp. 201–24.

J.C. Sainty, 'The secretariat of the chief governors of Ireland, 1690–1800', *Proceedings of the Royal Irish Academy*, series C, lxxvii (1977), pp. 1–33.

J. Shy, *Towards Lexington: The role of the British army in the coming of the American Revolution* (Princeton, 1965).

P.D.H. Smyth, 'The Volunteer Movement in Ulster' (PhD. thesis, Queen's University, Belfast, 1974).

L. Sutherland, 'The City and the Pitt/Devonshire Ministry of 1757', in A. Newman (ed.), *Politics and Finance in Eighteenth Century England* (London, 1984), pp. 67–115.

P.D.G. Thomas, 'New Light on the Commons Debate of 1763 on the American Army', *William and Mary Quarterly*, xxxviii (1981), pp. 110–12.

M. Wall, 'The Positions of Catholics in mid-18th century Ireland', in G. O'Brien (ed.), *Catholic Ireland in the Eighteenth Century: The Collected Essays of Maureen Wall* (Dublin, 1989), pp. 93–101.

M. Wall, 'Government policy towards catholics during the viceroyalty of the Duke of Bedford, 1757–61', in O'Brien (ed.), *Catholic Ireland in the Eighteenth Century*, pp. 103–6.

K. Wilson, 'Empire, Trade and Popular Politics in Mid-Hanoverian England: The case of Admiral Vernon', *Past and Present*, cxxi (1988), pp. 74–10.

——, *Sense of the People: Politics, Culture and Imperialism in England, 1715–1785* (Cambridge, 1995).

Index